CURBING THE COURTS

CURBING THE COURTS

THE CONSTITUTION AND
THE LIMITS OF
JUDICIAL POWER

GARY L. McDOWELL

LOUISIANA STATE UNIVERSITY PRESS
BATON ROUGE AND LONDON

Designer
Sylvia Loftin
Typeface
English Times
Typesetter
Focus Graphics
Printer
Thomson-Shore, Inc.
Binder
John H. Dekker & Sons, Inc.

10 9 8 7 6 5 4 3 2 1

Library of Congress Cataloging-In-Publication Data
McDowell, Gary L., 1949–
    Curbing the courts : the Constitution and the limits of judicial
power / Gary L. McDowell.
        p. cm.
    Includes indexes.
    ISBN 0-8071-1339-5
    1. Courts—United States. 2. Political questions and judicial
power—United States. 3. United States—Constitutional law.
4. Legislative power—United States. I. Title.
KF8700.M37 1988
347.73'1—dc 19
[347.3071]   87-24139
                                                              CIP

Grateful acknowledgment is made to the publishers of the following journals and
monographs, wherein parts of this work first appeared: *Public Interest*, LXVII
(Spring, 1982); *Journal of Contemporary Studies*, VII (Summer, 1984); *The Legal
System Assault on the Economy* (Washington, D.C., 1986); and *Constitutional
Commentary: The Constitution and Contemporary Constitutional Theory*
(Washington, D.C., 1985).

FOR
HENRY J. ABRAHAM
Teacher and Friend

It is jealousy and not confidence which prescribes limited constitutions to bind down those whom we are obliged to trust with power. . . . In questions of power, then, let no more be heard of confidence in man, but bind him down from mischief by the chains of the Constitution.

— THOMAS JEFFERSON

CONTENTS

Contents

PREFACE
AND ACKNOWLEDGMENTS

During the past thirty years or so two remarkable developments have been taking place in the way people think about the role of the judiciary under the Constitution. On one hand, the Supreme Court has grown increasingly bold in proclaiming itself to be the ultimate interpreter of the Constitution; the belief seems to be that there is no meaningful distinction between the Constitution and constitutional law. The Constitution has become in the eyes of many (as Charles Evans Hughes once quipped) merely "what the judges say it is."[1]

On the other hand, it is widely asserted today that judges and other public officials — but especially judges — are not bound by the text or original understanding of the Constitution. A common scholarly sentiment is that fidelity to text and intention need not be considered the touchstones of constitutional decisionmaking. Indeed, this scholarly sentiment has now been adopted by a growing number of jurists. Justice William Brennan, for example, has argued that the belief that a judge can divine the original intention of the Constitution is "little more than arrogance cloaked as humility." For Justice Brennan and his kind the main touchstone of constitutional interpretation is contemporary economic, social, and political realities. The Constitution, in this view, is unmoored and impermanent; it is a living constitution with an ideological vengeance.[2]

The practical consequence of these two doctrinal developments has been a judiciary increasingly immersed in what can only be called policy making. As the procedural requirements governing the judicial process — standing to sue, class actions, consent decrees, and so forth — have been loosened, judges have increasingly taken the plunge into the administrative minutiae of the policy process. And their opinions have reflected this substantive shift. Many judges have developed a knack, as Henry Monaghan has said, "of writing constitutional opinions that look like detailed legislative codes." Further, and more troubling, the Supreme Court has "fostered the impression that every detailed rule

---

1 Hughes quoted in Henry J. Abraham, *The Judicial Process* (4th ed.; New York, 1980), 324. See also *Cooper* v. *Aaron*, 358 U.S. 1 (1958).

2 William J. Brennan, "Construing the Constitution," *University of California, Davis Law Review*, XIX (1985), 4.

laid down has the same dignity as the constitutional text itself." More than a few commentators have now joined Monaghan in his belief that such an impression is simply a constitutional "illusion."[3]

Although throughout our history there have always been calls for radical political responses to what have been deemed judicial excesses and the presumption of judicial power, no period in our history has equaled either in duration or intensity the current period of antijudicial sentiment. What has been especially striking about this era, which began to emerge around 1954 with the advent of Warren Court activism, is the marked lack of success of political retaliations against this so-called government by judiciary. While judges have taken over the operation of school boards, mental health facilities, and prisons, their critics have fumed and fussed but little more. Judicial activism has come to be much like Charles Dudley Warner's weather: Everybody talks about it but nobody does anything.

This book is an effort to point toward an old but largely ignored way by which judicial power may be effectively curbed within the prudent guidelines provided by the Constitution itself. Article III of the Constitution provides that judicial power is subject not only to any exceptions Congress may see fit to make to appellate jurisdiction, but also to "such Regulations as the Congress shall make." While many critics of judicial activism have approached the problem from the perspective of carving out politically dramatic jurisdictional exceptions, few have looked to the power of Congress to regulate the procedures of the judicial process. However, the most effective way to curb the courts is through the various procedural arrangements that serve to guide and hem in the exercise of substantive judicial power.

As with any scholarly undertaking, a good many friends and colleagues lent their support along the way. Their willingness to read and criticize the manuscript — and, most of all, their persistence in attempting to convince me of the error of my ways in a good many instances — is greatly appreciated. Where their sharp eyes, clear minds, and good hearts prevailed, this book is much the better. I am especially indebted to Walter Berns, William A. Schambra, Eugene W. Hickok, Jr., Jeffrey L. Sedgwick, David Nichols, Nathan Glazer, Paul Peterson, Sotirios A. Barber, Ralph A. Rossum, George Friedman, Richard G.

3 Henry Monaghan, "Supreme Court 1974 Term Foreword: Constitutional Common Law," *Harvard Law Review,* LXXXVII (1974), 1, 2.

Preface and Acknowledgments

Stevens, David O'Brien, Peter Schultz, Charles J. Cooper, and Terry Eastland for their helpful comments on portions of the book.

In many ways, William Kristol's research and thinking on these issues made this project possible. Bill pointed me in directions I had not considered. The constant support—both moral and financial—of James McClellan and the Center for Judicial Studies made this a far easier task than it otherwise would have been.

John Agresto's careful reading of the entire manuscript provided me an especially rich opportunity for second thoughts. His many comments and suggestions taught me a great deal about the Constitution and constitutional law; my stubborn resistance no doubt deprived me of a good deal more.

Stephen J. Markman, then chief counsel of the Subcommittee on the Constitution of the Judiciary Committee of the United States Senate, was kind enough to read the sections dealing with the legislative history of court-curbing efforts. His encyclopedic knowledge of the subject and his suggestions were essential to the completion of the book.

My family offered unfaltering support and encouragement throughout this often seemingly endless project. Victoria Kuhn faithfully typed, read, and offered her usual gentle suggestions on the manuscript. Such a friend is rare indeed. Ron Tomalis and Eric Jaso were especially helpful in rendering the manuscript ready for publication.

This book grew from a paper I gave at a conference entitled "Judicial Power in the United States: What are the Appropriate Constraints?" sponsored by the American Enterprise Institute and held in Washington, D.C., on October 1 and 2, 1981. I am especially grateful to Bill Schambra for arranging for that invitation. As the project developed, it was generously supported by a grant from the Institute for Educational Affairs. Philip Marcus' early confidence in the ideas developed here is truly appreciated. The grant allowed me the luxury of spending a year as a Fellow in Law and Political Science at the Harvard Law School. Harold J. Berman, John Hart Ely, Paul Bator, and Abram Chayes made that year one of the most intellectually invigorating I have known. Although they obviously did not always convince me, they nevertheless made me see things and think about things in new ways. For that I am especially grateful.

The opportunity to conduct a study group on curbing the courts at the Institute of Politics at Harvard's Kennedy School of Government during the academic year 1981–82 was a rare opportunity to work

xiii

through a good many ideas at the most important, formative stages. Those who participated in that seminar—especially Nathan Glazer, Abram Chayes, Henry Abraham, Eugene Hickok, and Hrach Gregorian—contributed much to my efforts to think about the virtues and vices of judicial power under the Constitution.

I owe a special debt to Raoul Berger. His *Government by Judiciary: The Transformation of the Fourteenth Amendment* was the intellectual spark that first set fire to my scholarly interest in these matters. Since then, during the time this book was in progress, I have had the pleasure not only of his teaching but also of his friendship. For both, I am very grateful indeed.

Last but not least, this volume is dedicated to a man who has been a constant source of inspiration and direction to me, first through his books and essays, and then when I became his student at the University of Virginia in 1977. In the strictest sense, this work would not have been possible without him. Such is the influence of truly great teachers.

CURBING THE COURTS

INTRODUCTION
A MODEST REMEDY FOR
JUDICIAL ACTIVISM

I may not know much about law but
I do know that one can put
the fear of God in judges.

— THEODORE ROOSEVELT

We are a lost people when the
Supreme Tribunal of the law
has lost our respect.

— ABEL STEVENS

The issue of judicial activism is hardly new to American politics. Every Supreme Court since that which handed down the ruling in *Chisholm* v. *Georgia* (1793) that led to the Eleventh Amendment has found itself immersed in the animating political issues of its age. Although there is a strong tendency in American political thinking to view the judiciary as "exterior to the state" and, as an institution, removed from the "sweaty crowd" and rancid stuff of everyday political life, the fact of the matter is that, by the nature of its business, the federal judiciary is preeminently a political institution.[1]

Because the judiciary is a political institution, it has frequently been the object of a good deal of political wrath. Thomas Jefferson complained that in the hands of Chief Justice John Marshall the Constitution was "nothing more than an ambiguous text, to be explained by his sophistry into any meaning which may subserve his personal malice." Abraham Lincoln argued that Chief Justice Roger Taney in his opinion in the case of *Dred Scott* v. *Sandford* had done "obvious violence" to the "plain unmistakable language" of the Declaration of Independence. During the Progressive era, Senator Robert M. La Follette characterized all federal judges as "petty tyrants and arrogant despots." President Dwight Eisenhower reportedly concluded that his appointment of Earl Warren as Chief Justice of the Supreme Court was "the biggest damn fool mistake" he made during his presidency.[2]

1 Joseph Story, *Commentaries on the Constitution of the United States* (3rd ed.; 2 vols.; Boston, 1858), II, Sec. 1577. See also Alpheus T. Mason, "Judicial Activism: Old and New," *Virginia Law Review*, LV (1969), 385.
2 Thomas Jefferson to John Tyler, May 26, 1810, quoted in Charles Warren, *The*

There is a problem, however, in recognizing the Court's political position. That very recognition often serves only to blur the important line between proper and improper exercises of judicial power. Too often the debate over judicial activism and judicial restraint is dismissed as empty and as being spawned by rather superficial considerations of whose political ox is being gored. This is a mistake, for judicial power can be abused. When it is, it is important to be able to articulate how and why, and, most importantly, what should be done about it.

The past several years have seen an ever-increasing outpouring of congressional proposals to curb the courts. Most of the proposals differ little in form or substance from those that have been a fairly regular feature of each Congress since the early controversial decisions of the Warren Court. In general, the proposals are aimed at single issues such as abortion or school prayer and are attempts to curtail the jurisdiction of the federal courts in those areas. Such an ad hoc approach to the problem is ultimately inadequate for two reasons. First, Congressional efforts to deal with judicial activism by addressing particular decisions treat symptoms at the expense of curing causes. Second, attacks on particular decisions imply that the authority of the Court is not binding, that its decisions can be lightly dismissed or ignored. In the end, this approach can only serve to undermine public respect for both the role of the judiciary in American politics and the very idea of the rule of law. However wrong one might think the Court has been in deciding certain cases, no one would wish to lose the all-important veneration for the institution itself and thus sacrifice what Alexis de Tocqueville called the "moral force" of the government.[3]

The fundamental defect of most proposals to curb the courts is that they are imprudent. They are insufficient in that they fail to treat the causes of judicial activism at a level deep enough to make a permanent difference, and they are excessive in that they go so far as to seriously impair the proper functioning of the judiciary within the American

---

Supreme Court in United States History (3 vols.; Boston, 1924), I, 401 n. 1; Abraham Lincoln, speech delivered at Springfield, Illinois, June 26, 1857, in Gary L. McDowell (ed.), *Taking the Constitution Seriously: Essays on the Constitution and Constitutional Law* (Dubuque, Iowa, 1981), 249; Robert M. La Follette, "Address Before the Annual Convention of the American Federation of Labor" (Cincinnati, June 14, 1922), 2; Eisenhower quoted in Walter Murphy and C. Herman Pritchett (eds.), *Courts, Judges and Politics* (3rd ed.; New York, 1979), 155.

3   Alexis de Tocqueville, *Democracy in America*, trans. G. Lawrence, ed. J. P. Mayer (New York, 1966), 139.

political order. A more modest and ultimately more efficacious approach is to address the issue at the level of cause and to restructure the judicial process in such a way as to confine it to those issues with which it is best equipped to deal. The most successful remedy for judicial activism will be a procedural remedy.

Historically there have been two great periods of sustained judicial activism. The first, the era of substantive due process or the old activism, lasted from roughly 1890 until 1937. The second, the era of substantive equal protection or the new activism, has been going on since 1954. Between them lay a period that was characterized by a concern for efficiency in judicial administration. Although this interim period is distinct from both the old and the new activism, what occurred then has served as a bridge by which the two periods are connected.

The era of the old activism was a time of vigorous proscriptive judicial activity. Between 1898 and 1937 the Supreme Court issued some 50 decisions invalidating acts of Congress and about 400 invalidating state laws (as compared to 12 and 125 respectively for the period 1874–1898). It seemed as though no progressive social or economic legislation was constitutionally permissible.

Since 1954, the federal judiciary, with the Supreme Court leading the way, has been more prescriptively active than at any other time in the nation's history. Not only does the contemporary judiciary decree what the government may not do, but it has taken it upon itself increasingly to decree what the government must do to achieve what a majority of the Court holds to be the good life under the Constitution. This new activism differs from the old activism in being far more positive in its assertions.

Yet even though the new activism is markedly more prescriptive than the old, they are united on a deeper level. Like the old, the new activism issues from a judicial reliance on the so-called Rule of Reason. The negative activism against the Progressives and the New Dealers and the positive activism of the Warren and Burger Courts (and especially of such lower federal judges as Minor Wisdom, Frank Johnson, Arthur Garrity, and Frank Battisti) have more to do with the individual notions of justice embraced by the justices and judges than with the Constitution. In both instances a concern for social justice has replaced a concern for constitutionality in the judicial process.

The prescriptive activism of recent years has grown as a result of the procedural reforms of the 1930s coupled with a general willingness in Congress to delegate its constitutional prerogatives over the procedures and practices of the judiciary to the judiciary itself. The result is courts that are largely unbound by the procedural niceties that traditionally served as a source of restraint on the expressions of the judicial will. Without such procedural fences the judges have been left (in the memorable language of James Kent) to "roam at large in the trackless fields of their own imaginations."[4] Bolstered by substantial academic support, it is no wonder that federal judges decree the things they do.[5]

The period that lay between the old activism and the new, from 1938 to 1954, was a time characterized by a concern for efficient judicial administration. Although at first glance concerns over judicial procedure and administration may seem to have no immediate connection with concerns over activism, the procedural and administrative reforms of this period were prompted by the older activism from 1898 to 1937. This period of institutional reform is significant because some of the procedural reforms of the period would allow and encourage the extreme *prescriptive* activism of the post-1954 era.

A major accomplishment of the period was the adoption of the Rules of Civil Procedure of 1938, which merged actions of law with actions in equity into a unified civil action in the federal judiciary. The effort was designed to render the administration of the law more certain, uniform, and objective by reducing the gross subjectivity of judicial discretion.

The effort was not new in American politics, for judicial discretion had often seemed to many observers to be at odds with the logic of limited government under written law. There had been, for example, a series of attempts during the Jeffersonian and Jacksonian periods to reduce the mystical qualities of the law to simple rules that would be "legible to every reader," as Thomas Jefferson put it. And in 1848 David Dudley Field had successfully led a codification movement in

4 James Kent, *Commentaries on American Law* (4vols.; New York, 1826), I, 321.
5 See, in particular, Owen Fiss, "The Supreme Court 1978 Term Foreword: The Forms of Justice," *Harvard Law Review*, XCIII (1979), 1; Fiss, *The Civil Rights Injunction* (Bloomington, Ind., 1978); Abram Chayes, "The Role of the Judge in Public Law Litigation," *Harvard Law Review*, LXXXIX (1976), 1281; Jack B. Weinstein, "Litigation Seeking Changes in Public Behavior and Institutions—Some Views on Participation," *University of California, Davis Law Review*, XIII (1980), 231; Louis Jaffe, "The Citizen as Litigant in Public Actions," *University of Pennsylvania Law Review*, CXVI (1968), 1033.

New York, streamlining the civil procedures there. Thus the effort to simplify the law in the thirties was merely the culmination of a long struggle to trim judicial "excrescances."[6]

The reform impulse of the thirties had another objective as well, however. Whereas the merger of law and equity was rooted in a traditional distrust of judicial power, many of the twentieth-century reformers were also legal realists who sought to make the law a more efficient instrument of social reform and political change. And this meant a great expansion of the public role of the courts.[7] With the passage of the Declaratory Judgments Act of 1934 and the liberalization of requirements concerning class actions in the 1938 rules, the reformers sought to open up the judicial process. Bolstered by the Judges Bill of 1925, which allowed the Supreme Court its certiorari procedure whereby it could determine which cases it should hear, the Court was now procedurally capable of participating more fully in the resolution of social and political questions.

During the same period, efforts were also made to reform the administrative organization of the judiciary. Although efficiency was the reason most often cited for reforming the administrative structures, there was a political reason as well. The political branches of the government had been making forays against the courts, and the Administrative Office Act of 1939 was the judges' response to those political attacks. In particular, the act was part of the judiciary's substitute for Franklin D. Roosevelt's court-packing plan of 1937. Such administrative reform was an effort to defuse political antagonisms toward federal courts while leaving "intact and untouched the substantive heart of the judicial decision-making process."[8]

This preservation of the "substantive heart" of the judicial decision-making process, combined with looser procedural requirements for the administration of that process, would contribute greatly to increased judicial intrusion into areas of sensitive public policy. This judicial intrusion would lead to increased efforts to curb the courts, but most of the efforts so far have been misplaced and ineffective.

6 Gary L. McDowell, *Equity and the Constitution: The Supreme Court, Equitable Relief, and Public Policy* (Chicago, 1982), 34, 35, 87.

7 See William Kristol, "The American Judicial Power and the American Regime" (Ph.D. dissertation, Harvard University, 1979), 40–118.

8 Peter G. Fish, *The Politics of Federal Judicial Administration* (Princeton, 1973), 20, 427, 428–29; Fish, "Crises, Politics, and Federal Judicial Reform: The Administrative Office Act of 1939," *Journal of Politics*, XXXII (August, 1970), 625, 626.

Congress has been reduced to a role akin to a shepherd, who, having taken down his fences, is shocked to find that his flock has wandered off; instead of simply putting the fences back up and returning the wanderers to the fold, he chooses to condemn them for doing what comes naturally. In both instances, the effort will be in vain.

Controlling the Court through putting back up some of the procedural fences is an idea amply supported by American legal theory and experience — it makes sense in principle, and it works in practice. From Alexander Hamilton to Joseph Story to James Kent to Felix Frankfurter, it has been recognized that proper procedures are necessary to a proper exercise of judicial power. In his famous defense of the judiciary in *The Federalist*, Hamilton stated: "To avoid an arbitrary discretion in the courts, it is indispensable that they should be bound down by strict rules and precedents which serve to define and point out their duty in every particular case that comes before them."[9]

By turning its attention away from the more politically dramatic proposals for jurisdictional exceptions and focusing on the more mundane business of procedures and practices, Congress can direct its energies where they will be most successful. Through tightening up the judicial process, Congress can effect a legitimate and safe restraint on the exercise of judicial power. For the current spate of judicial intrusiveness is the result of a looseness in procedural arrangements that has allowed — even encouraged — a movement of the exercise of judicial power from a level of deciding concrete cases to a level of pondering abstract principles, from clearly defined particular controversies that admit of judicial decision to considerations of broad policy questions that admit more of political deliberation.

A steady movement from the concrete to the abstract has occurred in six basic procedural areas. In the area of *standing* there has been a movement from the traditional demand for a concrete legal interest toward the more abstract standards of "zones of interest" and "injury in fact." In the area of *class actions* there has been a shift from the standard of a clearly defined class with a strictly defined common legal interest toward more loosely defined classes presenting more abstract claims. In the area of *intervention* or *joinder* there has been an

9   Jacob E. Cooke (ed.), *The Federalist* (Middletown, Conn., 1961), No. 78, p. 529, hereinafter cited as *The Federalist*.

effort to liberalize the procedure to such an extent that nearly any person or especially any group with an "interest" in the outcome of the case may intervene in a lawsuit. In the area of *declaratory relief* the movement has been away from concrete standards of what constitutes a case or a controversy (an economic claim, for example) for the purposes of judicial resolution to more abstract standards (a violation of equal protection by a malapportioned legislative district). In the area of *consent decrees,* there has emerged a line of thinking that argues that such settlements be construed according to the spirit rather than the letter of the agreement. And in the area of *equitable relief* there has been a drastic movement away from a rather narrow understanding of equity jurisdiction as a proper means of vindicating concrete property rights (generally dealing with accidents, mistakes, frauds, and trusts) to a more amorphous understanding that equity jurisdiction is somehow competent to vindicate more abstract rights such as equality. In each instance Congress has the power—and, one could argue, the political responsibility—to return the Court to a more concrete exercise of its powers.

In order to move in this direction, however, it is essential that we first sharpen our view of the problem of judicial activism by ridding ourselves of the all too prevalent apothegm that the Constitution is only what the judges say it is, that its words are "empty vessels into which nearly anything can be poured."[10] We need to recover the older view that the Constitution has a meaning deeper and more permanent than the fluctuating opinions of the judges. In this light the Constitution is understood to embrace a theory of politics that serves as a standard against which the exercise of all powers of the government may be measured.[11]

At the heart of the Constitution's theory of politics lies a fundamental truth about popular government: All power—judicial as well as legislative and executive—is of an encroaching nature. Left to themselves, all political men will go as far as they can in pursuit of their view of the political good; the judiciary is subject to error of judgment no less than the other branches of the government. The

10 Arthur S. Miller, "The Human Element on the Bench," Chicago *Tribune,* July 16, 1981, Sec. 1, p. 4.

11 See the introduction to Ralph A. Rossum and Gary L. McDowell (eds.), *The American Founding: Politics, Statesmanship and the Constitution* (Port Washington, N.Y., 1981), 3–11.

judges were no more expected to be members of that "philosophical race of kings wished for by Plato" than any other officer. The framers of the Constitution suffered no delusion that the judiciary was in any way an apolitical institution, though they believed it could be rendered largely immune to ordinary partisan political impulses. Thus they sought to construct the judicial power within an institutional framework that would allow the politically indispensable judicial functions to be safely and fairly administered while any judicial excesses could be trimmed.

The question of judicial activism must be addressed within the context of the doctrine of separation of powers. The idea of separating the powers of government in the Constitution had two objectives: To prevent tyranny by avoiding the unhealthy concentration of power in any one department and to promote efficiency in the administration of the powers necessary to any government. Within this context the judiciary was to serve as a buffer against those ill humors that occasionally grip the population and can be translated into law. The judicial power was understood to be a necessary guard for the rights of individuals and minorities against the crushing political weight of what James Madison called "an interested and overbearing majority."[12] Yet the judiciary was only one of several auxiliary precautions designed to check the inevitable tendency in popular governments toward legislative tyranny. In spite of all the contrivances, the government was still considered to be, first and foremost, popular if not simply democratic. All of the institutional devices were meant to direct and tame popular opinion, not block it. The hope was that through institutional filters a qualitative rather than merely a quantitative majority will would come to be expressed as law.

Constitutionally, the judiciary is, as Alexander Hamilton claimed in *The Federalist*, the branch "least dangerous to the political rights of the Constitution."[13] But it is only the *least* dangerous (Hamilton did not naïvely suggest that it was simply not dangerous) if it exercises its legitimate function—judgment. Admittedly, the line between the exercise of the will and the exercise of the judgment is at best a blurred

12 *The Federalist*, No. 10, p. 57.

13 *Ibid.*, No. 78, p. 522. A fact often overlooked is that Hamilton's essays on the judiciary were written in response to the incisive commentary on that branch by the New York anti-Federalist Brutus. See Ann Stuart Diamond, "The Anti-Federalist *Brutus*," *Political Science Reviewer* VII (1976), 249. The essays by Brutus are in Herbert J. Storing (ed.), *The Complete Anti-Federalist* (7 vols.; Chicago, 1981).

one. But what Hamilton had in mind is unambiguous. The function of the Court was to patrol the constitutional boundaries of the other branches (the legislature especially) and of the states and to keep them within their prescribed limits. The purpose of an independent judiciary was to ensure that the limited and supreme Constitution remained so. As another leading founder, James Wilson, put it, the courts were intended to be "noble guards" of the Constitution.[14] Thus, the essence of the judicial power was originally understood to be *proscriptive*. Should the Court endeavor to take any "active resolution" it would be engaging in an illegitimate activity. Instead of being proscriptive and marking out the limits of the Constitution, the Court would be behaving in a *prescriptive* way and redefining the limits of the Constitution. Instead of being a bulwark of a limited constitution, it would become the vanguard of an unlimited one.

Despite the dangers of legislative power, it was still considered by the framers to be the cardinal principle of popular government. Basic to this principle is the belief that it is legitimate for the people through the instrumentality of law to adjust, check, or enhance certain institutions of the government whenever it is deemed necessary and proper. This includes the power of the legislature to exert some control over the structure and administration of the executive and judicial branches.

The qualified power of the legislature to tamper with the judiciary is not as grave a danger to the balance of the Constitution as the friends of judicial activism in every age attempt to make it. The framers were not blind to the problem of making the judiciary too much dependent upon "popularity." Even when a judicial decision runs counter to particular — and perhaps pervasive — political interests, the institutional arrangements of the Constitution are such as to slow down the popular outrage and give the people time for "more cool and sedate reflection."[15] And given the distance between the people and legislation that such devices as representation (with its multiplicity of interests), bicameralism, and the executive veto afford, an immediate backlash to judicial behavior is unlikely. Experience demonstrates that any backlash is likely to be "weak and ineffectual."[16] But if the negative response is not merely transient and is widely and deeply felt, then the

14   Robert G. McCloskey (ed.), *The Works of James Wilson* (2 vols.; Cambridge, Mass., 1967), II, 330.
15   See especially *The Federalist*, No. 81, and Nos. 68, 70, 71.
16   Kristol, "The American Judicial Power and the American Regime," 12.

Constitution wisely provides well-defined mechanisms for a deliberate political reaction to what the people hold to be intolerable judicial excesses.

If the history of court-curbing efforts in America teaches anything, the lesson is this: The American political system operates to the advantage of the judiciary. Presidential court-packing schemes are notoriously ineffective as a means of exerting political influence over the courts. Impeachment is properly too difficult to use as an everyday check against unpopular decisions.[17] Not since John Marshall saw fit to defend his opinion in *McCulloch* v. *Maryland* (1819) in the public press has any justice or judge felt obliged to respond to public outrage over a decision.[18] And it is very difficult — usually impossible — to build a coalition sturdy enough to pass court-curbing legislation.

Political responses to what are perceived to be excesses of judicial power take one of two forms. The response is either a policy response — against a particular decision or line of decisions — or an institutional response — against the structure and powers of the courts. In either event, the response may either be partisan or principled. Usually a policy response will take the form of a constitutional amendment or a piece of legislation designed to overrule a decision. An institutional response will generally make an effort to make jurisdictional exceptions, to create special courts with specific jurisdiction, or to make adjustments regarding the personnel, policies, and procedures of the judicial branch. Whatever the response, court-curbing is difficult for two reasons. First, no matter how badly a particular decision or line of decisions may "gore your ox" (to borrow Al Smith's phrase) that same decision will undoubtedly have benefited a clientele at least as large and politically vociferous. While a majority of one of the houses of Congress may object to particular cases of "judicial impertinence" (as Representative James Falconer Wilson viewed Justice David Davis' controversial opinion in *Ex Parte Milligan* [1867]) there will certainly be a variety of objections that will issue in different views of what should be done. James Madison's multiplicity of interest theory works well. The second reason court-curbing is not an easy business is that

17 Consider the ill-fated attempt to impeach Justice William O. Douglas. For an interesting history of such efforts see J. Borkin, *The Corrupt Judge* (New York, 1962); and Wrisley Brown, "The Impeachment of the Federal Judiciary," *Harvard Law Review*, XXVI (1913), 684.

18 See Gerald Gunther (ed.), *John Marshall's Defense of McCulloch v. Maryland* (Stanford, Calif., 1969).

there is an underlying appreciation in American political thought for a properly independent judiciary. There seems to be a general consensus that tampering with judicial independence is a serious matter and the consequences of rash reprisals against the court as an institution may upset the original constitutional balance that has worked so well for so long. Underlying the occasional outbursts of angry public sentiment against the Court is that "moral force" of the community of which Tocqueville spoke. On the whole, the American people continue to view the judiciary as the "boast of the Constitution."[19]

For any political attempt to adjust or limit the judicial power to be successful it is necessary that it be—and be perceived to be—a principled rather than a merely partisan response. Only then will the issue of judicial activism be met on a ground high enough to transcend the more common—and generally fruitless—debates over judicial liberalism and judicial conservatism. The deepest issue is not whether a particular decision or even a particular Court is too liberal for some and too conservative for others; the point is whether the courts are exercising their powers capably and legitimately. Together the standards of institutional capacity and constitutional legitimacy are far more helpful in thinking about the nature and extent of judicial power than the ideological stamps of liberal and conservative. Keeping the courts constitutionally legitimate and institutionally capable benefits both the liberal and the conservative elements in American politics.

Since the Constitution only creates judicial power, it is left to the more representative institutions to fashion the judicial process. In truth, the courts "live and move and have their being through the legislation of Congress." In the final analysis, judicial activism is not so much a case of judicial usurpation as it is of congressional abdication. In light of this, Congress would do well to recover a bit of wisdom offered over half a century ago by Felix Frankfurter and James Landis: "The happy relation of States to Nation—constituting as it does our central political problem—is to no small extent dependent upon the wisdom with which the scope and limits of the federal courts are determined."[20] Our current state of judicial affairs is largely the result of Congress failing to exercise such wisdom.

19 Tocqueville quoted in Warren, *The Supreme Court in United States History*, II, 22.

20 Felix Frankfurter and James Landis, "The Power of Congress Over Procedure

But the political and constitutional waters are muddier than such a statement reveals. For in many ways the debate over the proper scope and limits of judicial power is as much if not more an academic debate than a political one. That political action on this front seems nonexistent may be the result of the fact that there have come to be so many theories and justifications of judicial power that the "conscientious legislator" (to borrow Paul Brest's term) does not know where to turn. The result is a kind of constitutional poverty amidst theoretical plenty.[21]

Before plunging into yet another academic offering, it seems appropriate to survey critically the existing theoretical landscape on the question of judicial power.

---

in Criminal Contempts in 'Inferior' Federal Courts — A Study in Separation of Powers," *Harvard Law Review*, XXXVII (1924), 1010, 1020; Frankfurter and Landis, *The Business of the Supreme Court*, 2.

21   Paul Brest, "The Conscientious Legislator's Guide to Constitutional Interpretation," *Stanford Law Review*, XXVII (1975), 585.

ONE

THE CONSTITUTION AND CONTEMPORARY CONSTITUTIONAL THEORY

It would be hard to overstate the impact of the Supreme Court under Earl Warren on the course of American politics. In a series of cases, the Warren Court transformed the structure and process of the federal government and, to an even greater extent, the political processes within the states. In *Watkins* v. *United States*, for example, the Court curtailed the power of Congress to investigate subversive or un-American activities; in *Miranda* v. *Arizona*, it pressed a protective judicial thumb on the criminal side of the scales of justice by demanding that the police "read" the suspect his constitutional rights so as to inform him (among other things) that should he not be able to afford a lawyer one would be provided for him, courtesy of the Court in *Gideon* v. *Wainwright*. In *Reynolds* v. *Sims*, the Court restructured the basis of representation in state legislatures; perhaps most significantly, in *Brown* v. *Board of Education of Topeka, Kansas* it outlawed racial segregation in public schools (and, in later cases, extended that prohibition to all public facilities). In each instance, Chief Justice Warren followed his progressive instinct for what was fair, decent, and humane, regardless of constitutional text, original intention, or judicial precedent.[1]

Combining "an ethical gloss on the Constitution with an activist theory of judicial review," Warren's theory of judging made him more a legislator or policy-planner than a judge. Given Warren's belief that his appointment to the Supreme Court was a "mission to do justice," concepts such as separation of powers and federalism proved to be no match for his sense of decency and his demand for democratic fairness. Warren was never much concerned with constitutional text or intention. Rather, he believed his job as a judge lay in discovering and articulating the "ethical imperatives" he felt were (or should be)

---

1 *Watkins* v. *United States*, 354 U.S. 178 (1958); *Miranda* v. *Arizona*, 384 U.S. 436 (1966); *Gideon* v. *Wainwright*, 372 U.S. 335 (1963); *Reynolds* v. *Sims*, 377 U.S. 533 (1964); *Brown* v. *Board of Education of Topeka, Kansas*, 347 U.S. 483 (1954), 349 U.S. 294 (1955).

embedded in the Constitution. He pursued concrete political results without feeling any need to tote along much "theoretical baggage." His feelings were enough.[2]

But whatever effect the Supreme Court under Earl Warren had on the institutional arrangements of the American constitutional order, his legacy has proved to be far deeper and far more pervasive. As Judge J. Skelly Wright has pointed out, the greatest legacy of the Warren Court has been its "revolutionary influence" on the thinking of law students. Inspired by the "dignity and moral courage" of Warren and his Court, they have been taught to recite the "language of idealism" and to endeavor to act on those "ideals to which America is theoretically and rhetorically dedicated." Thus the Supreme Court under Earl Warren successfully taught several generations of law students (now professors and judges) that there need be "no theoretical gulf between law and morality."[3]

The jurisprudential quest of the Warren Court struck a particularly responsive chord in the juridical community. The current generation of legal scholars has taken as a nearly unquestioned truth Ronald Dworkin's view that rights cannot be taken seriously until there has been a "fusion of constitutional law and moral theory."[4] The veritable industry of constitutional theorizing that has resulted is not constitutional theorizing in any traditional sense (such as that of John Marshall or Joseph Story). The new constitutional theorizing is aimed not so much at the explication of the theoretical foundations of the Constitution as it is at the creation of new theories of constitutionalism that are in turn superimposed on the Constitution (if, indeed, the Constitution is considered at all).

The arguments offered by this new generation of theorists have struck more than a few observers as being sufficiently innovative to suggest, as Leonard Levy has, that they "have been concocted to rationalize a growing satisfaction with judicial review among the liberal intellectuals and scholars." Raoul Berger has been even more blunt; such theorizing, Berger argues, "is a very recent phenomenon,

---

2   G. Edward White, *Earl Warren: A Public Life* (New York, 1982), 350–69.

3   J. Skelly Wright, "Professor Bickel, the Scholarly Tradition, and the Supreme Court," *Harvard Law Review*, LXXXIV (1971), 769, 804.

4   Ronald Dworkin, *Taking Rights Seriously* (Cambridge, Mass., 1977), 149. See also Dworkin, *A Matter of Principle* (Cambridge, Mass., 1985); and Dworkin, *Law's Empire* (Cambridge, Mass., 1986).

seeking to justify judicial exercise of ungranted power by moral theories that have no constitutional roots in order to undergird judicial governance that supports activist aspirations." The juridical result has been the dominance of a "political jurisprudence." As Paul Brest has confessed, such efforts in fact are not political theory at all, but "advocacy scholarship—amicus briefs designed to persuade the Court to adopt our various notions of the public good."[5] Most of the new advocates are not as candid as Brest; they are inclined to support their "advocacy scholarship" by appeals to a higher law or moral justification. "In consequence," Berger concludes, "activists wander in a jungle of moral philosophy theories."[6] To better understand their project, it is necessary to clear out something of a path through their tangled undergrowth of theory.

ALEXANDER BICKEL AND THE SCHOLARLY TRADITION

In many ways the contemporary schools of constitutional jurisprudence can trace their origins to the work of the late Alexander M. Bickel. Bickel's work was at once seminal and paradoxical. On the one hand, Bickel sought to establish the legitimate grounds for a kind of judicial activism; on the other, he offered praise for a kind of judicial restraint. His first book, *The Least Dangerous Branch*, celebrated what he termed the "passive virtues" of the judicial process, techniques to be used by the courts to escape the opprobrium that too much meddling in the political process of policy making would bring. Doctrines such as standing, political questions, ripeness, and so forth provided the Court a safe shield from the mudslinging of the political arena. But from behind that shield Bickel expected the Court to go forth in defense of fundamental values. Indeed, the judges were to be "teachers to the citizenry"; it was their task, Bickel wrote, to "mold the peoples' view of durable principles of government." Thus Bickel argued for a curious kind of judicial restraint; in his view the Court was obliged to show restraint because the American polity was "dedi-

---

5   Leonard Levy (ed.), *Judicial Review and the Supreme Court* (New York, 1967), 24; Raoul Berger, *Death Penalties: The Supreme Court's Obstacle Course* (Cambridge, Mass., 1982), 194; Martin Shapiro, "Judge as Statesman, Judge as Pol," *New York Times Book Review*, November 21, 1981, p. 42; Paul Brest, "The Fundamental Rights Controversy: The Essential Contradictions of Normative Constitutional Scholarship," *Yale Law Journal*, XC (1981), 1063, 1109.

6   Berger, *Death Penalties*, 181.

cated both to the morality of government by consent and to moral self-government."[7]

It is from this theoretical distinction between the morality of government by consent and moral self-government that the main strands of contemporary jurisprudence begin to develop. On one hand is a dedication to procedural concerns, to the maintenance of those institutional contrivances—representation, separation of powers, and so forth—that are deemed essential to popular government; on the other is a dedication to substantive concerns, to the evolution and articulation of fundamental values and human rights. But by declaring that it was "decidedly the Court's function to proclaim principled goals," Bickel skewed his theory in favor of those who would be more inclined to confuse "fundamental values" with policy choices that were the result of their personal predilections.[8]

By 1969, when he delivered the Holmes Lectures at Harvard Law School (which would be published the next year as *The Supreme Court and the Idea of Progress*), Bickel was clearly disillusioned with the performance of the Warren Court since 1962. Thus by 1970 he had retreated from his passive defense of the Supreme Court as the source of principled rule. Indeed, he concluded, the judges were inevitably too "principle-prone and principle-bound" to be effective agents for formulating public policy.[9]

In *The Supreme Court and the Idea of Progress*, Bickel indicted the egalitarian impulses of the Warren Court he had praised as a general judicial posture in *The Least Dangerous Branch*. The jurisprudence of the Warren Court, he argued, aspired "to a groupless society, to politics without faction, and a theoretic preference, as Madison said, for 'reducing mankind to a perfect equality in their political rights'—a preference sustained by a prophetic judgment that the United States is now, or soon will be, so nearly a classless a society that Madison's analysis is dated." The political problem posed by such a jurisprudence born of good intentions, to Bickel's way of thinking, was that

---

7 Alexander M. Bickel, *The Least Dangerous Branch: The Supreme Court at the Bar of Politics* (Indianapolis, 1962), 69, 235, 240, 199.

8 *Ibid.*, 141; Robert K. Faulkner, "Bickel's Constitution: The Problem of Moderate Liberalism," *American Political Science Review*, LXXII (1978), 925.

9 Alexander M. Bickel, *The Supreme Court and the Idea of Progress* (New York, 1970), 175.

judges possessed of "roving commissions to do good" cease to be judges in the proper constitutional sense.[10]

There is no doubt that Bickel paid a rather hefty price in the liberal camp for his jurisprudential back stepping. Bickel and others who doubted not only the prudence but the propriety of judicial politics — most notably Philip B. Kurland — were condemned as "self-appointed scholastic mandarins." Even more than Bickel, Kurland's work, especially his 1964 foreword to the *Harvard Law Review*, "Equal in Origin and Equal in Title to the Legislative and Executive Branches of the Government," was indicted as "haughty derision merging into almost scurrilous disrespect" for the Court. To the liberal defenders of the Warren Court, Bickel was worse than a defector; he was a traitor. In their opinion, the "ultimate test of the Justices' work . . . must be goodness, not a cynically defined success." Bickel's new doubts as to the capacity of the Court to develop "durable principles" and the propriety of the Court to dabble in "broad areas of social policy" had led him — and the scholarly tradition he was alleged to lead — into the seamy moral underworld of the "western conservative tradition."[11]

The year after his death in 1974, Bickel's final book appeared; *The Morality of Consent* was, in many respects, his most theoretical work. In it, Bickel sought to portray "a contemporary crisis of practical judgment that originates in a crisis of theory." He concluded his scholarly career by warning that American politics had come to be undermined simultaneously by "a dictatorship of the self-righteous" and by a moral relativism and permissiveness that inevitably "eats away at the moral fabric." His final message was clear and chilling. "Our problem," he said, "has been, and is most acutely now, the tyrannical tendency of ideas and the suicidal emptiness of a politics without ideas."[12]

The most remarkable thing about *The Morality of Consent* was Bickel's rediscovery of Edmund Burke. Provoked, as Robert Faulkner has noted, by the "zealous moralism and despairing relativism" of our day, Bickel sought to resurrect Burke and with his philosophic assistance to teach the republic how to avoid the "opposite evils" of "intol-

---

10 *Ibid.*, 174, 134.
11 Wright, "Professor Bickel, the Scholarly Tradition, and the Supreme Court," 777, 778, 797, 795. See Philip B. Kurland, "Equal in Origin and Equal in Title to the Legislative and Executive Branches of the Government," *Harvard Law Review*, LXXVIII (1964), 143.
12 Faulkner, "Bickel's Constitution," 925; Alexander M. Bickel, *The Morality of Consent* (New Haven, Conn., 1974), 142, 12.

erance and indifference." Rather than appealing to the social contract theorists such as Locke and Rousseau who sought to measure particular societies and nations against the standard of universal natural rights, Bickel appealed to Burke; that appeal was an explicit rejection of the "contractarians" whose "premises cannot be questioned closely" in favor of a tradition that "begins not with theoretical rights but with a real society" and "with human nature as it is seen to be."[13] But the morality of consent that he sought to explicate really amounted to "hardly more than a generalized loyalty or law-abidingness, important to a good citizen and fair person, but hardly the whole of citizenship and virtue." Whatever his doubts about the sort of activism that characterized the Warren Court (and, it seemed in light of *Roe* v. *Wade*, also characterized the Burger Court), Bickel could not let go of the idea of the Constitution—even his "manifest constitution"—as a document of "open texture and evolving principle."[14]

Bickel's shift from his early stand in *The Least Dangerous Branch* to his last stand in *The Morality of Consent* was not as great as it might at first glance appear. This last effort was more a movement on the continuum between the poles of the morality of government by consent and moral self-government that he had first created in *The Least Dangerous Branch*. At its deepest level, perhaps, Bickel's judicial and legal theories were too inextricably linked to his reliance on history to allow a complete break from his early work in his last work. This notion of the manifest constitution of open texture and evolving principle served only to replace the fixed rights and powers of traditional constitutional jurisprudence "not with other definite powers, but with an indefinite legal intellectual colloquy by which principles (and thus principled powers) are evolved."[15]

There is a fundamental problem posed for the idea of constitutionalism by rooting constitutional interpretation in an appeal to fundamental values that are the product not of the Constitution—neither of its text nor of its intention—but are the product of "moral philosophy and political theory." Bickel obviously knew this; but in his search for a middle ground between a historically rigid meaning of constitutional language and a philosophically loose meaning, he erred too far in the direction of the latter. In his quest for a safe path between

13 Faulkner, "Bickel's Constitution," 930; Bickel, *The Morality of Consent*, 12, 4.
14 Faulkner, "Bickel's Constitution," 930; Bickel, *The Morality of Consent*, 29–30.
15 Faulkner, "Bickel's Constitution," 935.

"moral absolutes" and "moral relativity," Bickel sought a morality of process. But his morality of consent, with its too-easy acceptance of a constitution of open texture, reduces to "traipsing abjectly after an open and indefinite historical process."[16] Bickel's teachings, from *The Least Dangerous Branch* through *The Morality of Consent,* provide the most durable foundation for the contemporary ideology of a living constitution. Bickel left it to others to draw out the full implications of his juridical thinking.

RONALD DWORKIN AND THE
MORAL REVOLUTION OF RIGHTS

Most liberal critics of Bickel and his scholarly tradition have focused on the intellectual confusion they saw being spawned by Herbert Wechsler's famous call in 1959 for "neutral principles" in constitutional law. To advocate "neutral principles" in theory was one thing; to give them practical effect was quite a different matter. The entire quest for a principled neutrality presupposed a belief that "constitutional adjudication could remain a rigorously reasoned process while at the same time making and enforcing constitutional value choices." The inability of Bickel and those of his tradition to explain how such a "synthesis of 'value-free' values comes about" was, to their critics, their fatal flaw.[17]

Failing to work this problem out, Bickel opted for a "new skepticism" about the power of judicial reason and neutral principle; his new logic, his morality of consent, was nothing more than a rediscovery of an older faith in "the pluralistic political process — and in the adequacy of reliance on that process to protect fundamental values." This was insufficient; constitutional protections, especially of rights and liberties, were deemed to have a meaning beyond what Bickel and his so-called conservative critics would allow. Thus the intentionally "vague" language of the Constitution imposed a moral duty on "both judges and scholars" to "determine what that meaning might be." In brief, any solidly "liberal theory of law" demanded that judges and

16 Bickel, *The Supreme Court and the Idea of Progress*, 86; Faulkner, "Bickel's Constitution," 938, 936.

17 Herbert Wechsler, "Toward Neutral Principles of Constitutional Law," *Harvard Law Review*, LXXIII (1959), 1; Wright, "Professor Bickel, the Scholarly Tradition, and the Supreme Court," 775, 780.

scholars begin to take rights seriously.[18] Ronald Dworkin was more than willing to show them how to do that.

In *Taking Rights Seriously*, Dworkin set out to "define and defend" his liberal theory of law. More than any other book on constitutional law, *Taking Rights Seriously* was offered as an unrelenting *moral* defense of judicial activism. Believing that constitutional law and theory could make "no genuine advance" until there would come to be a "fusion of constitutional law and moral theory," Dworkin endeavored to effect that fusion. Resting his notion on the theoretical foundation that John Rawls had laid in his *Theory of Justice*, Dworkin sought to demonstrate that although "judicial activism involves risks of tyranny," those risks simply have to be taken, for the morality of individual rights demands nothing less. "A claim of right," Dworkin asserts, "presupposes a moral argument and can be established in no other way."[19]

To make his moral argument, Dworkin was first obliged to refound, in effect, the Constitution. Whereas the framers of the Constitution were confident that the security of American civil and political liberty lay in the Constitution's "design of government with powers to act and a structure to make it act wisely and responsibly," Dworkin and his followers (soon to be an army) were not.[20] Besides the fact that those internal contrivances of the Constitution that had been defended by the likes of James Madison were no real security against majority tyranny, there was the deeper moral issue. Human rights are dynamic, not static; or, perhaps more precisely, our understanding of what constitutes human rights is essentially evolutionary in character. In the same way the natural sciences have progressed so must the social sciences; it makes no more sense to be bound to an eighteenth-century conception of rights than it does to be bound to an eighteenth-century conception of physics. To Dworkin, any theory of rights that truly takes rights seriously must not be shackled by the chains of historical understanding. A true moral theory of rights is and must be progressive.

"Our constitutional system," Dworkin writes, "rests on a particular moral theory, namely that men have moral rights against the state.

18 Wright, "Professor Bickel, the Scholarly Tradition, and the Supreme Court," 783.

19 Dworkin, *Taking Rights Seriously*, vii, 143, 147. See John Rawls, *A Theory of Justice* (Cambridge, Mass., 1971).

20 Herbert J. Storing, "The Constitution and the Bill of Rights," in M. Judd Harmon (ed.), *Essays on the Constitution of the United States* (Port Washington, N.Y., 1978), 48.

The difficult clauses of the Bill of Rights, like the due process and equal protection [sic] clauses, must be understood as appealing to moral concepts rather than laying down particular conceptions; therefore a court that undertakes the burden of applying these clauses fully must be an activist court, in the sense that it must be prepared to frame and answer questions of political morality." The Constitution, Dworkin argues, was intentionally designed to provide vague standards of restraint against government in the name of individual rights. Those restraints, the drafters of the Constitution believed, "could be justified by appeal to moral rights which individuals possess against the majority." The Constitution was thus intended, Dworkin believes, to "recognize and protect" these moral rights of individuals. It is this understanding that provides his moral defense for judicial activism: "The program of judicial activism holds that courts . . . should work out principles of legality, equality, and the rest, revise those principles from time to time in the light of what seems to the Court *fresh moral insight*, and judge the acts of Congress, the states, and the president accordingly." Dworkin concludes that "the policy of judicial activism presupposes a certain objectivity of moral principle; in particular it presupposes that citizens do have a moral right to equality of public education or to fair treatment by the police. Only if such moral rights exist in some sense can activism be justified as a program based on something beyond the judge's personal preference."[21]

There is something ennobling about Dworkin's account of both moral certainty and judicial power; however, it is ennobling but wrong. His logic assumes a truly philosophic disposition on the part of a judge not simply to know those moral rights but, more important, to be able and willing to distinguish those moral certainties from his own prejudices and ideological inclinations. The problem of such an assumption is basic: a tendency of all mankind is to confuse *justice* with one's *perception of justice*. The defects of the human economy being what they are, we should doubt anyone's ability to distill his undefective reason from the swirling confusion of his opinions, passions, and interests. To assert, as Dworkin does, that judges above all other mortals are capable of such virtue is a case of the moral wish being father to the constitutional thought.

In the jurisprudential tradition created by Dworkin, taking rights

---

21 Dworkin, *Taking Rights Seriously*, 147, 133, 137, 138.

seriously means nothing less than creating new rights. "Unfortunately," as Walter Berns has argued, "this way of taking rights 'seriously' treats the Constitution frivolously and ultimately will undermine its structure." The legacy of this approach has been to make the fundamental issue of contemporary jurisprudence, as Thomas Grey has put it, the question of whether it is legitimate for judges to "define and enforce fundamental human rights without substantial guidance from constitutional text and history."[22]

This question is not raised, however, in an ideologically neutral way. The pervasive theme of recent constitutional jurisprudence, since the first days of the current activism in the Warren Court, has been what Philip Kurland has termed the "egalitarian ethos." The impulse toward a greater egalitarianism within American society has dominated the writings of those who have sought to construct broad new theories to defend particular Court decisions in which they take ideological comfort. The literary tradition spawned by the Warren Court's activism proves Archibald Cox right. "Once loosed," he wrote of the Warren Court in 1968, "the idea of equality is not easily cabined."[23]

In considering the claims of morality raised in defense of judicial activism, the bottom line is this: the founders anticipated that the judges would be the "faithful guardians of the Constitution." Their job—their constitutional duty—was to preserve and perpetuate the Constitution as it had been written. There would be unrelenting efforts, the founders knew, on the part of public officials to read out of the document any restraints it placed on their powers. As they knew all too well, "power is of an encroaching nature." The role of the judge would be to show that the Constitution meant what it said and said what it meant—no more, no less. For anyone to have suggested that it would be appropriate for a judge by construction any more than for a legislator by statute to change the meaning of the Constitution would have struck most if not all of that generation as absurd. That is precisely what Chief Justice Marshall meant when he argued that the

---

22 Walter Berns, "The Constitution as a Bill of Rights," in Robert Goldwin and William A. Schambra (eds.), *How Does the Constitution Secure Rights?* (Washington, D.C., 1984), 67; Thomas Grey, "Do We Have an Unwritten Constitution?" *Stanford Law Review*, XXVII (1975), 703, 714.

23 Philip B. Kurland, *Politics, the Constitution, and the Warren Court* (Chicago, 1970), xx; Archibald Cox, *The Warren Court* (Cambridge, Mass., 1968), 6.

judges must never forget that it is a constitution they are expounding.[24]

As Dworkin sought to bolster what Bickel had described as a dedication to moral self-government, so others stepped forth to counter Dworkin's theory by bolstering the claims accompanying the morality of government by consent. The most penetrating of these efforts was a demand that constitutional interpretation must be linked not only to the words or so-called inherent logic of the document but to the intentions of the framers. With the publication of *Government by Judiciary: The Transformation of the Fourteenth Amendment* in 1977, Raoul Berger fundamentally restructured the nature of the debate over judicial activism.

RAOUL BERGER AND THE
RETURN TO ORIGINAL INTENTION

Raoul Berger has never been one to shy away from the heat and glare of public debate. Indeed, since his retirement from the practice of law in 1965, he has actively helped to fuel the fires of controversy in the camps of both legal scholarship and popular opinion. His major works include *Congress v. The Supreme Court*; *Impeachment: The Constitutional Problems*; *Executive Privilege: A Constitutional Myth*; *Government by Judiciary: The Transformation of the Fourteenth Amendment*; and *Death Penalties: The Supreme Court's Obstacle Course*.[25] He has antagonized conservatives and liberals alike by his historical studies that have led him to condemn executive privilege on the one side and government by judiciary on the other. At the base of such intellectual diversity has been an unfaltering and unblushing commitment to popular government—a commitment to the belief that our "democratic system is bottomed on the legislative process." Throughout his writings, Berger, the quintessential liberal, has hammered out the same message: "In a Republican government, the legislative authority necessarily predominates."[26]

---

24 Jacob E. Cooke (ed.), *The Federalist* (Middletown, Conn., 1961), No. 78, p. 528; *No.* 48, p. 332, hereinafter cited as *The Federalist*; *McCulloch v. Maryland*, 4 Wheaton 316 (1819).

25 Raoul Berger, *Congress v. the Supreme Court* (Cambridge, Mass., 1969); Berger, *Impeachment: The Constitutional Problems* (Cambridge, Mass., 1973); Berger, *Executive Privilege: A Constitutional Myth* (Cambridge, Mass., 1974); Berger, *Government by Judiciary* (Cambridge, Mass., 1977); Berger, *Death Penalties*.

26 Berger, *Executive Privilege*, 3; *The Federalist*, No. 51, p. 322.

Behind this confidence in republican institutions lies an even deeper belief that the original intention of the framers — both of the Constitution and its subsequent amendments — is the first rule of constitutional interpretation. This dedication to pursuing what he believes to be the first principle of the rule of law has caused him no little public turmoil. Berger recognizes the problem that too often "rigorous constitutional analysis halts at the door of particular predilections." To avoid that scholarly pitfall he has pushed his point of discovering original intention so far as to offend many, for original intention is not always noble. But in his view, "intellectual honesty demands that the 'original understanding' be honored across the board."[27]

Berger's most controversial work by far has been *Government by Judiciary*, wherein he traced the judicial transformation of the Fourteenth Amendment from a rather limited constitutional vehicle for securing the provisions of the Civil Rights Act of 1866 against invalidation by judicial review into a "thing of wax." To demand fidelity not only to the language of the Constitution but to its framers' intentions is a demand that flies in the face of most contemporary legal, historical, and political scholarship. One commentator, outlining the different modes of constitutional interpretation, has put it more brazenly than most. "The framers, after all, are dead, and, in the contemporary world, their views are neither relevant nor morally binding." With this attitude rather firmly entrenched as academic orthodoxy it is little wonder that its proponents disparage those like Berger who would encourage "judicial autopsies on the framers' minds."[28]

Against this powerful, ideological trend, Berger has put forth something of an old-fashioned view of constitutional affairs:

> The Constitution represents fundamental choices that have been made by the people, and the task of the Courts is to effectuate them, 'not [as Robert Bork has pointed out], to construct new rights.' When the judiciary substitutes its own value choices for those of the people it subverts the Constitution by usurpation of power. . . . Substitution by the Court of its value choices for those embodied in the Constitution violates the basic principle of government by the consent of the governed. . . . [T]he Supreme Court has no authority to substitute an 'unwritten Constitution' for the written Constitution the Founders gave us and the people ratified.[29]

27 Berger, *Government by Judiciary*, 411.
28 Craig Ducat, *Modes of Constitutional Interpretation* (St. Paul, Minn., 1979), 103; William Harris, "Bonding Word to Polity: The Science of American Constitutionalism," *American Political Science Review*, LXXVI (1982), 34, 44.
29 Berger, *Government by Judiciary*, 292, 296, 289.

Taking the constitutional logic of James Madison, Alexander Hamilton, John Marshall, and Thomas Jefferson, among many others, as his scholarly point of departure, Berger focused *Government by Judiciary* on the transformation of the Fourteenth Amendment. Given that that amendment has become "probably the largest source of the Court's business," and certainly the source of its most controversial decisions, such attention was well placed. Berger's target was those of the scholarly tradition who, in defense of the Warren Court's achievements, had begun to celebrate the "open-ended" phrases of the Fourteenth Amendment—"Privileges or Immunities," "Due Process of Law," and "Equal Protection of the Laws"—as having been so shrewdly crafted as not to "foreclose a different application in the future." The defense that the Fourteenth Amendment had allegedly been drafted in "language capable of growth" struck Berger as preposterous; his research convinced him that such a position was absurd. "The Founders," Berger concluded of those who framed and ratified the Constitution, "were deeply committed to positivism, as is attested by their resort to written constitutions—positive law. . . . That commitment sprang from an omnipresent dread of the greedy expansiveness of power." This commitment had not been lost by the time the Civil War amendments were drafted to finish the unfinished constitutional business that the presence of the "peculiar institution," slavery, had prevented in 1787. The framers of the Fourteenth Amendment, Berger discovered, "had no thought of creating unfamiliar rights of unknown, far-reaching extent by the use of the words 'equal protection,' and 'due process.' Instead, they meant to secure familiar 'fundamental rights,' and only those, and to guard them as of yore against deprivation except by (1) a non-discriminatory law, and (2) the established judicial procedure of the State." Those "familiar" fundamental rights were nothing more abstract than the rights "to make contracts, own property, sue and be sued, and be subject only to equal punishment."[30]

Among Berger's primary targets are those who would smuggle "natural law" and "natural rights" concepts into the Constitution through its so-called open-ended provisions, especially the due process clause of the Fourteenth Amendment, which "has come to be the main provision through which natural law theories are made a part of current constitutional law." Archibald Cox, among many others, finds such a development cause for praise; "the very persistence of such evocative,

30 *Ibid.*, I, 113, 27, 53, 252, 19; Lino Graglia, "Was the Constitution a Good Idea?" *National Review*, July 13, 1984, pp. 34–36.

rather than sharply definitive, phrases attests to the strength of our natural law inheritance as authority for legal change." But as Berger knows, any judicial reliance on natural law as a guide to judicial decision is a matter, as Roscoe Pound once put it, "purely personal and arbitrary." At least since James Iredell took up his rhetorical arms to do juridical battle with Samuel Chase in *Calder* v. *Bull* in 1798, the dangers of imposing a natural law construction on a written constitution have been clear.[31] The reliance on such abstractions, although in principle ennobling, in practice too often pushes a judge into what can only be called murky moralizing.

Such philosophic or ideological meandering is not, to Berger's way of thinking, the job of the Court. In a more recent work, *Death Penalties,* Berger endeavored to illuminate still further — by example of the death penalty cases — the political, legal, and constitutional dilemmas posed by a Court that presumes the power to rewrite the Constitution, "identifying its own predilections with constitutional imperatives." The underlying theme of *Death Penalties* is much the same as that of *Government by Judiciary*: "the judicial takeover of government."[32]

In a sense, *Death Penalties* is aimed at reminding the Court, no less than teaching the public, of an old fact of popular constitutional government. That fact is that "laws may be unwise, may be dangerous, may be destructive, and yet not be unconstitutional." To think otherwise, and to assume "that the rights of man in a moral sense are equally rights in the sense of the Constitution and the Law," can only result, as Justice Oliver Wendell Holmes saw it, in "confusion of thought." As Chief Justice Marshall summed it up, defending his positions in *McCulloch* v. *Maryland*, the "peculiar circumstances of the moment may render a decision more or less wise, but cannot make it more or less unconstitutional."[33] But this is precisely what the contemporary Court has assumed: that the changing public conceptions of justice or changing juridical attitudes have more to do with determining questions on constitutionality than does the Constitution itself.

31 Berger, *Government by Judiciary*, 257, n. 38; Archibald Cox, *The Role of the Supreme Court in American Government* (New York, 1976), 113; Roscoe Pound, "Common Law and Legislation," *Harvard Law Review*, XXI (1908), 383, 393. See *Calder* v. *Bull*, 3 Dallas 386 (1798).

32 Berger, *Death Penalties*, 158, 186 n. 20.

33 Max Farrand (ed.), *The Records of the Federal Convention of 1787* (4vols.; New Haven, Conn., 1936), II, 73; Oliver Wendell Holmes, Jr., *Collected Legal Papers* (Boston, 1920), 171–72; Gerald Gunther (ed.), *John Marshall's Defense of McCulloch v. Maryland* (Stanford, Calif., 1969), 190–91.

It is often argued that it is the job of the judiciary to "adapt" the Constitution in order to keep it "current."[34] Such judicial finagling, we are assured, is all that has enabled the Constitution of 1787 to remain in effect. But when one closely analyzes this position, as Raoul Berger obviously has, one reaches an inescapable conclusion: the argument makes no sense. To argue that a written constitution is made viable only by ignoring both its literal text and original purpose is, in effect, to argue that the *idea* of a written constitution is meaningless. The truth of the matter is that the idea of a written constitution is not meaningless — but it is occasionally frustrating. And therein lies the permanent conflict. For a written constitution will always impede each generation's quest for moral and political progress: it is the means whereby political principles can hedge in popular passions.[35]

The contemporary willingness to justify judicial activism because of the good that it has done is to deny the fundamental wisdom of the American founding. The aim of those who framed the Constitution was to produce a document that they hoped would "last for ages." Their belief was that safe republican government depended upon a constitution that would be venerated by the people as "fundamental" and "paramount." To achieve such popular veneration, the framers recognized that the constitution would have to be a *written* one, and that there would have to be a popular presumption of the textual permanence of the document. Original intention and original meaning were held to be the primary means by which the written constitution could be kept limited. In this belief, men as politically opposed as Thomas Jefferson and John Marshall could stand united. A written constitution, Jefferson said, was "our peculiar security"; to Marshall, it was the "greatest improvement on political institutions."[36]

The idea of a written constitution of limited powers was considered a great improvement on political institutions because one cannot trust the good intentions of those who wield power. The entire point of a written document of clear, common language was to serve as a stumbling block to keep those in power from imposing their independent

34 In *Harper* v. *Virginia Board of Elections*, for example, Justice William O. Douglas argued that "the Equal Protection Clause is not shackled to the political theory of a particular era" (383 U.S. 663, 669 [1966]).

35 See *The Federalist*, Nos. 10, 51, 78-83.

36 Farrand (ed.), *Records of the Federal Convention*, I, 422; *The Federalist*, No. 53, p. 361, No. 78, p. 525; Thomas Jefferson to Wilson C. Nicholas, September 7, 1803, in A. Lipscomb (ed.), *The Writings of Thomas Jefferson* (20 vols.; Washington, D.C., 1905), X, 419; *Marbury* v. *Madison*, 1 Cranch 137, 178 (1803).

will on the society as a whole. The notion of a written constitution was the result of more than a few harsh experiences that had taught the founders a fundamental fact about human nature: "The disposition of mankind whether as rulers or as fellow citizens, to impose their own opinions and inclinations as a rule of conduct upon others, is so energetically supported by some of the best and some of the worst feelings incident to human nature, that it is hardly ever kept under restraint by anything but want of power."[37] A written constitution was considered to be the best defense to keep the good intentions of those who rule from running amok.

When the Constitutional Convention partitioned itself into the Committee of Detail and the Committee of Style to actually put these political principles into constitutional form, there was no confusion as to how to proceed. The provisions of the document — a document intended to be read and understood by governors and governed alike — had to be expressed in clear and common language. There would be no advantage in being vague. In order to make the Constitution as precise as possible, the framers opted for "common law terms of established and familiar meaning." Such terms, the framers thought, would serve very well to "*delimit* delegated power."[38]

That is not to say that the Constitution incorporated the common law *in toto*. When James Wilson and George Mason on different occasions sought to rely too heavily on the common-law tradition, the ever-vigilant James Madison urged caution, and delegates to the Convention followed suit. To rely on the common law alone, Madison thought, was both "vague" and "defective." No foreign law, he insisted, "should be a standard farther than is expressly adopted." To Madison's way of thinking, recurrence to the common law as a *general* standard for defining the specifics of the new document would not secure either "uniformity or stability in the law." To allow the common law to hover over the republic as an omnipotent spirit to be summoned down and invoked at will by Congress or the courts was to deny the desirability of an emphatically limited government. "Particular parts of the common law," Madison argued, "may have a sanction from the Constitution so far as they are necessarily comprehended in the technical phrases which express the powers delegated to the government," but to

37 John Stuart Mill, *On Liberty*, in Robert M. Hutchins (ed.), *Great Books of the Western World* (Chicago, 1952), 273.
38 Berger, *Death Penalties*, 61, 64.

go further would be to "sap the foundation of the Constitution as a system of limited and specified powers."[39] But when "technical phrases" from the common law were employed — such as habeas corpus, *ex post facto*, or cruel and unusual punishment — they were employed to give precise technical definition to the lines and limits of political power.

In *Death Penalties*, as in *Government by Judiciary*, Berger argues that a jurisprudence unanchored in the literal text of the Constitution is not merely a matter of rejecting old meaning for a new one; as an ideology, the logic of a living constitution strikes at the very heart of republican government. The Constitution is more than a mere bundle of compromises. It is a document that articulates a theory of politics under which the governed have consented to live, and its language reflects the principles to which the governed have consented. "Substitution by the Court of its own meaning for that of the Framers," Berger concludes, "changes the scope of the people's consent, displaces the Framers' value choices, and violates the basic principle of government by the consent of the governed." The result in his view has been the "dismal triumph of result-oriented jurisprudence over constitutionalism." The result is not justice; it is nothing more than a self-righteous judicial attempt at making an "end-run around popular government."[40]

Between them, Alexander Bickel, Ronald Dworkin, and Raoul Berger have created the terms of the debate in contemporary constitutional jurisprudence. To borrow the terms of Bickel, Dworkin stands at the forefront of a scholarly tradition dedicated to the achievement of moral self-government; Berger, in opposition, stands at the head of those who seek to perpetuate the morality of government by consent. On this jurisprudential battle line hangs the fate of the Constitution: does it matter or does it not?

THE QUEST FOR THE MORALITY
OF GOVERNMENT BY CONSENT

The most prominent commentators among those seeking the morality of government by consent have offered a "functional justification" for

39 Madison quoted in Gary L. McDowell, *Equity and the Constitution: The Supreme Court, Equitable Relief, and Public Policy* (Chicago, 1982), 55, 59, 60.

40 Berger, *Death Penalties*, 66, 22; William Rehnquist, "The Notion of a Living Constitution," in Gary L. McDowell (ed.), *Taking the Constitution Seriously: Essays on the Constitution and Constitutional Law* (Dubuque, Iowa, 1981), 78.

judicial review. They do not dismiss the Constitution out of hand, but neither are they willing to be inextricably bound to its historical meaning. The primary focus of these writers tends to be, as the foremost proponent of this school puts it, policing the processes of representation. "The tricky task," John Hart Ely has observed in his widely read, hotly debated, and frequently cited *Democracy and Distrust: A Theory of Judicial Review*, "has been and remains that of devising a way or ways of protecting minorities from majority tyranny that is not a flagrant contradiction of the principle of majority rule."[41]

But the solution is not to be found in a strict adherence to historical circumstance or the presumed intentions of the framers. The Constitution does not consist of self-contained units; the document, rather, "proceeds by briefly indicating certain fundamental principles whose specific implications for each age must be determined in contemporary context." Thus, a "clause-bound interpretivism" is simply impossible; the open-ended provisions of the document present an "invitation to look beyond their four corners [that] cannot be construed away."[42]

The privileges or immunities clause of the Fourteenth Amendment, for example, in Ely's hands becomes "a delegation to future constitutional decision-makers to protect certain rights that the document neither lists . . . nor even in any specific way gives directions for finding." Similarly, the equal protection clause of that amendment "amounts to a rather sweeping mandate to judge . . . the validity of governmental choices. And the content of the Equal Protection Clause — the answer to the question of what inequalities are tolerable under what circumstances — will not be found anywhere in its terms or in the ruminations of its writers." The Ninth Amendment, Ely insists, "was intended to signal the existence of federal constitutional rights beyond those specifically enumerated in the Constitution."[43] Recognizing, however, that to argue in behalf of "open-ended" provisions risks opening a constitutional Pandora's box, Ely seeks to find a legitimate source for discovering those fundamental values that the convenient silence of the Constitution demands each age to discover for itself.

Natural law as a source is at least problematic and at worst tragic. "Our society," Ely finds, "does not, rightly does not, accept the notion

41 John Hart Ely, *Democracy and Distrust: A Theory of Judicial Review* (Cambridge, Mass., 1980), 8.
42 *Ibid.*, 12, 1, 13.
43 *Ibid.*, 28, 32, 38.

of a discoverable and objectively valid set of moral principles . . . that could plausibly serve to overturn the decisions of our elected representatives." The argument for neutral principles also fails to satisfy; "requirements of generality of principle and neutrality of application do not provide a source of substantive content." They are, at best, a requirement for judicial behavior, not a source of constitutional judgment. To argue in behalf of reason is simply to urge making constitutional law into moral philosophy, and to assume that "judges are better than others at identifying and engaging in it."[44]

To believe, as Edmund Burke believed, that tradition provides the firmest foundation for law and legal meaning is too shallow a belief to aid in the contemporary quest for fundamental values. To believe that tradition is an adequate source is to believe that "yesterday's majority, assuming it was a majority, should control today's." Nor is mere popular consensus sufficient; indeed, to argue in behalf of consensus is to lose the quest at once. As Ely states, "It makes no sense to employ the value judgments of the majority as the vehicle for protecting minorities from the value judgments of the majority."[45]

Thus, it seems, this quest for fundamental values "with which to fill in the Constitution's open texture" is simply misbegotten; the argument for fundamental values is but the argument that the Court be transformed into a "council of legislative revision." The quest must not be a *substantive* quest for "goods or values deemed fundamental"; it must be a *procedural* one for a judicial broadening of "access to the processes and bounty of representative government."[46]

In Ely's view, "the original Constitution was principally dedicated, indeed . . . overwhelmingly dedicated to concerns of process and structure and not to the identification and preservation of specific substantive values." In sum, "The theme of the Colonists that justice and happiness are best assured not by trying to define them for all time, but rather by attending to the governmental processes by which their dimensions would be specified over time, carried over into our critical constitutional documents."[47]

In Ely's constitutional scheme, then, judicial review need not be feared; it is only a rather mechanical function. "Unblocking stoppages

44 *Ibid.*, 54, 55, 56.
45 *Ibid.*, 62, 69.
46 *Ibid.*, 73, 74–75.
47 *Ibid.*, 92, 89.

in the democratic process is what judicial review ought preeminently to be about," he concludes. Ely's constitutional jurisprudence, his jurisprudence of procedure, takes its life from no deeper a constitutional source than the famous footnote four that Justice Harlan Stone saw fit to append to his opinion in *United States* v. *Carolene Products Co.* The concerns Justice Stone expressed there over "legislation which restricts those political processes which can ordinarily be expected to bring about repeal of undesirable legislation," and legislation that is directed by "prejudice against discrete and insular minorities," form the substantive heart of Ely's procedural jurisprudence.[48] Ely explains that "the whole point of the approach is to identify those groups in society to whose needs and wishes elected officials have no apparent interest in attending. If the approach makes sense, it would not make sense to assign its enforcement to anyone but the courts. . . . We are a nation of minorities and our system thus depends on the ability and willingness of various groups to apprehend those overlapping interests that can bind them into a majority on a given issue; prejudice blinds us to overlapping interests that in fact exist."[49]

Ely espouses a "utilitarian theory of democracy" that, in his view, "will yield a brand of judicial review that is richer on the subject of equality than would be yielded by a theory of democracy that is geared to equality *simpliciter*." In the end, it seems, Ely's jurisprudence puts him more in the theoretical camp of John C. Calhoun than of James Madison. "Calhoun showed a keen understanding of the physics or mechanics of group politics. . . . The groups or portions have a kind of tangible relevance, easily detectable in their marchings and countermarchings across the political landscape. If there was a whole or entity, what could it be if not the sum of all these discrete groupings?" Further, Ely's process-oriented jurisprudence, like Calhoun's theory of concurrent majority rule results in a process of government being itself elevated to the common good. "Given a whole that is the arithmetical sum of its parts, given parts that are engrossed in the single-minded pursuit of their self-interest, narrowly conceived, it is hardly cause for amazement that the highest common denominator — the *only* common denominator — is an agreement to persist with the game."[50]

48 *Ibid.*, 117. For the history of this footnote see Alpheus Mason, *Harlan Fiske Stone: Pillar of the Law* (New York, 1956), 512–15.
49 Ely, *Democracy and Distrust*, 151, 153.
50 John Hart Ely, "Democracy and Judicial Review," The Rocco J. Tresolini Lecture in Law, Lehigh University, March 8, 1982; Ralph Lerner, "Calhoun's New Science of Politics," *American Political Science Review*, LV (1963), 918.

Along with Ely, Jesse Choper has also offered a new "functional" theory of judicial review. Like Ely's *Democracy and Distrust,* Choper's *Judicial Review and the National Political Process* seeks to take us back to the central issue: the problems and prospects presented by the doctrine of judicial review in a government based upon a limited written Constitution. Unlike other writers who have focused on the manner in which American politics has been influenced by the exercise of judicial power, both Choper and Ely endeavor to offer explicitly a reconsideration of the core of judicial power, judicial review.

Like Ely, Choper's primary concern is with the processes of government and the role of the judiciary in protecting the rights of minorities against the often crushing weight of majority rule. But unlike Ely, Choper goes further than merely arguing for the Court to preserve minority access to the political arena from which they might otherwise too easily be excluded. At the heart of Choper's work are his federalism, separation, and, most importantly, individual rights proposals.[51]

Choper's unifying theme is that because of its political isolation, the Supreme Court is the "most effective guarantor" of the rights of minorities. He believes it should bolster this role by refusing to enter disputes that arise between national power and states' rights (his federalism proposal), and between the president and Congress (his separation proposal). By restricting the exercise of its power to what Choper sees as its legitimate functional province (his individual rights proposal), the Court will strengthen its position in the national political processes.

Although he does not support the judiciary's expressing its will in the areas falling under either the federalism or the separation proposals, Choper has no qualms about judicial activism in the area under the individual rights proposal. As he puts it, "It is the very rare Supreme Court decision that affirmatively mandates the undertaking of government action. And even when it does—as when the judiciary fashions a reapportionment scheme or institutes a school desegregation plan—it substitutes its own program for a popularly sponsored one that it finds constitutionally deficient." But this is precisely the point—is it ever legitimate for judicial power to be exercised in a *prescriptive* rather than a merely *proscriptive* manner in the areas of constitutional adjudication? Further, even though such occurrences may be rare (and there are many who would disagree), they also tend to be

51 Jesse Choper, *Judicial Review and the National Political Process* (Chicago, 1980), 1–59.

33

among the most politically divisive actions that the Court undertakes. If the purpose of this work is to strengthen what Tocqueville called the "moral force" of the Court in the community, this question needs to be seriously considered.[52]

Although Choper rightly stresses the necessity of judicial restraint in the areas of federalism and separation of powers, his defense of these doctrines is weak. Apparently, in such civil liberties cases as *Brown* v. *Board of Education, Baker* v. *Carr,* and *Miranda* v. *Arizona,* the limiting features of federalism must yield; similarly, in such cases as *Wesberry* v. *Sanders* and *United Steelworkers* v. *Weber,* the doctrine of separation of powers is equally mutable.[53] A basic weakness of Choper's work stems from his half-hearted defense of the principles of federalism and separation of powers. This, in turn, stems from his understanding of the political theory of the Constitution.

Choper's entire project, not unlike that of Ely, is aimed at defending the institutional presence of judicial review within the context of "traditional democratic philosophy." That is difficult to do; it may be impossible. The difficulty is that Choper's analytical perspective blurs a fundamental theoretical distinction that to the framers of the Constitution was of deepest practical significance: the distinction between *democratic* theory and *republican* theory.[54] The problem arises from that which Choper's language obscures. For the framers, the Constitution rested upon a republican rather than a democratic foundation. And in light of republican political theory, the notion of an independent judiciary exercising judicial review appears far less suspect. An independent judiciary, like a unitary executive and an indirectly elected Senate, is an integral feature of sound republican government.

This confusion over democratic and republican principles leads Choper to lose sight of another premise that is central to the framers' science of politics. The problems they saw as inherent in popular government — especially majority tyranny — did not lead them to abandon the cause of a popular form of government resting upon majority rule. It did, however, lead them to seek a "republican cure for the diseases most incident to republican government." Their cure was a set of institutional arrangements that would "filter" popular opinion so that it

52   *Ibid.,* 25; Alexis de Tocqueville, *Democracy in America,* trans. G. Lawrence, ed. J. P. Mayer (New York, 1966), 139.

53   347 U.S. 483 (1954); 349 U.S. 294 (1955); 369 U.S. 186 (1962); 384 U.S. 436 (1966); 376 U.S. 1 (1964); 443 U.S. 193 (1979).

54   *The Federalist,* No. 10, pp. 61–64; No. 51, pp. 350–51.

would be more likely to issue in *qualitative* rather than merely *quantitative* majority rule. It was the entire system, as James Madison explained, that was to work to "secure the public good and private rights" against the "superior force of an interested and overbearing majority."[55]

Ultimately, the deepest problem with Choper's analysis, like Ely's, Bickel's and Dworkin's, to name but three, is that it perpetuates the notion that the protection of individual rights depends more upon the judicial power than upon the entire constitutional system. It is not clear that this notion is correct, nor is it clear that it is safe. In his quest to restrain and bolster judicial power, Choper leaves open, perhaps inadvertently, the door the Court repeatedly has used to enter the political arena in order to dabble in the most sensitive areas of public policy.

Believing, as perhaps most do, that since 1937 the Supreme Court has been the "citadel of American freedom, equality and justice," Louis Lusky set out to "justify virtually everything the Court had done since . . . 1937." But once embarked on the task, he found such a justification impossible. On review, it struck Lusky that "the justices have given serious cause for suspicion that they have come to consider the Court as above the law." With the decision regarding abortion in 1973, *Roe* v. *Wade*, Lusky became convinced that a vast majority of the justices were "ready to engage in freehand constitution-making in order to combat what they viewed as basic injustice, in any field where they thought the Court's intervention would be helpful and effective."[56] His intended justification for judicial power became a sharply critical attack on judicial activism.

In *By What Right?*, Lusky shows himself to be of the camp of Alexander Bickel: a solid liberal who believes deeply in the rule of law and the necessary role of the Court and who cannot tolerate judicial pretensions that undermine both the rule of law and the role of the Court. Benjamin Cardozo once remarked that there is a tendency in ideas to expand to the limits of their logic; Lusky, like Bickel, grew alarmed as the logic of liberal jurisprudence began to pass its rightful constitutional limits.

At the bottom of Lusky's criticism is the damage judicial activism does to the principle of the rule of law. Like Herbert Wechsler, Lusky

55 *The Federalist*, No. 10, pp. 57, 64.
56 Louis Lusky, *By What Right?* (Charlottesville, Va., 1975), vii, 14.

is a proponent of "neutral principles." The very idea of the rule of law, he argues, reflects "a preference for objectively understandable rules that lead to similar results on similar facts." Thus, judicial decisions must rest — and must be known to rest — "on analysis and reasons quite transcending the immediate result that is achieved."[57]

This view embraces the belief that there is "a great difference between interpretation of the constitutional *text* and exercise of implied judicial power to make new constitutional rules." Cases like *Roe* v. *Wade* pose a serious threat to this logic of judicial restraint. Indeed, that case was "a spectacular display of constitution-making." Further, and most important, *Roe* v. *Wade* is an opinion that cannot be discounted as "casual error"; rather, it reveals "the *deliberate* determination to impose on the nation the will of seven men who have not been elected by the people."[58] In Lusky's view, the *Marbury* v. *Madison* conception of judicial review no longer fits the way judicial power is exercised.

Far tougher than Ely and Choper, Lusky is willing to call a spade a spade: "If a textual provision of the Constitution (including its preamble and its amendments) sets forth in explicit terms neither an objective of the Constitutors [framers] relevant to the case at hand, nor an applicable standard of conduct, but the court . . . articulates a constitutional objective or prescribes a constitutional standard of conduct, we have a case, not of judicial lawmaking but of constitution-making." Modern constitutional adjudication includes "announcement of rules plainly (and sometimes admittedly) not derived from constitutional text, and creation of new legal rights whose adjudication provides an occasion for promulgation of new legal rules. In short, the *power* of judicial review is now broader than the *duty* to enforce the expressed will of the Constitutors."[59]

Reviewing the history of the Court since 1937 was a particularly troublesome task for Lusky. In 1938, at the time of the footnote to the *Carolene Products* decision, Lusky had been the law clerk to Justice Stone.[60] Recognizing in retrospect that the "*Palko* concept of the Court's responsibility for ordered liberty, and the *Carolene Products*

---

57 *Ibid.*, 2, 4.
58 *Ibid.*, 22, 15, 19.
59 *Ibid.*, 67, 73.
60 See Berger, *Government by Judiciary*, 275–78.

justification of the Court's special role, facilitated liberation from the hobbles of precedent," Lusky is not as willing as Ely to find the essence of American government in that by-now-infamous footnote. Indeed, it was from this source that the recent trend toward constitutional change without constitutional amendment has gained so much of its moral force.

> The *Carolene Products'* footnote . . . contained the germs of two distinct theories for expanding the Court's protection of individual freedoms and immunities. One is the *implied power theory,* which accepts the necessity of justification in terms of the Court's special fitness to reach desirable goals. It is a rational theory in the sense that it calls for measurement of the Court's performance against objective standards. The other has come to be known as the *preferred position theory*, which affirms that certain rights are in some sense more important than others—so important that the Court should protect them against impairment by any governmental organ—and that the Court's power to select them is limited only by its ability to manipulate words contained in the Constitution. It dispenses with the need for justification in terms of explained necessity, and assumes that any meaning the Court chooses to ascribe to the sacred text will be accepted as revelation. Faith, not reason, is to be the foundation of public acquiescence.

Ultimately, Lusky's answer to the question, by what right does the Court revise the Constitution? is no more limiting than the theories of Ely or Choper or Bickel. Judicial revision is legitimate "if and only if the Court submits to the restraint imposed by overriding principles and does not proceed on an *ad hoc* basis to implement the Justices' personal views of national policy. The overriding principles, and the limits upon them, are prescribed by the concept of implied judicial power."[61] The problem is that Lusky's answer is no answer at all; by his theory, constitutional restraint on judicial power is nearly nonexistent.

The dilemma faced by those who most prominently have sought to develop theories consistent with the morality of government by consent is that they refuse to go so far as to embrace firmly the original intentions that lay behind the language of the Constitution. The reason, it seems, is that to do so would demand sacrificing certain decisions with which they agree but that would be rejected by a theory as absolute as that of Raoul Berger. To the degree to which they fail to embrace so strict a view, they open the door to those who seek not the morality of government by consent but moral self-government.

61 Lusky, *By What Right?* 114, 111–12, 21.

THE QUEST FOR MORAL SELF-GOVERNMENT

The greatest obstacle to those who argue in behalf of moral self-government is the Constitution; it often simply gets in the way of so-called moral progress. The reason is clear: "moral progress" is but another phrase for "new rights," rights not in the letter of the Constitution and usually not even in its original spirit. The Constitution, however, poses no insurmountable obstacle to these moral advocates; they simply explain it away. What is important to constitutionalism is not following procedures established by the Constitution but the achievement of substantively just ends. In short, their jurisprudence — "result-oriented jurisprudence" — boils down to this: the end justifies the means. And in their jurisprudential view, the primary means is first and foremost a liberated judicial power.

Laurence Tribe, perhaps the most prominent (certainly the most public) of the defenders of this constitutional faith, has described the development of contemporary constitutional jurisprudence this way: "No longer content with securing justice by defining the inherent limits and internal boundaries of governmental institutions, after the Depression, judges and advocates were consumed by the search for an alternative conception of the just in matters of governmental power. The years since 1937 are best understood in terms of that search; its triumphs and failures mark the history of modern constitutional thought." Tribe argues that constitutional theorizing since 1937 has been characterized by "a shift from the minimal state to the affirmative state." In thinking about the new understanding of the affirmative, positive state, Tribe argues that "without judicial prodding, whatever positive constitutional duties might exist would too often and too easily be ignored by public authorities short-sightedly wedded to the status quo."[62]

Like Ely, Tribe views the Constitution as characterized if not by "open-ended provisions" then, worse, by "gaping holes left by constitutional text and history." But unlike Ely, Tribe sees no reason to stick with a procedural defense of judicial power; for Tribe the role of the Court is not merely keeping open the channels of representative government. The Courts have an obligation to fill those "gaping holes" with "a substantive vision of the needs of the human personality." To Tribe, it is neither the text nor the intention of the Constitution that

62 Laurence Tribe, *American Constitutional Law* (Mineola, N.Y., 1978), 6-7, 9.

gives guidance on these matters. It is the "social context of asserted rights" that is "crucial to the formation of the 'substantive judgment' the judges are called upon to exercise."[63]

At its deepest level, Tribe's jurisprudential quest is for a substantive defense of the ideologically pleasing notion of a living Constitution:

> The Constitution is an intentionally incomplete, often deliberately indeterminate structure for the participatory evolution of political ideals and governmental practices. . . . The best we can hope for is to encourage wise reflection—through strict scrutiny of any government action or deliberate omission that appears to transgress what it means to be human at a given time and place. . . . "[N]eutral" principles of structure are worth embracing only to the extent that the substantive human realities they help bring about are worth defending. . . . [A] fairly common characteristic of the evolution of a substantive constitutional ideal is that its "optimal" structural embodiment is likely to undergo significant change from one era to the next. . . . [T]he structural norms through which a substantive value is best preserved may be expected to vary over time and from one setting to the next.[64]

The argument is clearly designed to diminish whatever lingering importance the literal Constitution still has in the minds of "judges and advocates." The "highest mission" of the Court, Tribe concludes, is to form a more perfect union; to achieve this, judges—and those who persuade the judges, the advocates—have a moral obligation to exploit the Constitution's "necessarily evolutionary design" in order to nurture and direct "the living development of constitutional justice." At a minimum, the Courts must free themselves from the shackles of the status quo that tends to be "insufficiently sensitive to human rights and needs." This is nothing more than what Philip Kurland called the "egalitarian ethos"—with a vengeance.[65]

The underlying premise that has come to dominate the quest for moral self-government is that judges, more than other officials, are best suited to discover the "public values" that are "the necessary accompaniment of the moral freedom of the individual." Individual liberty of the sort that informed the social contract theory on which the Constitution was originally deemed to rest is no longer sufficient. The quest is for a morality essentially communitarian in its ethos. The public values sought as a source of principled content for the open-ended Constitution have little if anything to do with institutional ar-

63 *Ibid.*, 12, 889, 891.
64 *Ibid.*, 111, 892, 1137-39.
65 *Ibid.*, iv, iii, v.

rangements or conventional understandings of freedom. What is sought are values that constitute nothing less than the "moral ambience of the social world we can only inhabit together."[66] The movement for moral self-government has inspired something analogous to evangelical fervor among its leaders.

One of the most remarkable efforts—both for its candor and its radical approach—has been that of Michael Perry. In a series of essays, but most clearly in his book *The Constitution, the Courts, and Human Rights*, Perry has pushed his arguments for a functional justification for "noninterpretive" judicial review especially in cases involving human rights. Unlike most others, Perry is willing to put his constitutional cards on the table. While others contrive elaborate theories that attempt to connect noninterpretive review with the Constitution, either to its letter or its spirit, Perry is forthright. There is "neither a textual nor a historical justification . . . for *any* noninterpretive review, including that exercised by the Court in human rights cases."[67]

The justification for such "constitutional policy-making by the Supreme Court" is, and can only be, a functional one. As Perry puts it, "If noninterpretive review serves a crucial governmental function, perhaps even an indispensable one, that no other practice can realistically be expected to serve—and serves it in a manner that accommodates the principle of electorally accountable policy-making—then that function constitutes the justification for the practice."[68] Put a bit more simply, the end justifies the means.

At the bottom of Perry's jurisprudence is his unfaltering commitment to the belief in moral progress. Perry finds that the commitment to "moral evolution" is approaching a nearly "religious" level in American political life. His central thesis bears out his belief. The basic function of noninterpretive review, he argues, is to deal with

> those political issues that are also fundamental moral problems in a way that is faithful to the notion of moral evolution . . . not simply by invoking established moral conventions but by seizing such issues as opportunities for moral reevaluation and possible moral growth. . . . My essential claim . . . is that noninterpretive review in human rights cases enables us to take

66 Frank Michelman, "Politics and Values or What's Really Wrong with Rationality Review?" *Creighton Law Review*, XIII (1979), 487, 509, 402.

67 Michael Perry, *The Constitution, the Courts, and Human Rights* (New Haven, Conn., 1982), 91–92.

68 *Ibid.*, 2.

seriously—indeed is a way of taking seriously—the possibility that there are right answers to political-moral problems. As a matter of comparative institutional competence, the politically insulated federal judiciary is more likely, when the human rights issue is a deeply controversial one, to move us in the direction of a right answer (assuming there is such a thing) than is the political process left to its own devices, which tends to resolve issues by reflexive mechanical reference to established moral conventions.[69]

Like Tribe, Perry's quest is to move beyond the status quo—those "established moral conventions"—to something better. Thus, as with Tribe, Perry has no affection for appeals to tradition or consensus. The Court, in moving toward the desired result in a given case, may well make appeals to tradition and consensus; however, such claims are "little more than rhetorical points of departure and quite malleable points at that." The process of judicial thinking must be "dialectical," moving inexorably forward toward a new and higher moral ground. The Court, in Perry's view, has an obligation to resolve "moral problems not simply by looking backward to the sediment of old moralities, but ahead to emergent principles in terms of which fragments of a new moral order can be forged."[70]

The heart of Perry's jurisprudence is not merely the fusion of moral philosophy with constitutional law that Dworkin had called for; it is the replacement of constitutional law by moral philosophy. Reliance on consensus or established moral conventions to guide judicial decisions is inadequate because the "moral sensibilities of the pluralistic American polity typically lag behind, and are more fragmented than, the developing insights of moral philosophy and theology."[71] Thus, it seems, academic musings should count for more in the determination of constitutional rights than does the Constitution itself. James Madison is replaced by John Rawls.

Divorced from the text and intention of the document, the judges' decisions are to be guided by nothing more than their "own moral vision" and their "own values." This, however, obviously poses something of an institutional dilemma; if the old *Marbury* v. *Madison* standard of judicial review struck many as undemocratic, Perry's scheme is far beyond the democratic pale. Thus, there is a need to establish that this judicial philosophizing is not simply freewheeling. To his

69 *Ibid.*, 93, 99.
70 *Ibid.*, 101–102, 98, 112.
71 *Ibid.*, 111.

credit, Perry attempts to make the case that his notion of judicial review is politically safe.

> The tension between noninterpretive review and the principle of electorally accountable policy-making seems especially acute in light of the fact that the decisional norms the Court elaborates and enforces in the exercise of such review are derived not from some authoritative source of value external to the Court, to which "the people" subscribe, but from the justices' own values. [T]he course of significant political control to which . . . the Court's exercise of noninterpretive review is subject [is] the legislative power of Congress . . . to define, and therefore to limit, the appellate jurisdiction of the Supreme Court and the original jurisdiction of the lower federal courts. . . . [T]he national legislative power over the jurisdiction of the federal judiciary is, in Charles Black's apt phrase, "the rock on which rests the legitimacy of the judicial work in a democracy," and so the Court must not subject jurisdiction-limiting jurisdiction to noninterpretive review; that is, it must not measure such legislation by its own value judgments.[72]

The problem with his solution is that once judges are unleashed to exercise noninterpretive review, it is not clear that they could be called back from exercising it over legislation that would seek to limit their jurisdiction. Surely, the debate over the power of Congress to tamper with jurisdiction is such to reveal even to Perry the fact that there are powerful advocates who would argue against him. Ely, for one, has suggested that congressional power over the jurisdiction of the Court is "so fraught with constitutional doubt" as to render it an unlikely weapon against alleged judicial usurpations. Herman Pritchett has gone so far as to suggest that it "is generally believed that any legislation seriously curtailing the appellate jurisdiction of the Supreme Court would be declared unconstitutional by the Court, for such action would challenge its standing as head of the judicial branch and its authority to make final interpretations of the Constitution."[73]

But the reason Perry's solution is inadequate is because he does not seem to intend it as a solution at all. "Interpretivists," he suggests, "are dogmatists for whom there are clear orthodoxies and heresies." For most people, he alleges, it is the "experience of what works . . . and not the text of the Constitution or some original understanding [that] is the ultimate criterion of the propriety, the legitimacy, of any governmental function, including any judicial function." What Perry seeks is obviously not a restrained Court in any conventional sense.

---

72 *Ibid.*, 118, 123, 125, 128.
73 Ely, *Democracy and Distrust*, 46; C. Herman Pritchett, *The American Constitutional System* (5th ed.; New York, 1981), 70.

He writes, "Noninterpretive review cannot serve the function I have attributed to it unless the Court is staffed by persons capable of subjecting established moral conventions to critical reevaluation — thoughtful, deliberate individuals not wedded to a closed morality, but committed to the notion of moral evolution and are themselves open to the possibility of moral growth."[74]

The ultimate failure of Perry's jurisprudential enterprise is the result of his assumption that the meaning of "moral growth" or "moral evolution" is self-evident; it is not. As Peter Schultz has said of Perry's effort, it fails to recognize that the meaning of "moral growth" is the subject of intense debate. It is not clear, for example, why a woman's right to abortion is necessarily a higher or more morally evolved principle than the right to life of the unborn. Perry fails to realize that "the question of 'moral evolution' like that of 'social progress' [that encouraged progressives such as Roscoe Pound, Oliver Wendell Holmes, and Benjamin Cardozo] is ultimately a political question. To disjoin moral evolution and political philosophy, as Perry suggests, is necessarily unsatisfactory. Put differently, any adequate defense of 'human rights' must be, ultimately, a political defense, a defense of a particular kind of society." In the end, Perry's morally evolutionary jurisprudence is the motion of good intentions but is without direction. A limited form of *constitutional* government demands more. Without the presence of authoritative restraints that are external to their own values judges will be left "to roam at large in the trackless field of their own imaginations."[75]

Following somewhat in the Perry tradition, though without Perry's candor, is Philip Bobbitt. Like Perry — and Dworkin and Tribe — Bobbitt's goal is to develop a system of constitutional ethics; and, like the others, it soon becomes clear that the emphasis is on ethics and not on the Constitution. In his book *Constitutional Fate,* in order to develop his "theory of the Constitution," Bobbitt first breaks contemporary constitutional jurisprudence down into the essential arguments that are most often put forward to justify particular decisions. The primary arguments — historical, textual, doctrinal, structural, and prudential — Bobbitt finds at once useful and insufficient.

The historical argument, the intentions of the framers, is, he believes, ultimately "more effective as rhetoric, than as decision proce-

74 Perry, *The Constitution, the Courts, and Human Rights,* 142–43, 187, 143.

75 Peter Schultz, Review of Michael Perry's *The Constitution, the Courts, and Human Rights* in *Benchmark,* I (1984), 56–58; James Kent, *Commentaries on American Law* (4 vols.; New York, 1826), I, 321.

dure." Thus, with a quick brush, that old stumbling block is pushed aside. The textual argument — that concerning the present sense of the language of the Constitution — Bobbitt finds more useful. Falling back on the open-endedness of the document, he finds the primary virtue of this approach is that it "provides a valve through which contemporary values can be mingled with the Constitution." Going even further beyond the Constitution, the doctrinal argument — an argument whereby principles of judicial decision are derived from precedent or commentary on precedent — allows the "ideology of the common law" to guide constitutional interpretation. It is not what the founders said or meant in the Constitution but what earlier judges said — and, one presumes, what professors have said they meant. The goal here is not the explication of the original intention of those who framed the provision in question, but rather the creation of doctrines that can serve the "general purposes sought by the drafters."[76]

The structural argument is "largely factless"; it depends upon "deceptively simple logical moves from the entire constitutional text rather than from one of its parts." The structural argument gathers its rhetorical force from "general assertions about power and social choice." It seems this "potent" line of constitutional theorizing is somewhat akin — to borrow Justice Holmes's words — to the "brooding omnipresence" of the Constitution; something that hovers above our constitutional world but is not, strictly speaking, of it. The final traditional argument, the prudential argument, is, like the structural argument, a step or so removed from the Constitution's text or the framers' intentions. What is demanded by this line of thinking is less principle than prudence. "Prudential argument," Bobbitt concludes, "is constitutional argument which is actuated by the political and economic circumstances surrounding the decision."[77] Like Holmes's common law, the argument here reflects the "felt necessities of the times."

In the end, the typology of arguments offered in *Constitutional Fate* reveals a steady movement away from the Constitution toward rather unfettered judicial opinion. From the historical to the textual to the doctrinal to the structural to the prudential arguments, the Constitution fades in significance. Thus the logical next step: the ethical argument. The object of this line of argument is simple: it is an effort to "help justify particularly difficult and otherwise troublesome deci-

76 Philip Bobbitt, *Constitutional Fate* (New York, 1982), 24, 36, 77.
77 *Ibid.*, 74, 61.

sions," decisions that without recourse to this ethical argument are simply "incomprehensible."[78]

To be sure, these ethical arguments are not moral ones. Although they are often "expressions of considerable passion and conviction," they are not merely a matter of personal predilection or ideological commitment. Ethical arguments are, in a sense, the deepest of possible constitutional arguments. An ethical argument, Bobbitt explains, is a "constitutional argument whose force relies on a characterization of American institutions, and the role within them of the American people. It is the character, or *ethos*, of the American polity that is advanced in ethical argument as the source from which particular decisions derive. . . . [E]thical arguments [are] appeals to an ethos from which rules may be derived, whether they are embodied in the text or not."[79]

At first glance this theory of constitutional ethics would seem to exert a delimiting influence on judicial power insofar as one might think our ethos as a people sprang from a distrust of all governmental power that had something to do with our original understanding that as we are not angels, neither are angels to govern us. But this ethos of individual liberty against political power is not the ethos of which Bobbitt speaks; indeed, the constitutional ethos that lies behind his proposed ethical argument is nothing so fixed as the ethos of limited government. For the "ethical argument . . . changes through time as the constitutional ethos changes."[80]

Thus, Bobbitt's intention becomes clear. The ethical argument is not a way to limit judicial power but is intended to expand it. The ethical argument, he states, "is an important resource to the creative judge." However much he would have it seem that ethical arguments can serve to "confine" judges and lawyers, it is not confinement in any ordinary sense. It "confines" lawyers and judges to a process that is inherently liberating. Although it might keep them tied to a common "legal grammar," that grammar is itself endlessly evolutionary and progressive in its essential character. For example, in making the ethical argument a text is often used "not for its own force, but rather as evidence of a more general principle from which a nontextual argument was derived." Thus, "the textual provision of the Eighth Amendment which forbids cruel and unusual punishment is evidence of a

78 *Ibid.*, 93, 169.
79 *Ibid.*, 94, 125.
80 *Ibid.*, 221.

more general constitutional ethos, one principle of which is that government must not physically degrade the persons for whose benefit it is created."[81] The object of the ethical argument is, simply, to create new "nontextual" rights.

The "constitutional" basis for the ethical argument turns out to be nothing other than the line of logic Justice William O. Douglas employed in *Griswold* v. *Connecticut*. Rights, it seems, emanate from the cracks and crevices of the constitutional text and form penumbras. The Ninth Amendment, it is alleged, makes it "quite clear that the Bill of Rights and the body of the Constitution do not exhaustively enumerate the specific rights of persons." Substantive due process is essential, "given the necessarily partial list of rights which is the Bill of Rights." In the final analysis, the constitutional grammar that is supposed to confine lawyers and judges is but the imprecise grammar of moral ambiguity.[82]

What is most important in Bobbitt's jurisprudence of constitutional ethics is the spirit it exudes: "The particular Bill of Rights we have serves, and seems chosen to serve, as more than a text for exegesis. It acts to give us a constitutional motif, a cadence of our rights, so that once heard we can supply the rest on our own. . . . Constitutional decisionmaking has . . . an expressive function. . . . The Constitution is our Mona Lisa, our Eiffel Tower, our Marseillaise. . . . [I]f we accept the expressive function of the Court, then it must sometimes be in advance of and even in contrast to, the largely inchoate notions of the people generally." The quest is to make the Constitution more democratic by making it more "participatory." It is made more participatory by replacing the literal text and the framers' intentions by the various creative arguments that "come to be proffered by counsel who would otherwise lose or risk loss in the competition of previously accepted arguments." Thus, it is up to the judicial process to save popular government from its own moral naïveté. What is needed is less a sweaty, bustling marketplace of ideas than a chic boutique of academic theories. "In our theories," Bobbitt warns, "shall be our fates."[83]

One of the most ideologically revealing testaments to appear in behalf of moral self-government is Arthur Selwyn Miller's *Toward Increased Judicial Activism: The Political Role of the Supreme Court.*

---

81 *Ibid.,* 137, 169, 175, 142, 143.
82 *Ibid.,* 144, 147, 153.
83 *Ibid.,* 177, 185, 211, 225, 242.

46

This is an effort at home with the constitutional moralism of Ronald Dworkin and Michael Perry. Its message is simple: "More judicial activism is both necessary and desirable . . . if it furthers the attainment of human dignity."[84] Miller's thesis is hardly new and never shocking; it is, on the whole, merely a reconsideration of the old, result-oriented argument for judicial activism, but stripped of its sheeplike clothing. What others have said, Miller shouts.

The problem with *Toward Increased Judicial Activism* is far deeper, however, than its tone; the dilemma here is a substantive one. The basic weakness with Miller's line of reasoning is that it takes too lightly (totally disregards is probably more accurate) the fundamental purpose for which the Constitution was written. The purpose of a *written* constitution, those who wrote it understood, was to limit all governmental power. Although the most obvious political danger would be power wielded by a factious majority or a clique of shrewd mercantile manipulators, the framers were not blind to the fact that a good bit of injustice could be inflicted in the name of justice as well. Power wielded in a spirit of altruism or in defense of ideological beneficence could be equally disastrous to the liberty of individuals and balanced popular government. As a result of this harsh fact of political life, the framers sought to create a government that would be, as James Madison put it, obliged to control itself. There was too great a likelihood of institutional self-righteousness to leave power too unencumbered. The founders knew all too well that men in power often confuse (in Thomas Sowell's words) "broader powers with deeper insight." Good intentions are not sufficient for good government.[85]

When the founders declared that power is of an encroaching nature, they meant all political power, judicial no less than executive or legislative. Transgressing the lines of constitutional limitations can be tolerated no more in pursuit of allegedly just ends than in pursuit of demonstrably unjust ends. For it is precisely the adherence to politics within those limits imposed by the Constitution that the regime is pushed into a position that will generally be deemed *just* because it will not be arbitrary.

The main thrust of Miller's argument is that the procedural notion

84 Arthur Selwyn Miller, *Toward Increased Judicial Activism: The Political Role of the Supreme Court* (Westport, Conn., 1982), 9.

85 *The Federalist*, No. 51, p. 349; Thomas Sowell, *Knowledge and Decisions* (New York, 1980), 303.

of justice inherent in the institutional balance created by the Constitution is an insufficient basis for securing a just regime; what must be had is a dedication to justice that transcends the institutional contrivances of the founding generation — "men long dead," Miller reminds us. What Miller sees as justice, however, is in fact but an ideological stance; it is perhaps the Constitution's greatest achievement that it keeps such opinions, passions, and interests as Miller's ideology in check.[86]

Miller has long been known as one of the foremost advocates of the ideology of a living constitution as opposed to what the founders understood to be a constitution of fixed principles. To the founders, the Constitution's principles, though fixed, were of a nature sufficient to allow for political change under them. What the ideology of a living constitution argues is not that the Constitution — by its own terms and language — allows political solutions to the exigencies time inevitably will bring, but that the terms and the language of the Constitution itself must be understood as changing. The means of achieving this is to celebrate the Court as a continuing constitutional seminar. But this is really nothing more elevated than suggesting that the judges are properly considered seers and soothsayers pondering the darkest mysteries of nature and making the Constitution and its polity to so conform. The dilemma posed by such a line of thinking is that to those cautious men who framed and ratified the document, judges were no more expected to be Platonic guardians than any other governmental official.[87] They knew something that Miller and the others of this school ignore: political tyranny can issue from any office where men unfettered by constitutional chains wield great power over the lives of other men — judges no less than anyone else.

The value of *Toward Increased Judicial Activism* is that it lays bare the truth behind the various theories proffered in pursuit of moral self-government. From Dworkin to Tribe to Perry to Bobbitt, the message is the same as Miller's; in putting so starkly what the others have sought to obscure, Miller provides an important insight into the underlying ideology of the moral self-government theorists.

What each of these jurisprudential constructions has in common is the belief in an unwritten but morally controlling Constitution, one that must take precedence over the written Constitution of 1787. At

---

86 Miller, *Toward Increased Judicial Activism*, 5.
87 *The Federalist*, No. 49, p. 340.

their deepest level, the various theories seek to resuscitate and legiti-mate the notion of a higher-law background to the Constitution whereby to elevate the spirit above the letter of the document as *the* source for judicial decision making. The strongest theoretical and his-torical foundation for the moral self-government school is perhaps to be found in the work of Thomas Grey. Grey first explicitly posed the question of whether we have an unwritten Constitution in 1975; by 1978 he had embarked on answering affirmatively.[88]

The question of greatest importance in contemporary jurisprudence has come to be whether the Constitution left in judicial hands "the considerable power to define and enforce fundamental rights without substantial guidance from Constitutional text and history." For Grey, no less than the others, the answer must be yes. But Grey cuts deeper than the others to offer some semblance of a historically justifiable grant of such judicial power. "For the generation that framed the Constitution," he argues,

> The concept of a "higher law," protecting "natural rights," and taking prece-dence over ordinary positive law as a matter of political obligation, was widely shared and deeply felt. An essential element of American constitu-tionalism was the reduction to written form — and hence to positive law — of some of the principles of natural rights. But at the same time, it was generally recognized that written constitutions could not completely codify the higher law. Thus in the framing of the original American constitutions it was widely accepted that there remained unwritten but still binding principles of higher law. The Ninth Amendment is the textual expression of this idea in the fed-eral Constitution. As it came to be accepted that the judiciary had the power to enforce the commands of the written Constitution when these con-flicted with ordinary law, it was also widely assumed that judges should en-force as constitutional restraints the unwritten natural rights as well.[89]

But the problems of Grey's theoretical and historical foundation — and thus the problem of those whose theories rest either explicitly or implicitly on his — is that he does not properly understand "the doc-trine of modern natural rights and natural law from which . . . we derive our understanding of constitutionalism." For what the modern constitutional theorists assert as natural law, natural rights, human rights, or a constitutional ethos are not assertions of modern natural rights as they were understood by the philosophic forefathers of the

88   Thomas Grey, "Origins of the Unwritten Constitution: Fundamental Law in American Revolutionary Thought," *Stanford Law Review*, XXX (1978), 843.
89   Grey, "Do We Have an Unwritten Constitution?" 714, 715–16.

American Constitution, especially Thomas Hobbes and John Locke. There can be in American constitutionalism an "unwritten constitution" to which the judges especially, or perhaps only, are privy only at the expense of limited constitutional government. Such assertions of what the "unwritten Constitution" demands, in the end, "can only be private opinions of what is unwritten"; modern constitutionalism, deriving as it does from modern natural rights theories, demands that such private opinions be rendered politically impotent lest such private judgment — isolated as it is from the deliberative political processes — replace the adequately "refined and enlarged" public opinion as the force of popular government. To allow the ascendance of private opinions as the rule of law, whether by legislators, presidents, or judges, is to risk tyranny.[90]

The search for fundamental constitutional values as the source of legitimacy for judicial activism has not been limited to those who seek to formulate new constitutional theories strictly speaking. Going beyond the effort to justify the judicial creation of new rights has been a scholarly effort to justify the judicial power to create innovative remedies whereby those innovative rights are given concrete application; it is meaningless to argue, for example, that the cruel and unusual punishment clause of the Eighth Amendment is a constitutional expression of the value of human dignity unless the judges can order prisons and other public facilities to make their policies — from water temperature to dietary balance — conform.

FROM MORAL SELF-GOVERNMENT
TO SUBSTANTIVE CIVIL PROCEDURE

One branch of the new constitutional theorizing has come to surround what has been called the new "public law litigation" or, perhaps more accurately, structural or institutional reform litigation.[91] Whatever the name, the object is the same: to reform a public institution — a school system, a prison, or a mental hospital, for example — that is seen as threatening some constitutional "value." The willingness on

90 Walter Berns, "Judicial Review and the Rights and Laws of Nature," in Philip B. Kurland *et al.* (eds.), *The Supreme Court Review: 1982* (Chicago, 1983), 58.

91 See Abram Chayes, "The Role of the Judge in Public Law Litigation," *Harvard Law Review*, LXXXIX (1976), 1281; Chayes, "Public Law Litigation in the Burger Court," *Harvard Law Review*, XCVI (1982), 4; Owen Fiss, "The Forms of Justice," *Harvard Law Review*, XCIII (1979), 1; Fiss, *The Civil Rights Injunction* (Bloomington, Ind., 1978).

the part of the courts to entertain such suits has led to a not-so-subtle transformation of the traditional lawsuit and the rise of what may be called substantive civil procedure.

Abram Chayes, one of the leading forces in the new procedural movement, has neatly outlined the differences between the traditional lawsuit and the new institutional suit. The old lawsuit was characterized by the following attributes:

> First, litigation is bi-polar: two parties are locked in a confrontational, winner-take-all controversy. Second, the process is retrospective, directed to determining the legal consequences of a closed set of past events. Third, right and remedy are linked in a close, mutually defining logical relationship. Fourth, the lawsuit is a self-contained entity. It is bounded in time: judicial involvement ends with the determination of the disputed issues. It is bounded in effect: the impact is limited to the [two] parties before the court. Finally, the whole process is party initiated and party controlled. The judge is passive, a neutral umpire.

The new public lawsuit stands in striking contrast:

> First, the party structure and the matter in controversy are both amorphous, defined ad hoc as the proceedings unfold rather than exogenously determined by legal theories and concepts. Second, the temporal orientation of the lawsuit is prospective rather than historical. Third, because the relief sought looks to the future and is corrective rather than compensatory, it is not derived logically from the right asserted. Instead, it is fashioned ad hoc, usually by a quasi-negotiating process. Fourth, prospective relief implies continuing judicial involvement. And because the relief is directed at government or corporate policies, it will have a direct impact that extends far beyond the immediate parties to the lawsuit.

The result is a lawsuit that becomes a sprawling judicial enterprise with a life of its own. It is characterized by an "array of competing interests and perspectives organized around a number of issues." And in the middle of this political swirl sits the judge, who of necessity in the new suit has become a political power broker.[92]

This transformation of the lawsuit has necessitated a transformation in the procedural arrangements that had for quite a long time governed the judicial process. The loosening of the procedural requirements for standing, class actions, intervention, declaratory judgment, and equitable relief was essential to the development of public-law litigation. As the claims raised in a lawsuit became less concrete

---

92 Chayes, "Public Law Litigation in the Burger Court," 4–5.

and more abstract, and as the lawsuit itself moved away from being a strictly judicial exercise and edged toward becoming a legislative one, the channels of access to, and the procedures of, the judicial process had to be made to accommodate the new role of the courts. Bickel's "passive virtues" were taught to be "active vices."

These procedural modifications were made possible only by the diminution of the importance of the "case or controversy" requirement of the Constitution. For this explicit requirement is the constitutional key to understanding the forms and limits of judicial power. Simply put, the doctrine historically had restricted the jurisdiction of the federal courts to matters that were considered justiciable, disputes that would admit of judicial resolution. Thus a strict interpretation of what constitutes a case or controversy necessarily limited the exercise of judicial power; a judiciary willing to flex its political muscle first had to loosen its procedural shackles.

Traditionally, the case or controversy requirement was understood to include a judicial power to resolve abstract legal and constitutional issues "but only as a necessary by-product of the resolution of particular disputes between individuals."[93] This traditional understanding has been reversed so that the resolution of abstract legal or constitutional issues is very often the primary objective and the resolution of a particular dispute between individuals merely a by-product. The focus of litigation is less often an individual who seeks to vindicate a constitutional *right* than a group that seeks to have a constitutional *value* declared. As a result, the individual adverse litigant pressing his claim is often lost in the judicial shuffle to remedy a "social condition," such as limited urinal space in a prison, that is held to threaten "important constitutional values" such as the humane treatment of those incarcerated.

The theoretical cornerstone of this strand of contemporary constitutional jurisprudence, substantive civil procedure, justifies judicial power not as a necessary means of resolving concrete disputes but as a necessary political power to oversee and, when necessary, transform society in light of abstract principles. The new jurisprudence holds that the "central function" of judicial power is the "determination of the individual's claim to 'just' treatment."[94] The intellectual force of this procedural jurisprudence has been sufficient in lawsuits dealing

93 Lea Brilmayer, "The Jurisprudence of Article III: Perspectives on the Case or Controversy Requirement," *Harvard Law Review*, XCIII (1979), 297, 300.
94 *Ibid.*

with public questions to shift the emphasis from the character of the parties to the character of the claim; the issue has become more important than the litigants.

The desire is to achieve social reform through the judicial resolution of ideological challenges to the status quo. Indeed, some confess that institutional reform litigation "is premised on a skepticism about the existing distribution of power and privilege in American society." Such litigation "reflects doubt as to whether the status quo is in fact just." The object is thus simple: "The goal of this new mode of litigation is the creation of a *new* status quo."[95]

Central to this new mode of litigation is the belief that "widespread access to the courts for people as well as ideas is desirable." This belief, followed through to its logical end, has demanded a transformation in the way the plaintiff to a suit is viewed. The traditional plaintiff (defined, at least in part, by traditional procedural rules), characterized by a concrete and vested legal interest in a particular dispute, has been replaced by the "ideological" plaintiff. The new plaintiff in public law litigation comes without the traditional personal stake in the case; he comes primarily with an ideological interest in its outcome. The primary motivation of this plaintiff is to bring his theoretical weight to bear on the courts as they pursue their "task of evolving a principled conception of lawful society." A kind of social and political altruism is the motive force behind the ideological plaintiff. Like judges when they make law and scholars when they propose new rules of law, the ideological plaintiff, in seeking to influence a judicial decision, is guided by his "vision of society as it is and as it might be." The "sociological realities" of contemporary constitutional litigation demand nothing less. If the courts are going to endeavor to restructure society, then it is in the courtroom rather than in the legislative chamber that competing ideologies must clash.[96]

The demise of any constitutionally rooted view of what constitutes a case or controversy has allowed the emergence of — indeed, the dominance of — the new public-law litigation. In such lawsuits the trial

95 Owen Fiss, "The Social and Political Foundations of Adjudication," in Goldwin and Schambra (eds.), *How Does the Constitution Secure Rights?*, 8.

96 Louis Jaffe, "The Citizen as Litigant in Public Actions," *University of Pennsylvania Law Review*, CXVI (1968), 1033, 1034; Jack Weinstein, "Litigation Seeking Changes in Public Behavior and Institutions — Some Views on Participation," *University of California, Davis Law Review*, XIII (1980), 231; Mark Tushnet, "The Sociology of Article III," *Harvard Law Review*, XCIII (1979), 1698, 1726.

judge has "increasingly become the creator and manager of complex forms of ongoing relief." The result has been a transformation in kind of the judicial decree; it has become "pro tanto, a legislative act." The decree has become the hallmark of the new jurisprudence and constitutional litigation: "The decree seeks to adjust future behavior, not to compensate for past wrong. It is deliberately fashioned rather than logically deduced from the nature of the legal harm suggested. It provides for a complex, ongoing regime of performance rather than a simple, one-shot, one-way transfer. Finally, it prolongs and deepens, rather than terminates, the court's involvement with the dispute." Thus the role of the judge has been transformed as well as the decree and the mode of litigation generally. In "actively shaping and monitoring the decree, mediating between the parties, developing his own sources of expertise and information, the trial judge has passed beyond even the role of legislator and has become a policy-planner and manager."[97]

This jurisprudence of substantive civil procedure, with its new model of public-law litigation, celebrates litigation as a "political forum" and the court as a "visible arm of the political process." And the new looser procedural arrangements are applauded for enabling greater citizen participation in the judicial decision-making process. Thus judicially included in the processes of government, the individual citizen will presumably no longer suffer the sense of "helplessness" and "exclusion" our vast and bureaucratic government tends to make him feel.[98] Paradoxically, popular, democratic government is somehow enhanced by the denigration of the more popular institutions as the loci of political decision making.

The legitimacy of this procedural jurisprudence and reform litigation hinges to a great degree on the acceptance of its fundamental maxim that it is the proper role of a judge to declare constitutional *values* as much as to protect constitutional *rights*; and this is what those advocates of moral self-government actually mean when they urge that rights be taken "seriously." A constitutional right differs from a constitutional value in that a right is more concrete than a value. A constitutional right, for example, is the right to be secure against cruel and unusual punishments; constitutional values are, as one federal judge put it, "broad and idealistic concepts of dignity, civi-

---

97 Chayes, "The Role of the Judge in Public Law Litigation," 1284, 1297.
98 *Ibid.*, 1298; Jaffe, "The Citizen as Litigant in Public Actions," 1044.

lized standards, humanity, and decency." The problem is that a punishment may be neither cruel nor unusual but still offend the moral sensibilities of those who seek humane treatment. This shift in emphasis from rights to values has had a significant impact on constitutional litigation. Such "particularized and discrete events" as "the black child turned away at the door of the white school, or the individual act of police brutality" are no longer the stuff of most constitutional litigation. While such traditional plaintiffs are still necessary to trigger the lawsuit or "may be" of "evidentiary significance" (living examples of the challenged "social condition") their true value is little more than openers of the door for the courts to enter the realm of political deliberation and public choice.[99]

The courts, it is believed by proponents of this new jurisprudential view of the world, are the institutions best suited to respond to grievances about public programs that threaten constitutional values. The courts possess "a special kind of substantive rationality" that enables them to declare constitutional values and to make the polity conform.[100] There is a superficial attractiveness to the proposition that the federal courts and the Supreme Court in particular should see their primary task as the giving of meaning to constitutional values rather than as the mundane business of resolving ordinary disputes. There is something to be said for a "feeling" of national commitment to legality and constitutionality that is typically associated in the public mind with the judicial determination of issues. It is a grand scheme of judicial power, one that gives a certain degree of political comfort. Unfortunately, this scheme is totally at odds with the Constitution. For a Court that understands its primary function as the declaration of constitutional or public values is a Court that has come to believe that the Constitution is only what it says it is.

On one hand, the new remedial jurisprudence insists that "the task of the judge is to give meaning to constitutional values, and he does that by working within the constitutional text, history, and social ideals. He searches for what is true, right, or just." Lest the judge think he may do whatever he pleases, the new jurisprudence carries the admonition that "the judicial role is limited by the existence of constitutional values." Since it is the function of the judge to give meaning

99 *Jackson* v. *Bishop*, 404 F. 2d. 571, 579 (8th Cir. 1968), as quoted in *Estelle* v. *Gamble*, 429 U.S. 97, 102; Fiss, "The Forms of Justice," 18.
100 Fiss, "The Forms of Justice," 34.

to the values that are in turn the limitations on his power to declare those values, it is clear that in the new jurisprudence the only restraint upon a judge is his sense of self-restraint. But self-restraint is no restraint at all. As the anti-Federalist Brutus warned so long ago, political men rendered independent of "every power under heaven . . . generally soon feel themselves independent of heaven itself."[101] This is the reason the new constitutional jurisprudence of substantive civil procedure not only has very little to do with the Constitution but is actually destructive to its fundamental principles.

In the end the new constitutional remedial or procedural jurisprudence is nothing more than an attempt to "do justice" at the expense of the idea of a written constitution intended to endure for the ages unless specifically altered by the solemn and authoritative act of formal amendment. This new constitutional jurisprudence is indeed the idea of a "living constitution with a vengeance"; it is nothing more than a "formula for making an end-run around popular government."[102]

THE QUEST FOR JUDICIAL STATESMANSHIP

The problems raised by most of the contemporary constitutional theorists and the judicial interpretations they seek to support have struck a growing number of commentators as far deeper than merely institutional or political problems; they reflect, at their deepest level, "a philosophic degeneracy in American society at large . . . that is ultimately destructive of the very idea of a constitution." The rise of the idea of "noninterpretive judicial review," both from those who advocate the morality of government by consent and those who seek to develop a scheme for moral self-government, has led to a scholarly tradition that denies any need for "fidelity to an objective, intelligible Constitution." Thus, a constitutionalism bereft of a Constitution has arisen. As one observer has put it, "while they may be rivulets of genuine constitutionalism in the profession of legal scholarship, those rivulets hardly constitute the mainstream."[103]

---

101 *Ibid.,* 9, 11; Brutus in Herbert J. Storing (ed.), *The Complete Anti-Federalist* (7 vols.; Chicago, 1981), 2. 9. 145. Storing employs a unique system of citation followed in these notes. 2. 9. 145 represents Volume 2, item number 9, paragraph 145. 9, paragraph 145.

102 Rehnquist, "The Notion of a Living Constitution," 78.

103 Paul Peterson, "Is the Constitution Really What the Judges Say It Is?" (Paper presented at the annual meeting of the American Political Science Association, New York, N.Y., September, 1981), 1, 2.

To counter this aconstitutional constitutionalism, the newer critics have sought to restore a belief in the literal, objective, and intelligible Constitution of 1787. The argument, simply put, is that the language of the document matters, the intentions of those who framed and ratified the Constitution and its amendments matter — and that both text and intention matter more than any unleashed judicial opinion that seeks to infuse the Constitution with contemporary morality. The thrust of this school of thought is to refute Charles Evans Hughes's oft-quoted aphorism that while we are under a Constitution, "the Constitution is what the judges say it is."[104] In this jurisprudence of judicial statesmanship, the Constitution is understood to embrace a theory of politics far more substantial and permanent than the fleeting opinions of judges and justices. The task of judicial statesmanship is to explicate that political theory, not to ignore it.

Judicial statesmanship is not merely a crabbed literalism. This approach recognizes that there will inevitably be disagreements over what the Constitution means. Constitutional truth is more than a simplistic assertion of historical intention. Paul Peterson states: "To believe in an objective, intelligible Constitution is not to deny that there may be room for discretion. It is not to deny that there is room where reasonable people may disagree. But belief in an objective, intelligible Constitution maintains that such disagreement is based within the Constitution. While there may be legitimate rival interpretations of particular clauses, there can also be interpretations so groundless, from the perspective of the Constitution, that they are neither reasonable nor legitimate."[105] The advocates of judicial statesmanship appreciate the power of the Constitution to have separated the likes of Marshall and Jefferson, of Hamilton and Madison. But even as those celebrated members of the founding generation stood divided over constitutional meaning, they stood, and understood each other to be standing, on *constitutional* grounds. For both the "strict constructionists" and the "loose constructionists" were *constructionists*; "noninterpretivism" under a written constitution would have struck both camps as an absurdity.

Those who argue in behalf of judicial statesmanship seek to effect a fusion — in their view, a rejoining — of the two dominant strands of

104 Hughes quoted in Henry J. Abraham, *The Judicial Process* (4th ed.; New York, 1980), 324.
105 Peterson, "Is the Constitution Really What the Judges Say It Is?," 3-4.

57

contemporary constitutional jurisprudence; they see morality of government by consent as ultimately inseparable from moral self-government. Protecting the representative institutional arrangements and procedures of the Constitution is insufficient to achieve good government; however, moral decisions wrenched free of those representative institutions and procedures are not only politically suspect, they are constitutionally illegitimate. The proper political goal is not simply popular government or good government in some moral sense detached from the Constitution: the quest is for good popular government under the terms of an "objective and intelligible Constitution."

This jurisprudence of judicial statesmanship is, in effect, an attempt at the political restoration of the Court. On one hand, it is urged that the Court abandon any aconstitutional activism; on the other, it is demanded that the Court shun any demand for aconstitutional restraint. The Court, no less than the other more representative branches of the government, was intended to have a *political* role in the American constitutional order. For the Court to assume itself to be politically autonomous and morally empowered to revise the Constitution is intolerable. But it is equally intolerable for the Court to blindly defer to the representative branches: the justices and judges have no constitutional obligation to let the people go to hell if they choose, as Holmes once quipped. The role of the judge or justice is to bring the principles of the Constitution to bear on the particular circumstances that may confront him in the various cases and controversies that he is called upon to decide, but he must never forget, as Marshall said, that it is a Constitution he is expounding. The proper judicial function is for the Court "to think through for the nation the meaning of the fundamental principles or values of the American political order." While this task will inevitably eventuate in activism, it will be a *constitutional* activism that does not lead to a "depreciation of the Constitution." Such constitutional activism, its proponents argue, is ultimately consistent with an understanding of constitutional limitations on the Court's power.[106]

At the heart of this line of constitutional theorizing is the belief that

106   Peter Schultz, "Activism, Restraint, and Judicial Statesmanship: The Role of the Supreme Court in the American Political Order" (Paper presented at the annual meeting of the Pennsylvania Political Science Association, Shippensburg State College, Shippensburg, Pa., April, 1982), 7–8; Sotirios Barber, *On What the Constitution Means* (Baltimore, 1984), 218; John Agresto, *The Supreme Court and Constitutional Democracy* (Ithaca, N.Y., 1984), 134.

"the Constitution is and must be partially open to higher political values and that it should be construed accordingly where possible." Thus the original intention is not limited to the "immediate wants and fears" of those who framed the Constitution and its amendments; original intention, properly understood, extends to the "political aspirations of the framers," to their ideals and values more than to their immediate interests.[107] The object of this jurisprudence is to restore to the judiciary its originally intended role as an "active but checked, not self-restrained and passive instrument of government." There is a meaning to the Constitution that is deemed independent of what anyone might want it to mean. There is, then, beyond constitutional language or the original, immediate intentions of the framers, a discernible constitutional logic; the Constitution not only was designed to express the aspirations of the framers, it was designed to move the polity toward those aspirations. And that is the proper role of judicial statesmanship.[108] The Constitution is no dead letter but a living, dynamic organ of governance. It is, as John Agresto describes it,

> more than a system of political organization or a catalogue of governmental restraints; it is an architectonic statement of laws and principles under which people bind themselves and their futures with the strongest of formal ties. . . . The highest and most complex attribute of judicial review is its potential ability to help the nation as a whole govern itself and direct its progress in the light of constitutional principles; not only principles that need to be applied to new circumstances, but principles that — like the colonial ideas of sovereignty and equal rights and even constitutionalism itself — might grow, develop, and expand.[109]

The purpose of the Court is to remind us of "our enduring civic principles." But this argument for judicial statesmanship is not an argument for government by judiciary. To argue that "judicial quiescence is a constitutional mistake" is not to suggest that judicial supremacy is tolerable or legitimate, or so the advocates of this theory argue. But to suggest that principles "unfold themselves in time" is to brush dangerously close to the full-blown ideological commitment to a living constitution whose meaning depends only upon time, circumstance, and judicial whim. Thus, judicial statesmanship must have its

---

107 Barber, *On What the Constitution Means*, 12, 36, 33, 37.
108 Agresto, *The Supreme Court and Constitutional Democracy*, 38; Barber, *On What the Constitution Means*, 23, 30.
109 Agresto, *The Supreme Court and Constitutional Democracy*, 54, 55.

roots, if not in the narrow, original literal intention of the framers, then in the principles or the spirit of the Constitution as that was recognized and celebrated by the framers. The development of our fundamental principles through the judicial process must be along lines charted by the original founding commitment to the principles of limited, republican government that issued in the Constitution of 1787. Our constitutional future, in a sense, was predestined by our revolutionary past.[110]

"Although change in our understanding of the Constitution will prove to be an essential part of living by the Constitution," Sotirios Barber points out,

> one cannot deny the difference between change that is and change that is not consistent with a foundational set of values. . . . If our present constitution is open to anything and everything, it does not make sense as the law it claims to be, and constitutionalism itself serves only as a salutary myth. . . . Looking for guidance in the Constitution requires only a belief in the possibility of ascertaining what the Constitution means; those who believe it can mean nothing in particular cannot take it seriously as law. Those who take it seriously as law must believe it means something, however much they may debate that meaning or oppose it politically.[111]

Thus the proper judicial task is not to transplant new principles and ideals in the well-tilled political soil of the Constitution; the proper task is to be found in "sheltering and nourishing" the original ideas and principles until they can be brought to complete constitutional fruition.[112]

To avoid what has been rightly called the "intellectual mushiness" of most contemporary constitutional scholarship, those who seek a resuscitation of judicial statesmanship look to the judicial statesmanship of John Marshall. For it was Marshall as chief justice who first undertook not only the resolution of cases but the judicial articulation of the fundamental principles of the Constitution. The cardinal tenet of this juridical faith was best captured by Marshall in *Marbury* v. *Madison*: "The judicial power of the United States is extended to all cases under the Constitution. . . . Could it be the intention of those who gave this power to say that in using it the Constitution should not be looked into? That a case arising under the Constitution should be

---

110 *Ibid.*, 97, 138, 143.
111 Barber, *On What the Constitution Means*, 36.
112 Agresto, *The Supreme Court and Constitutional Democracy*, 143.

decided without examining the instrument under which it arises? . . .
This is too extravagant to be maintained. . . . It is apparent that the
Framers of the Constitution contemplated that instrument as a rule
for the government of courts, as well as of the legislature."[113]

However much Marshall is understood to serve as the model of
judicial statesmanship, it is ultimately upon Abraham Lincoln and his
brand of *constitutional* statesmanship that this school of juridical
thought comes to depend. To understand the principles of the Constitution as aspirational and as unfolding themselves in time, and not
merely as matters of judicial predilection, demands a recovery of an
appreciation for the relationship between the Constitution and the
Declaration of Independence. For the Constitution is understood as
merely completing in concrete institutional terms the principled political work begun by the Declaration. Thus, to understand the inherent
logic of the Constitution and to explicate its ideals and principles, one
must first come to grips with the philosophic premises of the Declaration. And it was Lincoln, not Marshall or Jefferson or Madison, who
best understood this connection between the Constitution and the
Declaration.

The appeal to Lincoln and thus to the principled foundation of the
Constitution achieves two things for this school of constitutional theorists not available to Dworkin, Perry, Berger, Ely, Choper, Tribe, or
Bickel. First, it provides a standard whereby to offer a principled condemnation of occasionally errant exercises of judicial review; second,
it establishes a principled source for constitutional interpretation,
which, while not *explicit* in the Constitution, is at least not *external* to
the Constitution in the same way, say, the moral theory of John Rawls
is external to the Constitution. The Constitution *was*, after all, understood to derive logically from the principles of the Declaration; it *was*
an attempt to follow the maxim that governments are instituted
among men to secure those inalienable but insecure natural rights
granted to naturally equal men by their Creator. In this sense, the
jurisprudence of judicial statesmanship is an appeal to the original
philosophy of natural rights that the Constitution was understood to
embrace.

It was in reaction to the infamous *Dred Scott* decision of March 6,
1857, that Lincoln first had occasion to develop fully his theory of

113 Peterson, "Is the Constitution Really What the Judges Say It Is?," 10; *Marbury
v. Madison*, 1 Cranch 137 (1803).

constitutionalism. This theory celebrates at once popular government *and* those principles that lie beyond and check popular government. On June 26, 1857, in Springfield, Illinois, Lincoln spoke against Justice Taney's opinion in *Dred Scott* and against the defense of that opinion Stephen A. Douglas had offered in Springfield on June 12.

Chief Justice Taney, in his opinion in the Dred Scott case, admits that the language of the Declaration is broad enough to include the whole human family, but he and Judge Douglas argue that the authors of that instrument did not intend to include negroes, by the fact that they did not at once, actually place them on an equality with the whites. Now this grave argument comes to just nothing at all, by the other fact, that they did not at once, or *ever afterwards* actually place all white people on an equality with one or another. And this is the staple argument of both the Chief Justice and the Senator, for doing this obvious violence to the plain unmistakable language of the Declaration. I think the authors of that notable instrument intended to include *all* men, but they did not intend to declare all men equal in *all respects*. They did not mean to say all were equal in color, size, intellect, moral developments, or social capacity. They defined with tolerable distinctness, in what respects they did consider all men created equal — equal in "certain inalienable rights, among which are life, liberty, and the pursuit of happiness." This they said, and this meant. They did not mean to assert the obvious untruth, that all were then actually enjoying that equality, nor yet, that they were about to confer it immediately upon them. In fact they had no power to confer such a boon. They meant simply to declare the *right*, so that the *enforcement* of it might follow as fast as circumstances should permit. They meant to set up a standard maxim for free society, which should be familiar to all, and revered by all; constantly looked to, constantly labored for, and even though never perfectly attained, constantly approximated, and thereby constantly spreading and deepening its influence, and augmenting the happiness and value of life to all people of all colors everywhere. The assertion that "all men are created equal" was of no practical use in effecting our separation from Great Britain; and it was placed in the Declaration, not for that, but for future use. Its authors meant it to be, thank God, it is now proving itself, a stumbling block to those who in after times might seek to turn a free people back into the hateful paths of despotism. They knew the proneness of prosperity to breed tyrants, and they meant when such should re-appear in this fair land and commence their vocation they should find left for them at least one hard nut to crack. I have now briefly expressed my view of the *meaning* and *objects* of that part of the Declaration of Independence which declares that "all men are created equal."[114]

114 Roy Basler (ed.), *The Collected Works of Abraham Lincoln* (7 vols.; New Brunswick, N.J., 1953), II, 405–406. For the classic study of Lincoln's principled constitutionalism see Harry V. Jaffa, *Crisis of the House Divided* (Garden City, N.Y., 1959).

The crux of this constitutional jurisprudence of judicial statesmanship, as Lincoln said, is not limited to the meaning of the principles of the Constitution but extends to the objects those principles are, in time, intended to achieve. "It is the meaning of the ideas, not the particulars to which they were once attached that we must first understand when we interpret the Constitution."[115] It is not toward supplanting those ideas but toward fulfilling them that judicial statesmanship is directed.

The deepest problems with the quest for a theory of judicial statesmanship is that the line between statesmanship and partisanship in judicial matters is no more precise than in other political matters. It is difficult for this school to provide a very firm foundation from which to criticize judicial opinions so that the criticism does not sound simply like political disagreement toward judgments with which the critic does not agree. It is not sufficient to dismiss *Roe* v. *Wade*, for example, as "a transparent attempt to impose a constitutionally unfounded policy preference on the unwilling words of the Constitution."[116] Why is such an opinion deemed "unfounded"? Surely the logic of Justice Douglas in discovering the right to privacy in *Griswold* v. *Connecticut*, upon which the *Roe* v. *Wade* decision rests, is not as strikingly dissimilar to the historically unfolding principles of the judicial statesmanship school as its proponents would have us believe. In the end the arguments of the jurisprudence of statesmanship in behalf of their version of constitutional activism do little to restrict and much to encourage judicial activism of the more traditional Warren Court variety. The only difference between principled activism and unprincipled activism, apparently, is the partisan character of the creative judge in question. But judicial statesmanship has certainly been claimed for Justice Harry Blackmun in *Roe*, for Justice Douglas in *Griswold*, and even for Chief Justice Taney in *Dred Scott* — as well as for Chief Justice Marshall in *McCulloch* v. *Maryland*. The line between noninterpretive review and the fundamentally loose construction view of this school is not so broad and dark a demarcation as their theory of constitutionalism assumes. The jurisprudence of judicial statesmanship is but an invitation for a shrewd judge to step across.

To an extraordinary degree the work of Alexander Bickel remains the rubric under which most contemporary constitutional theorizing has

115 Agresto, *The Supreme Court and Constitutional Democracy*, 149.
116 *Ibid.*, 157.

taken place. Each theorist who has endeavored to provide a functional, moral, or political justification for judicial activism seems to have been doomed to stumble around in the intellectually darkened constitutional anteroom that Bickel left unlocked; that constitutional confusion has resulted is the most that could ever have been expected. In their rush to give legitimacy to the judicial tampering with the Constitution that has characterized constitutional law for the last quarter of a century, contemporary constitutional theorists have failed to take the Constitution as seriously as did the generation that framed and ratified it. Laboring as they all have along the continuum established by Bickel from the morality of government by consent to moral self-government, the most prominent new constitutional theorists (with the exception of Raoul Berger) have contributed a good deal to the political emergence and intellectual support of what Paul Mishkin has termed the "reforming judiciary."[117]

The problem of judicial activism that issues from this notion of a "reforming judiciary" can only be addressed adequately once the intended role of the judiciary in the political science of the Constitution is considered. For it is only under the rubric of the Constitution and its concerns to achieve republican justice that the judiciary's powers and limits can be understood. Ultimately, the practical role of the independent judiciary must be reconciled with the theoretical demands of limited republican government.

117 Paul J. Mishkin, "The Reforming Judiciary" (Paper presented at a conference entitled "Judicial Power in the United States: What are the Appropriate Constraints?" held at the American Enterprise Institute, Washington, D.C., October 1–2, 1981).

TWO

THE CONSTITUTION AND THE
REPUBLICAN IDEA OF JUSTICE

When James Madison proclaimed in no uncertain terms in *The Federalist* that "Justice is the end of government . . . the end of civil society," he did not mean the idea of justice that had moved the philosophical wheels of antiquity. He meant justice in the modern sense:
Justice not so much a *substantive* as a *procedural* matter. The substantive element of this idea of justice was limited to a concern for devising
a system of government that would secure individual liberty; the concern was more with natural rights than with natural right. The object
was not so much the cultivation of the good or excellent and fully
human life as it had been for antiquity; rather it was the modern vision
that was restricted to the protection of the conditions of mere (as opposed to the good) life. The necessity, Madison told the delegates to
the Constitutional Convention, was to provide "more effectually for
the security of private rights and the steady dispensation of Justice."
For Madison, as for most of his generation, justice had more to do
with due process of law than with virtue. It was an idea of republican
justice that demanded a "government with powers to act and a structure to make it act wisely and responsibly."[1]

Justice, in the sense in which it was most commonly used by the founding generation, was an idea that evoked visions of a government fairly,
safely, and decently administered. The great achievement of their science of politics, they thought, would be the reduction of arbitrariness
in the conduct of public affairs. The kernel of their understanding of
justice was the concept of *ordered* liberty. A regulated liberty was
sought, Richard Henry Lee said, "so that the ends and principles of
society may not be disturbed by the fury of a Mob or by the art, cun-

---

1 Jacob E. Cooke (ed.), *The Federalist*, (Middletown, Conn., 1961) No. 51, p. 352,
hereinafter cited as *The Federalist*; Max Farrand (ed.), *The Records of the Federal Convention of 1787* (4 vols.; New Haven, Conn., 1936), I, 134–35; Herbert J. Storing, "The
Constitution and the Bill of Rights," in M. Judd Harmon (ed.), *Essays on the Constitution of the United States* (Port Washington, N.Y., 1978), 48.

ning, and industry of wicked, vicious, and avaricious men."[2] The idea of republican justice was directed at avoiding the twin dangers of anarchy and despotism.

Regulated or ordered liberty meant to the founders *constitutional* liberty. A properly constructed constitution was necessary to achieve the central concern of their political science: The substitution of the rule of law for the rule of men. The ultimate effect of this change would be to distract man's attention from a concern for abstract justice and *natural* rights to a more pragmatic concern for legality or constitutionality and the security of *civil* rights. It was far safer politically, they thought, for public discourse to center on concrete (if occasionally ambiguous) provisions of the written law rather than on more fundamental and abstract principles.

The founders appreciated the fact that the quest for justice (in the ancient sense) in the conduct of human affairs had inspired man's most heroic efforts and noblest political accomplishments. But they knew also that it had often led societies blindly over the edge into the abyss of tyranny. Too many hands and heads had been lopped off, too many bodies battered and burned in the name of justice for them to try to found a durable regime on that noble cause. The philosophy of antiquity might have been inspiring, but its politics had been brutal and bloody. It was for this reason that the "American political order was deliberately tilted to resist . . . the upward gravitational pull of politics toward the grand, character-ennobling but society-wracking opinions about justice and virtue."[3]

But even the founders' more modest understanding of republican justice was not without its political difficulties. Man would still opine about justice; and those opinions could and probably would be politically divisive. As Madison said, "As long as the reason of man continues fallible, and he is at liberty to exercise it, different opinions will be formed. As long as the connection subsists between his reason and his self-love, his opinions and his passions will have a reciprocal influence on each other; and the former will be objects to which the latter attach themselves." But opinions and passions are only half the problem: "The diversity in the faculties of men from which the rights of

2   Richard Henry Lee to Thomas Lee Shippen, February 12, 1794, in James Curtis Ballagh (ed.), *The Letters of Richard Henry Lee* (2 vols.; New York, 1914), II, 576.
3   Martin Diamond, "Ethics and Politics: The American Way," in Robert Horwitz (ed.), *The Moral Foundations of the American Republic* (Charlottesville, Va., 1977), 56.

property originate, is not less an insuperable obstacle to a uniformity of interests. The protection of these faculties is *the first object of government*."[4] This first object of government — the protection of the diverse faculties among men — is, of course, inextricably linked to the true end of government, justice. Indeed, in the political science of the Constitution, justice is the protection of those different faculties.

In *The Federalist*, after his pronouncement that justice is the end of both government and civil society, Madison explained the connection between the first object of government and the end of government by noting that justice "ever has been, and ever will be pursued, until it be obtained or until liberty be lost in the pursuit." Thus, because "liberty . . . is essential to political life," justice is not possible in the absence of liberty.[5] The only just regime is the liberal regime. And to be liberal a regime must not only acknowledge but actively protect the natural differences among men.

This is the same understanding as that expressed in the Declaration of Independence. Because all men are created equal, and because they are endowed with the inalienable rights to exercise the powers and abilities with which they are blessed by nature, governments are instituted. According to both the Declaration and the Constitution the only legitimate function of government is to protect those rights. Convention is understood as being placed in service of nature, not to transform it but only to secure those things that nature has left insecure.

Paradoxically, the most aggravating practical problem of popular governments issues from the fundamental requirement of all just regimes. By protecting those faculties of men, government enhances the development of different interests, interests that can become contentious. It is clear, then, that the simple protection of the exercise of the diverse faculties of men is not sufficient to create a just regime. The reason for this, Madison explained, is that this "protection of difference and unequal faculties of acquiring property" results in "the possession of different degrees and kinds of property"; the various and unequal distribution of property has a pervasive influence on "the sentiments and views of the respective proprietors." The result is an inevitable "division of the society into different interests and parties." Thus, Madison concluded, "the latent causes of faction are sown in the nature of man."[6]

4 *The Federalist*, No. 10, p. 58.
5 *Ibid.*, No. 51, p. 352; No. 10, p. 58.
6 *Ibid.*, No. 10, p. 58.

Although the most common source of factions is economic there are other sources as well. Man's "unfriendly passions" are often kindled by the "most frivolous and fanciful distinctions" such as race and nationality; by a "zeal for the different opinions concerning religion, concerning Government and many other points, as well of speculation as of practice; an attachment to different leaders ambitiously contending for power; or to persons of other descriptions whose fortunes have been interesting to the human passions." The common denominator of all faction is man's ability and inclination to think and opine about the just and the good. For the most vexatious factions are not those made up of mercantile manipulators who shrewdly plot to disrupt or direct the commonwealth for their own narrow, selfish gain. Madison's teaching is deeper than that. Besides, such factions will generally always be a minority of the whole society, and thus the republican scheme of majority rule will be able to check such combinations. The most politically vexing factions are those made up of individuals who come to unite in common cause around a particular view of what constitutes the common good. The view may be distorted by economics, religion, a sense of benevolence and altruism, or any other subjective element, but the crucial point is that those participating *think* their view is right. The political dilemma of popular government is not that man is simply vicious or mean-tempered as much as he is self-interested. And self-interest goes well beyond economic interest; it includes man's attachment to his *ideas.* Man tends to mistake his *perception* of what is just for what actually *is* just. The greatest tyrants have usually been moved by a view of justice, however distorted or warped. As Alexander Hamilton argued, "people commonly *intend* the public good. This often applies to their very errors." The reason the distribution of property is the most prominent source of faction is that those who "labour under all the hardships of life and secretly sigh for a more equal distribution of its blessings" do so because they think a more equal distribution is more just.[7] It is not simple avarice that will prompt these demands; they will nearly always be justified as appeals to the moral principle of equality.

Man becomes so passionately attached to his opinions, simply because they are his, that compromise is difficult. When a sufficient

7 *Ibid.*, 59; No. 71, p. 482; Farrand (ed.), *Records of the Federal Convention*, I, 422.

number of men share a particular view of the public good, they can become politically disruptive; if their number should amount to a majority, they can become tyrannical. The reason is that the tendency in men is to impose their opinions on others as a general rule of conduct. Unfortunately, this tendency is so pervasive and persistent "that it is hardly ever kept under restraint by anything but want of power."[8]

A similar thought lay at the heart of one of Madison's famous teachings in *The Federalist*:

> When a majority is included in a faction the form of popular government . . . enables it to sacrifice to its ruling passion or interest, both the public good and the rights of other citizens. To secure the public good and private rights against the danger of such a faction, and at the same time to preserve the spirit and form of popular government, is then the great object to which our enquiries are directed. . . . Either the existence of the same passion or interest in a majority must be prevented; or the majority, having such co-existent passion or interest must be rendered, by their number and local situation, unable to concert and carry into effect schemes of oppression. If the impulse and opportunity be suffered to coincide, we well know that neither moral nor religious motives can be relied on as an adequate control.[9]

In addition to controlling the "mischiefs of faction" the founders were also dedicated to preserving the "spirit and the form of popular government." And in the structure and balance of their Constitution, they thought they had successfully devised a remedy inherently republican for "the diseases most incident to republican government." The framers recognized that fashioning a regime in which the citizens would not care and opine about justice and the common good was a task as impossible as it would ultimately be undesirable. In fashioning a *liberal* regime, it was impossible to preclude the citizens from concurring and acting on those opinions about justice and the common good. Thus the framers sought to build a government sturdy enough to take it. Their remedy was a scheme of representative government with institutions where those conflicting views could be safely hashed out. For in their view it is the "regulation of these various and interfering interests that forms the principal task of modern Legislation, and involves the spirit of party and faction in the necessary and ordinary operations of Government."[10] By creating an extensive constitu-

---

8   John Stuart Mill, *On Liberty*, in Robert M. Hutchins (ed.), *Great Books of the Western World* (Chicago, 1952), 27.

9   *The Federalist*, No. 10, pp. 60–61.

10   *Ibid.*, 65, 59.

tional republic that would embrace a great multiplicity of interests, public law and policy could only be the result of compromise and coalition. Such a regime would encourage a politics of moderation.

The essential feature of the framers' constitutional scheme was institutional deliberation. The deliberative processes that would characterize a carefully constructed representative government would safely supply the defect of human wisdom. The various and clashing opinions among the citizenry would be "refined and enlarged" by being passed through a body of representatives. And there would a further weighty advantage. By forcing deliberation on fundamentally divisive issues to be conducted *within* the context of constitutionally created institutions, the framers could confidently expect to achieve their goal: By making the Constitution the rubric under which public discourse would be carried out, the natural concern for justice would be transmuted into a conventional concern for constitutionality. For example, it is better that a law restricting some facet of business be debated as to whether it violates the Constitution's grant of the power to Congress to regulate commerce than debated as to whether such a restriction is abstractly right or abstractly wrong.

The founders' twin concerns of securing both the public good and private rights were the dominant strands of their theory of representative government. They recognized that among other matters, what was essential to achieving both of their objects was the generation of a sense of community among the people. They knew that the "enthusiastic confidence in their patriotic leaders" that the Americans had displayed during the Revolution and that had been sufficient to stifle "the ordinary diversity of opinions on great national questions" was fast fading. But they also believed that beneath the often "vindictive, rapacious, and ambitious" mood of naturally self-interested men lay an attachment to their country and to some notion of the public good.[11] They understood that in addition to man's more selfish and hostile inclinations, there is a streak in his nature that inclines him toward civil society and political community. Such generous motives as patriotism, pride in country, and unselfish devotion to the public welfare—the elements of what that generation called civic or republican virtue—were as much a part of the human economy as avarice and

11 *Ibid.*, No. 49, p. 341; No. 6, p. 28.

ambition. "Is there no virtue among us?" Madison demanded of the Virginia ratifying convention. "If there be not," he argued, "we are in a wretched situation. No theoretical checks, no form of government, can render us secure. To suppose any form of government will secure liberty or happiness without any virtue in the people, is a chimerical idea." There was, the founders firmly believed, "sufficient virtue among men for self-government."[12]

Although these more estimable attributes were too feeble to be the sole foundation of a stable political order, they could be appealed to, drawn out, and nurtured in such quantity as to at least shore up the foundations of the regime. There was, the founders knew and appreciated, that "mingled blood" of common citizenship that only recently had been shed in defense of their "sacred rights." Although such an attachment might weaken in ordinary times, it would not be completely obliterated by man's selfish side. The founders' appreciation was for that often indefinable political force that Abraham Lincoln would so eloquently appeal to in his first inaugural address as those "bonds of affection," those "mystic chords of memory" that stretch "from every battlefield, and patriot grave, to every living heart and hearthstone, all over this broad land."[13]

The framers were aware that because there is this deeper stratum, this sense of community and political attachment, there would always be two levels of opinion on those issues that would demand public resolution. The first level can be characterized as *popular opinion*; the second, deeper level, as *public opinion*.[14] Popular opinion is "inherently more superficial, ephemeral, and transitory" than public opinion; it is "more immediate or spontaneous, uninformed, and unreflective." Robert Nisbet explains, "Popular opinion is . . . shallow of root, a creation of the mere aggregate or crowd, rooted in fashion or fad and subject to caprice and whim, easily if tenuously formed around a single issue or personage and lacking the kind of cement that time, tradition, and convention alone can provide."[15]

12 Jonathan Elliot (ed.), *Debates in the Several State Conventions on the Adoption of the Federal Constitution* (2nd ed.; 5 vols.; Philadelphia, 1866), III, 536–37; *The Federalist*, No. 55, p. 378.

13 *The Federalist*, No. 14, p. 88; Roy Basler (ed.), *The Collected Works of Abraham Lincoln* (7 vols.; New Brunswick, N.J., 1953), IV, 271.

14 This distinction between popular opinion and public opinion is taken from Robert Nisbet, "Public Opinion versus Popular Opinion," in Nathan Glazer and Irving Kristol (eds.), *The American Commonwealth: 1976* (New York, 1976), 166–92.

15 *Ibid.*, 168.

In sharp contrast, public opinion is a reflection of those sentiments and attachments that transform a group of men into a political community. It is the political expression of those bonds of affection that issue from those "mystic chords" of memory: "What proves to be public opinion in a community is commonly generated by popular opinion, whether in majority or minority form; but it is only through a process of adaptation or assimilation — by the habits, values, conventions, and codes which form the fabric of the political community — that popular opinion ever becomes what we are entitled to call public opinion, that is at bottom a very reflection of national character."[16]

To the founders it was this deeper level of political opinion, this amalgam of shared sentiments and received traditions, that made up the "permanent and aggregate interests of the community." And it was this level of opinion that the institutional arrangements of the Constitution were designed to tap and then to be guided by. The theoretical core of the Constitution demanded no less. The "deliberate sense of the community," the framers believed, not breezes of passion and bursts of impulse among the people, was to guide the actions of those chosen to govern. But what that principle does not demand — indeed, what it clearly rejects — is that the representatives are obligated to "an unqualified complaisance to every sudden breese of passion, or to every transient impulse" that may grip the people.[17]

The essential difference between popular and public opinion is the difference between the inclinations of the people on one hand and their interests on the other. This is why representation is a much more complex part of the republican theory of the Constitution than merely an arrangement to obviate the numerical inconveniences of direct democracy. Those who would be chosen to fill the offices of public trust, it was hoped (though not demanded), would be those men who would "possess the most wisdom to discern, and the most virtue to pursue, the common good of society."[18]

By channeling all the opinions, passions, and interests that flow from the great body of the people through a filtering "medium of a chosen body of citizens," public views on important issues would come to be refined and enlarged. The various transitory and impulsive views would be refined and deepened by political debate until they

16 *Ibid.*, 169.
17 *The Federalist*, No. 10, p. 57; No. 71, p. 482.
18 *Ibid.*, No. 57, p. 384.

more accurately reflected the permanent interests of the community; simultaneously, narrow or partial views would be enlarged or stretched (by the process of coalition) until they came to approximate the aggregate interests of the community. This process of institutional distillation would eliminate most of the passionate and selfish vulgarities of opinion, leaving a broadened, refined, and elevated view of the issues.[19]

By a prudent reliance on judiciously empowered and strategically balanced institutions, the founders sought to redeem popular government — to preserve both its spirit and its form — against those who claimed that it was incompatible with liberty. Their intention was not to abandon democratic government but to improve it by enhancing the deliberative element that was inherent in it. Through institutional arrangements the founders believed that they could extract the "deliberate sense of the community" and make it the dominant force in the conduct of public affairs. The objective was to "tame" popular opinion so that under the Constitution the people would enjoy that ordered liberty that was the essence of the just regime. Such devices were necessary, they argued, because "it is the reason of the public alone that ought to controul and regulate the government. The passions ought to be controuled and regulated by the government."[20] Deliberation was the key to ensuring that public opinion would be more likely than popular opinion to govern; it was the means necessary to produce a *qualitative* rather than simply a *quantitative* majority rule.

Deliberation is necessary to sound democratic or republican government for another reason beyond extracting the deeply shared public opinion that reflects national character. It is also necessary to supply the defect of perfect wisdom. In most instances there will be "wise and good men on the wrong as well as on the right side of questions of the first magnitude of society."[21] Disarming the passions through institutional distillation is but one half of the problem; securing the reason of the public is the other half. The problem of politics is always the problem of knowledge.

Man's reasoning faculty, as the founders never hesitated to point out, is fallible. It is a difficult matter, in the conduct of ordinary personal affairs, for man to "contemplate and discriminate objects exten-

---

19 *Ibid.*, No. 10, p. 62. See also No. 51.
20 *Ibid.*, No. 49, p. 343.
21 *Ibid.*, No. 1, p. 4.

sive and complicated in their nature." Reflecting an epistemology akin
to David Hume's *Treatise on Human Nature*, Madison in *The Federalist* pointed out that not even the faculties of the human mind had ever
been "distinguished and defined with satisfactory precision," nor the
"boundaries between the great kingdoms of nature"; the apparently
obvious "line which separates the district of vegetable life from the
neighboring region of unorganized matter, or which marks the termination of the former and the commencement of the animal empire"
was itself still shrouded in mystery. But, Madison went on, no matter
how difficult it is to discriminate the different realms of the natural
world, it is even more so in trying to deal with human institutions.[22]

Attempting to understand the nature and limits of political institutions is a particularly ticklish business. Sketching with any degree of
certainty the contours of the judicial, executive, or legislative powers;
or marking with precision the lines that separate the different classes
of law, such as common, statute, and ecclesiastical; or even explaining
new laws that have been "penned with the greatest technical skill" are
all tasks usually characterized by "frequent and intricate discussions."
Madison's point was clear: It is very difficult to know much about
even those things so common to everyday political life that are generally taken for granted. But the problem is deeper:

> Besides the obscurity arising from the complexity of objects, and the imperfections of human faculties, the medium through which the conceptions of
> men are conveyed to each other, adds a fresh embarrassment. The use of
> words is to express ideas. Perspicuity therefore requires not only that the
> ideas should be distinctly formed, but that they should be expressed by
> words distinctly and exclusively appropriated to them. But no language is so
> copious as to supply words and phrases for every complex idea, or so correct as not to include many equivocally denoting many ideas. Hence it must
> happen, that however accurately objects may be discriminated in themselves, and however accurately the discrimination may be considered, the
> definition of them may be rendered inaccurate by the inaccuracy of the
> terms in which it is delivered. And this unavoidable inaccuracy must be
> greater or less, according to the complexity and novelty of the objects defined. When the Almighty himself condescends to address mankind in their
> own language, his meaning, luminous as it must be, is rendered dim and
> doubtful by the cloudy medium through which it is communicated. Here
> then are three sources of vague and incorrect definitions: indistinctness of
> object, imperfection of the organ of conception, inadequateness of the
> vehicle of ideas.[23]

22 *Ibid.*, No. 37, pp. 234–35.
23 *Ibid.*, 236–37.

Because of this radical inability of man to fully know about political things, and because of his tendency to confuse his perception of the just for what is just, institutional deliberation is the best alternative for reaching judgment on the most important issues. The natural equality of men means that no one opinion is per se politically more acceptable. But to say that all opinions are politically equal is not to say that no opinion is intrinsically stronger — that is, truer — than the others. Indeed, at the base of the political science of the Constitution is the belief that some opinions are more enlightened than others. The difficulty in a regime based upon the mechanical device of majority rule is to encourage the ascendance of the best ideas.

Representation is the first step toward encouraging such an ascendance. It creates the context conducive to reflection on the merits of different perspectives by first drawing out and displaying those different perspectives. Then, representation allows the proponents of the various measures a forum in which to fight a battle of persuasion. This deliberative process provides the opportunity for the truth to emerge — or, perhaps more accurately, to be dragged out. In deliberating on the merits of the various views on a particular issue, representatives will make certain choices because they strike a majority as *better*, or more *just*, than the alternatives. In the context of constitutionally created institutions, deliberation is more than collective wisdom. It is a dynamic political act that goes beyond merely the assembling of the parts. The core of deliberation is rational judgment. And in the end that judgment will move toward and approximate what one may call the public interest. The task the founders set for themselves was "to fashion a set of institutions that would strike just the right balance between responsiveness and restraint, that would foster the rule of the deliberative majority by protecting it against the dangers of unreflective popular sentiments." For their understanding was that "the deliberative sense of the community is created through the operation of the institutions; it does not usually exist outside the institutions in a way that can be measured and compared to governmental decisions."[24]

The founders were staunch republicans. It was this form of government alone that was "reconcilable with the genius of the people of America; with the fundamental principles of the revolution; or with

24 Joseph M. Bessette, "Deliberative Democracy: The Majority Principle in Republican Government," in Robert A. Goldwin and William A. Schambra (eds.), *How Democratic is the Constitution?* (Washington, D.C., 1980), 106, 111.

that honorable determination, which animates every votary of freedom, to rest our political experiments on the capacity of mankind for
self-government." But they were not simple-minded republicans who
placed their faith in any simple scheme of representation. Mere representation in a legislative council was woefully inadequate to the tasks
of refining and enlarging popular opinion or of establishing an institutional context that was sufficiently deliberative. When Richard Henry
Lee, expressing a common anti-Federalist complaint, grumbled that
the proposed House of Representatives, nominally the most representative body created by the new Constitution, provided but "a mere
shred or rag of representation," the Federalists could unite in a sound
refutation.[25] Even the most cursory glance at the political history of
America under the Articles of Confederation was enough to see that
an emphasis on representation in the legislative body was an insufficient means of securing the great ends of republican government.
Under the Articles the national council had shown itself to be fickle
and feeble; the state legislatures had been spectacles of turbulence and
tyranny. When the delegates from the twelve states convened in Philadelphia in May, 1787, they soon recognized that their primary difficulty lay in deciding how best to combat the most common defects of
popular government: democratic tyranny and democratic ineptitude.
Most of their deliberations centered on the questions of the nature and
proper extent of the legislative power.

One of the great advantages of the principle of representation, most
Federalists and anti-Federalists agreed, was that it withdrew consideration of public issues from the great mass of the people and placed it in
a body that would, by the character of its members and its public position, be more sober and deliberative. It was a common observation
that in "cases of great national discussion" it was normal that a "torrent of angry and malignant passions" would be let loose. It was normal
but hardly desirable. Representation would be the primary means of
avoiding that "danger of disturbing the public tranquillity by interesting
too strongly the public passions."[26] These problems would not be
checked in a regime where the legislative council was simply dominant.

The reasons for this were a matter of common sense. Given the fact

25 *The Federalist*, No. 39, p. 250; Richard Henry Lee to Edmund Randolph, October 16, 1787, in Herbert Storing (ed.), *The Complete Anti-Federalist* (7 vols.; Chicago,
1981), 5. 6. 2.
    26 *The Federalist*, No. 1, p. 5; No. 40, p. 340.

that the legislative department is the most numerous, and that its members are "distributed and dwell among the people at large [and that] their connections of blood, of friendship and of acquaintance, embrace a great proportion of the most influential part of the society," it is closer to the people, and to all the passions that poison popular opinion. As Madison pointed out, the legislative power is exercised by an assembly—"which is inspired by a supposed influence over the people with an intrepid confidence in its own strength"—that will be "sufficiently numerous to feel all the passions which actuate a multitude; yet not so numerous as to be incapable of pursuing the objects of its passions, by means which reason prescribes."[27]

Because the legislators are closest to the people, they will be the most likely to bend to any sudden breeze of passion that may strike the community. As such, the legislative branch alone cannot produce the deliberation necessary to draw out the opinions that more truly reflect the interests as opposed to the inclinations of the community. Left to itself, the legislative power, bolstered by its claim to speak most directly and most clearly in the name of the people, and endowed with "constitutional powers . . . at once more extensive and less susceptible of precise limits," will suffer an unavoidable tendency to extend the "sphere of its activity, and [draw] all power into its impetuous vortex." Indeed, raw, untempered legislative power is the very antithesis of the kind of deliberation necessary to sound republican government. "In all very numerous assemblies," Madison warned, "of whatever characters composed, passion never fails to wrest the sceptre from reason."[28]

Accepting this dismal fact, amply supported as it was by both theory and experience, the framers saw fit to introduce into the constitutional plan various "auxiliary precautions." Among them: federalism, the separation of powers, bicameralism, an energetic executive, and an independent judiciary. These were the "powerful means," Hamilton said, "by which the excellencies of republican government may be retained and its imperfections lessened or avoided."[29]

FEDERALISM

Although one should argue against Max Farrand's appraisal that the Constitution is nothing but a "bundle of compromises," federalism, as

27 *Ibid.*, No. 49, pp. 341-42; No. 48, p. 334.
28 *Ibid.*, No. 48, pp. 334, 333; No. 55, p. 374.
29 *Ibid.*, No. 9, p. 51.

we have come to know it, *was* a compromise between those in the Constitutional Convention of 1787 who sought to create a new nationalistic constitution and those who attempted to remain true to their charge merely to revise the Articles of Confederation.[30]

To the men who argued so eloquently in behalf of nationalism — most notably James Madison, James Wilson, and Gouverneur Morris — the problem with the Articles of Confederation was nothing less than the theory of government it embraced. The Articles failed to meet the exigencies of the Union not because it was not true to its animating principle, federalism (more precisely, *confederalism*), but because it was. As Martin Diamond has stated, the problem facing the nationalists was to show "not how to be federal in a better way, but how to be better by being less federal." When Madison boasted in *The Federalist* of having found a republican cure for the diseases most incident to republican government through a "judicious modification . . . of the *federal principle*," he meant *modification*.[31]

Against Madison and his cohorts, men such as George Mason, Patrick Henry, Richard Henry Lee, and Melancton Smith stood opposed. The modification of the federal principle, they thought, had been anything but judicious. Beneath the thin polemical veil of the Federalist writers the anti-Federalists saw an awesome concentration of powers all tending toward the same end: the complete dissolution of the states into one simple, consolidated republic. Certainly consolidation would not be the immediate result of the proposed constitution; the nationalists were too shrewd to think that, and the attachment of too many people to confederal principles was too strong. What the anti-Federalists fearfully pointed to was the *tendency* of the Constitution toward consolidation. "Ere too many years have passed," Lee cautioned, "we shall see a government far different than a free one" evolve from the new constitution. It would be, he said, "replete with power, danger, and hydra-headed mischief" and would eventually snuff out the lamp of liberty the revolutionary generation had fought so hard to light.[32]

30 See Herbert J. Storing, "The Federal Convention of 1787: Politics, Principles, and Statesmanship," in Ralph A. Rossum and Gary L. McDowell (eds.), *The American Founding: Politics, Statesmanship and the Constitution* (Port Washington, N.Y., 1981).

31 Martin Diamond, "*The Federalist's* View of Federalism," in George C. S. Benson (ed.), *Essays on Federalism* (Claremont, Calif., 1961), 233; *The Federalist*, No. 51, p. 353.

32 Ballagh (ed.) *The Letters of Richard Henry Lee*, II, 465.

A look in the literature of the founding period for a theoretical defense of the American notion of federalism is in vain, for there was no comprehensive defense. The Federalists argued against the old understanding while the anti-Federalists argued for it. No one really argued for the new idea *as a principle*. To the founding generation, the new formulation was merely a pragmatic compromise between the two old and warring principles of confederalism and nationalism. And the compromise of two old principles did not necessarily a new principle make. In short, the Constitution was as *national* as the Federalists could make it and as *confederal* as anti-Federalists could keep it.

Even though the most ardent Nationalists, such as Madison, could never accept in principle that both national legislative houses should not be apportioned according to population, and would continue to believe that a national veto over state laws was essential, they always recognized a place for the states as political entities under the Constitution.[33] On the eve of the Constitutional Convention, Madison gave George Washington a preview of his thinking on the federal question: "Conceiving that an individual independence of the States is utterly irreconcileable with their aggregate sovereignty; and that a consolidation of the whole into one simple republic would be as inexpedient as it is unattainable, I have sought for some middle ground, which may at once support a due supremacy of the national authority, and not exclude the local authorities wherever they can be subordinately useful."[34] A consolidated republic would have been inexpedient, Madison thought, because so large a nation as the one he and his partners envisioned would inevitably be characterized by regional differences. "Honest differences of opinion, political biases, and local interests" would be backed up by political weight.[35] This was no closet theory. As Madison would have occasion to point out, one of the most divi-

---

33 See *The Federalist*, No. 14, p. 86. In the convention Alexander Hamilton had argued similarly that "subordinate authorities . . . would be necessary. There must be district tribunals and corporations for local purposes" (Farrand [ed.], *Records of the Federal Convention*, I, 287).

34 James Madison to George Washington, April 16, 1787, in Robert A. Rutland and William Rachal (eds.), *The Papers of James Madison* (16 vols.; Chicago, 1974), IX, 382.

35 See Madison's speech of June 6, 1787, in Farrand (ed.), *Records of the Federal Convention*, I, 134-36. Madison's famous indictment of faction as the most serious threat to republican liberty was addressed, in theory, to all popular forms of government; by experience, it was addressed to the political turmoil that had occurred at the state, not the national, level under the Articles.

sive issues in the convention itself was not the conflict between large and small states but the regional issue of northern versus southern states. The political continuation of the states under the Constitution would provide the proper forums for the discussion and resolution of matters local in character and thereby free the national councils to deal with national concerns. But because it had been in the states under the Articles of Confederation where the glaring examples of legislative tyranny had occurred, it was absolutely necessary, in the political science of the Constitution, that the role of the states be clearly subordinate.

In their subordinate role, however, the states still provided a valuable check on the potentially hazardous consolidation of popular opinion. As Madison explained, the division of the power surrendered by the people between two distinct governments, national and state (each of which guarded against tyranny by an internal "division of the government into distinct and separate departments"), gives rise to a "double security" to the rights of the people: "The different governments will controul each other; at the same time that each will be controulled by itself." The mere presence of the states, bolstered by their institutional involvement in the national government itself, would tend to make popular opinion *federal* in nature.[36]

By giving the states a voice in the selection of the president, a significant role in the amending process, and direct representation in the Senate, the Constitution allows for regional opinions and interests to be introduced into the public forum. In this way, the prevailing popular opinion of each state is not excluded from national affairs: The dominant popular opinion of Mississippi, for example, has a chance to be heard along with the dominant popular opinion of Massachusetts. To see that this is so one need only consider the wearying pace of a presidential candidate as he trudges from state to state, or the fate of certain constitutional amendments, such as the Equal Rights Amendment. In both instances, federalism adds a dimension to the public debate that would be missing in any scheme of simple national representation. The result is a broadened deliberative process that enhances the likelihood that major issues such as constitutional amendments will reflect fairly evenly distributed consensuses.

36 *The Federalist*, No. 51, p. 351. See also Martin Diamond, *The Electoral College and the American Idea of Democracy* (Washington, D.C., 1977).

SEPARATION OF POWERS

The Constitution separates the powers of government for two reasons. The first is obvious—to avoid tyranny. Madison wrote, "The accumulation of all powers in the same hands . . . may justly be pronounced the very definition of tyranny."[37] The second reason, perhaps more subtle but equally important, is that the separation of powers leads to greater efficiency in the administration of the necessary powers of government. And this, according to the framers, was the true test of any government.

The Constitution of 1787, according to its proponents both during and after the convention, had to address two problems confronting any popular form of government: the just formulation of the laws and policies, and the sound administration of those laws and policies once formulated. Law obviously ought to be formulated in light of permanent public opinion rather than merely transient popular opinion, and the offices of the government must be so constructed as to achieve a steady and just administration of the laws regardless of prevailing popular sentiment. These objects were to be accomplished through a Constitution that would combine "the requisite stability and energy in Government, with the inviolable attention due to liberty, and to the Republican form."[38] The separation of powers in the Constitution was the means whereby the framers thought they could succeed.

Having shunned the hope that they could create a regime of perfect wisdom and virtue, the framers sought to design their institutions not to make men virtuous but to make them responsible. To accomplish this, the institutions had to be so contrived as to capitalize on human nature rather than work around it. Ambition would have to be made to counteract ambition in order to supply the "defect of better motives." By connecting the personal interest of the man to the constitutional powers of the office, the framers intended that "each department should have a will of its own."[39] With each department having a different mode of election, a different constituency, and different objects of concern, each would contribute to keeping the other departments in their places. The government would thus control itself.

Such a system of separated powers with an attendant system of checks and balances would lead to the development of a healthy and

37 *The Federalist*, No. 47, p. 324.
38 *Ibid.*, No. 37, p. 233.
39 *Ibid.*, No. 51, pp. 349, 348. See also Nos. 6, 10, 57, 70, 71, 63, 78.

creative tension between the branches of government. Agreement between the branches would be essential to get anything done, and such agreement presupposed a certain amount of compromise. Therefore, deliberation on the merits of an issue was required *between* as well as *within* the separate branches. The system would require that reason rather than passion be the motive force behind governmental decision making. The nature of the process made it more difficult to pass a proposal into law than to defeat one. Hence, only reasonable laws—seasoned by deliberation and debate and supported by broad majorities—would emerge. In the end, the laws and other public measures would "seldom take place on any other principles than those of justice and the common good."[40]

These separating arrangements were necessary because in a republican government "the legislative authority, necessarily, predominates."[41] Simple representation in a legislature of the various opinions, passions, and interests of the community is not a sufficient means for securing republican justice. And even with the separation of powers, more was needed. Bicameralism, an energetic executive, and an independent judiciary were further institutional embellishments on the republican principle.

BICAMERALISM

Because legislative power constituted the central threat to sound popular government, the framers recognized that simply separating the powers of government and bolstering the executive and judicial departments might not be sufficient to solve the problems of democratic tyranny and democratic ineptitude. At the bottom of the framers' theory of separation of powers was an appreciation for the fact that it would be impossible ultimately to give each branch an equal power of self-defense against the encroachments of the others. It was unrealistic to think that a "mere demarkation on parchment of the constitutional limits of the several departments" would be adequate to keep the legislature from drawing all power unto itself. Even when the three great departments were provided with a "partial agency" in the exercise of each other's powers, the legislature would still predominate. It was important, therefore, not only to fence in legislative power by external

40 Bessette, "Deliberative Democracy," 109–12; *The Federalist*, No. 51, p. 353.
41 *The Federalist*, No. 51, p. 350.

institutional walls but also to so construct the legislature as to make it more likely to be self-regulating. The remedy for the inconveniences of legislative power, Publius contended, "is to divide the legislative into different branches; and to render them by different modes of election, and different principles of action, as little connected with each other as the nature of their common functions, and their common dependence on the society, will admit."[42]

The most persistent weakness of legislative power that bicameralism was meant to mitigate was the tendency toward "improper acts of legislation." In particular, "facility and excess of lawmaking" struck the framers as the diseases to which the American republic was most liable. Tyrannical legislation was not the only concern; foolish or imprudent legislation was an equally weighty problem. The "blunders" of the state governments were evidence enough that something had to be done, institutionally, to encourage a more deliberative legislative process.[43] The Senate was an integral part of the framers' solution.

Bicameralism was "not a device to thwart majority rule but an institutional mechanism that would promote the effective rule of the deliberative majority." The Senate was devised to accomplish six things conducive to a more sober exercise of legislative power. First, on the most superficial level, the institutional presence of a second chamber whose assent was required to pass laws doubled the political security of the people by "requiring the concurrence of two distinct bodies in schemes of usurpation or perfidy, where the ambition or corruption of one would other wise be sufficient."[44] Such collusion was simply not likely.

A second purpose of the Senate was to reduce the chance that transient or impulsive measures would be enacted as law. Such was the unfortunate tendency of "all single and numerous assemblies."[45] A smaller, more select body would serve as a sufficient *republican* counterweight to the *democratic* impulses more likely to characterize the measures of the House of Representatives. Being closer to the people by their term of office and mode of election, the representatives would be the first to register whatever opinion, passion, or interest might surface in the community. By being a bit further removed from the peo-

---

42 *Ibid.*, No. 48, p. 338; No. 51, p. 350.
43 *Ibid.*, No. 62, p. 419.
44 Bessette, "Deliberative Democracy," 109; *The Federalist*, No. 62, p. 418.
45 *The Federalist*, No. 62, p. 418.

ple, the Senate would be better able to resist those popular inclinations whenever it seemed appropriate.

A third and crucial element in the creation of the Senate was the encouragement of a "due acquaintance with the objects and principles of legislation." The frequent turnover of representatives precluded much thoughtful and sustained reflection in the House on the nature and limits of legislation. The result of frequent elections in the states under the Articles of Confederation had been a multiplicity of confused and often contradictory legislation that "fill[ed] and disgrace[d]" their codes of law. Such a mess was a monument of "deficient wisdom."[46] The fundamental differences in the House and the Senate — age and tenure — were attempts to secure a degree of experience in the Senate that would contribute to deliberation and consideration of a sufficiently high quality so that the national legislature would not be as susceptible to such confusion and uncertainty.

In addition to the dangers posed by a multiplicity of legislation, the framers were equally wary of the political vices of legislation that was too mutable. "An irregular and mutable legislation is not more an evil in itself than it is odious to the people."[47] Believing that it was essential to good government that legislation be stable, the framers argued that frequent elections would lead to a frequent change of opinions in the legislature and thence to a frequent change of measures. Mutability would give an appearance of arbitrariness, and arbitrariness would lead, both at home and abroad, to a loss of confidence in the government.

A fifth object of the Senate was to establish a "sense of national character."[48] Through a system of stable and enlightened law making designed to avoid the dangers of multiple and mutable legislation would come policy and law reflective of those more "permanent and aggregate interests of the community." A well-constructed bicameral legislature would promote the kind of deliberation on the merits of the issues that would cut through the superficial level of popular opinion and reach the deeper level of public opinion. By encouraging the tapping of those sentiments that unite the people in a common bond as a nation, the Senate was essential to the kind of qualitative majoritarianism the framers sought.

The final purpose of the Senate was to further the framers' object of

46 *Ibid.*, 419.
47 *Ibid.*, 419–22.
48 *Ibid.*, No. 63, p. 422.

securing a government that was, in the most meaningful sense, responsible to the people. As Madison put it, by having "sufficient permanency to provide for such objects as require a continued attention, and a train of measures," the Senate would be "justly and effectually responsible for the attainment of those objects." But the Senate provided another kind of responsibility. A body like the Senate, Madison explained, "may be sometimes necessary as a defence to the people against their own temporary errors and delusions." He continued,

> As the cool and deliberate sense of the community ought in all governments, and actually will in all free governments ultimately prevail over the views of the rulers; so there are particular moments in public affairs, when the people stimulated by some irregular passion, or some illicit advantage, or misled by the artful misrepresentations of interested men, may call for measures which they themselves will afterwards be the most ready to lament and condemn. In these critical moments, how salutary will be the interference of some temperate and respectable body of citizens, in order to check the misguided career, and to suspend the blow meditated by the people against themselves, until reason, justice and truth, can regain their authority over the public mind?[49]

The Senate would foster a political responsibility to the *interests* of the people when those interests were at variance with the *inclinations* of the people. The object was *good* government; and, to the framers, good government implied two things: "first, fidelity to the object of government, which is the happiness of the people; secondly, a knowledge of the means by which that object can be obtained."[50] In the Senate, the framers believed they had gone far in their attempt to secure both the fidelity and the knowledge necessary for good republican government.

The ultimate purpose of the Senate was to introduce into the legislative process a more sober body than could be expected in the more popular House. Through a more stable and thoughtful law-making process would come better laws that would earn a sustained respect for the law and a veneration for the government and the Constitution. It was widely conceded that popular government depended upon an "attachment and reverence" for the polity in the hearts of the people. No system that displayed infirmity or confusion and arbitrariness would enjoy that attachment. "No government any more than an individual will be long respected," Publius warned, "without being truly

49 *Ibid.*, 425.
50 *Ibid.*, No. 62, p. 419.

respectable, nor be truly respectable without possessing a certain portion of order and stability." Popular veneration was a necessary ingredient in even the "wisest and freest government."[51]

Once the internal organization of Congress had been taken care of, the framers turned their attention to shoring up the constitutional powers of the two coordinate branches of the national government. Their science of republican politics led to two conclusions. First, executive power had to be energetic; second, judicial power had to be independent.

THE ENERGETIC EXECUTIVE

If the disasters of legislative power under the Articles of Confederation (weak at the national level, tyrannical at the state) presented the framers with a major task of constitutional design, the creation of the executive power nearly matched it.[52] Except in New York, the state executives between 1776 and 1787 had been weak and dependent; a national executive power simply did not exist. The efforts by the framers to fashion a competent, constitutionally distinct executive power sprang from the same concern that moved them toward the creation of a Senate and an independent judiciary. It was a concern for "combining the requisite stability and energy in Government, with the inviolable attention due to liberty, and to the Republican form." Publius explained: "Energy in Government is essential to that security against external and internal danger, and to that prompt and salutary execution of the laws, which enter into the very definition of good Government. Stability in Government is essential to national character, and to the advantages annexed to it, as well as to that repose and confidence in the minds of the people, which are among the chief blessings of civil society."[53]

In several respects, the president was the political key to the framers' conception of good government. "A feeble executive," warned Publius, "implies a feeble execution of the government. A feeble execution is but another phrase for a bad execution: And a government ill executed, whatever it may be in theory, must be in practice a bad government." As the sole representative of the entire people, the president,

51 *Ibid.*, 422; No. 49, p. 340.
52 See Charles Thach, *The Creation of the Presidency* (Baltimore, 1929).
53 *The Federalist*, No. 37, pp. 233–34.

armed with powers sufficient to his tasks, was the clearest institutional expression of the blend of energy in government with a due regard for the republican form. For all the powers the office possessed, it was ultimately both dependent upon, and responsible to, the people. This, in the framers' view, constituted "safety in the republican sense."[54]

The presidency, like the Senate and the judiciary, was intended to introduce stability into the government by standing a bit removed from the political hustle and bustle of the people. These offices were not, as is sometimes suggested, aristocratic as opposed to the more democratic House of Representatives. They, no less than the House, are *republican* and not *democratic* in their nature and structure. All the offices ultimately are popular. Their differences lie not in the animating principles of each office but in their practical organization. At the level of principle, they are united; they are republican.

Firmly believing that the people could be blind to their own interests, the framers sought to devise the office of the president, like the Senate and the Court, as a popular office with the institutional strength to resist vulgar popular pressure. Such a view did not wash well with everyone. The institutions of the presidency, Senate, and Supreme Court had monarchical, oligarchical, or aristocratic overtones that struck many observers and critics of the Constitution as antithetical to the principles of republican government. Publius offered these doubters a quick lesson in the new science of politics:

There are some, who would be inclined to regard the servile pliancy of the executive to a prevailing current, either in the community, or in the Legislature, as its best recommendation. But such men entertain very crude notions, as well of the purposes for which government was instituted, as the true means by which the public happiness may be promoted. The republican principle demands, that the deliberate sense of the community should govern those to whom they entrust the management of their affairs; but it does not require an unqualified complaisance to every breese of passion, or to every transient impulse which the people may receive from the arts of men, who flatter their prejudices to betray their interests. It is a just observation, that the people commonly *intend* the PUBLIC GOOD. This often applies to their very errors. But their good sense would despise the adulator, who should pretend they always *reason right* about the *means* of promoting it. . . . When occasions present themselves in which the interests of the people are at variance with their inclinations, it is the duty of the persons whom they have appointed to be the guardians of those interests, to with-

54 *Ibid.*, No. 70, pp. 471–72.

stand the temporary delusion, in order to give them time and opportunity for more cool and sedate reflection.[55]

The problem was that of partiality. "Each legislator represents only a portion of the whole; no one of them, whether in the House or Senate, can truly claim to speak for the entire nation."[56] By "commanding a view of the whole ground," as Thomas Jefferson remarked, the president more clearly represents the aggregate will of the community. As an additional spokesman for the will of the community, the president would inevitably clash with Congress over whether the legislative or the executive view was correct.

To be prepared for these republican battles, the presidency had to be "fortified" in order to resist the inevitable encroachment of legislative power. Even with a different mode of election, and with a more broadly based constituency, still more was needed to ensure the independence and energy of the executive. The office had to be armed with an explicit power to repel legislative invasions of executive turf. The power sufficient to thwart imprudent or tyrannical legislative designs was the qualified veto over legislation.

The presidential veto, however, is more than a means of curbing legislative excesses. It is designed, constitutionally, to force a dialogue between the most representative branches of the government. The two branches, each claiming to express the aggregate will of the community, thus engage in a kind of institutional debate over the virtues of particular measures. As Joseph Bessette has explained: "The Constitution itself requires that the president publicly give his reasons whenever he vetoes a bill. His objections are laid before the House or Senate as reconsideration begins. The clear intention of this process was to raise the conflict above a battle of wills to a genuine conflict of opinion and argument. Both the actual and the threatened use of the veto will foster a kind of deliberation *between* the branches of government."[57]

This institutional deliberation is a necessary ingredient in the Constitution's political theory because it is not always certain that the legislature is speaking with the voice of the people. There is a chance that the legislature will be overwhelmed with a democratic confidence that causes it to think it *is* the people. In fact, in many instances, the legis-

55 *Ibid.*, No. 71, pp. 482–83.
56 Bessette, "Deliberative Democracy," 109–10.
57 *Ibid.*, 110.

lature may stand in opposition to the will of the people or the people may be simply neutral on a certain issue. In either case, Publius argued, "it is certainly desirable that the executive should be in a situation to dare to act his own opinion with vigor and decision."[58]

With the executive properly empowered to resist legislative encroachments and to tame and educate popular opinion, the framers turned their attention to the creation of a department that more than any other would, they hoped, stand apart from the fray of politics and partisanship. The judiciary, the framers believed, was absolutely essential to the maintenance of a limited constitution. And to fulfill its constitutional function, it had to be as independent of the more political branches as was possible under the republican principle.

THE INDEPENDENT JUDICIARY

Alexander Hamilton's defense in *The Federalist* of the judicial department of the Constitution is justly considered the most profound treatment of the subject. Although the defense spans six essays (Nos. 78–83) it is upon No. 78 that attention is most frequently focused. But that essay was not a detached theoretical musing; it had a specific polemical purpose. Hamilton's defense of the judiciary was a carefully calculated response to the attack that had been leveled on that branch in the New York press by the anti-Federalist Brutus. The Federalist confidence in the judicial branch as being "peculiarly essential in a limited constitution"[59] is placed in political perspective by considering anti-Federalist concerns.

Brutus, like his fellow anti-Federalist the Federal Farmer, feared that the proposed judicial branch was too independent. In their view such independence in theory bordered on, and in practice would degenerate into, arbitrariness. Even after Publius' defense against the charges of Brutus, the Federal Farmer still insisted that his countrymen were "more in danger of sowing the seeds of arbitrary government in this department than in any other." And, to the critics of the Constitution, arbitrariness in the administration of any political power was simply "repugnant to the principles of free government."[60]

---

58 *The Federalist*, No. 71, p. 483.
59 Robert G. McCloskey (ed.), *The Works of James Wilson* (2 vols.; Cambridge, Mass., 1967), II, 330; *The Federalist*, No. 78, p. 524.
60 The Federal Farmer, in Storing (ed.), *The Complete Anti-Federalist*, 2. 8. 185.

The Constitution, Brutus pointed out, makes the judges "independent in the fullest sense of the word. There is no power above them, to controul any of their decisions. There is no authority that can remove them, and they cannot be controuled by the laws of the legislature. In short, they are independent of the people, of the legislature, and of every power under heaven." And, Brutus warned: "Men placed in this situation will generally soon feel themselves independent of heaven itself."[61]

With no effective power over them, the judges would not be "constitutionally accountable for their opinions." Given the nature of man, there would be a natural tendency among the judges to do justice, and this would lead them too often "to find in the spirit of the constitution, more than was expressed in the letter." This, Brutus argued, was tantamount to granting the judges power sufficient to "enable them to mould the government into most any shape they please." They would be able to decide the cases and controversies that came before them "as their conscience, their opinions, their caprice, or their politics might dictate."[62]

In the anti-Federalist view, not only was the judicial branch tainted by the possibility of exercising an arbitrary discretion, but it was also constructed in such a way as to make it superior to the legislative power. Should the legislature pass laws "inconsistent with the sense the judges put upon the constitution, they will declare it void; and . . . in this respect their power is superior to that of the legislature." There was another pernicious twist to the relationship between the judiciary and the legislature. Not only could the judges invalidate legislation, but by their interpretations regarding the spirit of the Constitution, they would effectively mark out the boundaries of legislative power, often going much further than the legislature had. The consequence would be for the legislature to expand its powers up to those limits. For this reason Brutus (and a good many other anti-Federalists) saw the Constitution and its judicial power as designed to "melt down the states into one entire government, for every purpose as well internal and local, as external and national."[63]

Brutus' assault undoubtedly deepened Publius' account and defense of the judicial provisions of the Constitution. Earlier, in *The Federal-*

61 *Ibid.*, Brutus, 2. 9. 189.
62 *Ibid.*, 2. 9. 196; 2. 9. 134–44; The Federal Farmer, 2. 8. 195.
63 *Ibid.*, Brutus, 2. 9. 139–42.

ist, No. 22, he had been content to remark that the "want of a judiciary power" was the crowning defect of the confederation. In that paper, in December, 1787, he voiced what was a commonplace: "Laws are a dead letter without the courts to expound and define their true meaning and operation."[64] Brutus' criticism, which appeared in March, 1788, went so far beyond the typical anti-Federalist complaints over such matters as jury trials in civil cases, and appellate jurisdiction both as to law and to fact, that Publius had to plumb the depths of his political theory to defend the independent judiciary as being not only compatible with but essential to limited republican government.

Publius had to demonstrate that the issue was not the presumed superiority of the judicial power to the legislative power but rather the natural tendency of legislative power to expansion and abuse. His task was to show how in a republican scheme of government the judiciary was "an excellent barrier to the encroachments and oppressions of the legislative body." The argument in behalf of the judiciary dove-tailed nicely with the arguments Publius had already presented to the public in defense of the separation of powers, bicameralism, and the energetic executive. It was legislative encroachments that posed the deepest threat to a limited constitution. For, Publius explained, a limited constitution was "one which contains certain specified exceptions to the legislative authority." These constitutionally based exceptions could be "preserved in practice no other way than through the medium of the courts of justice; whose duty it must be to declare all acts contrary to the manifest tenor of the constitution void."[65]

The Constitution, Publius pointed out, was to be the fundamental law insofar as it was understood to be the legal expression of the sovereign will of the people. The Constitution created all the powers of the government, as well as the primary offices, and provided for the creation of the secondary offices necessary to administer those powers. All the powers created by the Constitution — legislative, executive, and judicial — were powers delegated by the people to the government. The officers administering those powers were merely the agents of the people. Because there would be occasions when the legislature might enact legislation that would be contrary to the original grant of legislative power made by the Constitution (granting, for example, titles of

64 *The Federalist*, No. 22, p. 143.
65 *Ibid.*, No. 78, pp. 522, 524.

nobility) it was necessary that there be a coordinate power, drawing its legitimacy from the same source as the legislature — the Constitution — to check and condemn the legislation. The judiciary, being the least political branch in a partisan sense, was the best institution for the job. The judiciary was intended, Publius said, to serve as "an intermediate body between the people and the legislature, in order, among other things, to keep the latter within the limits assigned to it." This constitutional function in no way implies a superiority of the judiciary to the legislature: "It only supposes that the power of the people is superior to both; and that where the will of the legislature declared in its statutes, stands in opposition to that of the people declared in the constitution, the judges ought to be governed by the latter, rather than the former. They ought to regulate their decisions by the fundamental laws, rather than by those which are not fundamental."[66]

Because the judges were intended to be the "bulwarks of a limited constitution against legislative encroachments," it was necessary that they be properly independent of that body. The great advancement of the American judiciary over any previous form was that it derived its powers neither from the executive power nor the legislative power, but directly from the Constitution. This separate constitutional foundation was essential to overcome the "natural feebleness of the judiciary" and to enable it to defend itself against the attacks of the other branches.[67] Where Brutus had erred, Publius suggested, was in assuming that the judiciary was radically independent; it was not. No less than the other branches, the judiciary was limited by the Constitution.

In order to fulfill its constitutional functions, the judiciary would naturally have to "hazard the displeasure" of the other branches. In its role of marking the constitutional limits of the other branches, or in its role of protecting the rights of individuals and minorities from the "occasional ill humours in society" that could be translated into "unjust and partial laws," the judiciary would be frequently involved in fundamental political battles. It thus was necessary to construct the judicial branch in such a way that it would not suffer "too great a disposition to consult popularity" in the administration of its powers. But the framers had no delusion that the judiciary would be a self-regulating or apolitical institution. The judges were, after all, subject to the same defects of human nature that torment the rest of us. They

66 *Ibid.*, 525.
67 *Ibid.*, 526, 523.

were no more expected to be members of that "philosophical race of kings wished for by Plato" than any other official.[68] The framers did believe, however, that by institutional arrangements judges would be rendered less subject to the immediate and transient political pressures in the community and hence less partisan in their judgments. That the judges might on occasion presume to substitute their will for that of the people or the legislature was not a possibility the framers dismissed. Indeed, they sought to construct the judicial power within an institutional context that would allow for the politically indispensable judicial functions to be safely and fairly administered and any judicial excesses trimmed.

The judges were subject to impeachment, and the administration of the great bulk of judicial power was left largely to legislative discretion. Further, Publius conceded, it was expected that in order to "avoid an arbitrary discretion in the courts, it is indispensable that they should be bound down by strict rules and precedents, which serve to define and point out their duty in every particular case that comes before them." Thus empowered and controlled, the independent judiciary was an essential ingredient in the framers' constitutionalism. It was necessary to articulate the lines and limits of the other branches and to protect individuals from the crushing weight of tyrannical inclinations masquerading as duly enacted law. Its constitutional function demanded an "inflexible and uniform adherence to the rights of the constitution and of individuals." Only by institutional independence would the judges have sufficient fortitude "to do their duty as faithful guardians of the constitution where legislative invasions of it had been instigated by the major voice of the community."[69]

By fulfilling its constitutional mandate, the judiciary would be yet another voice in the deliberative process. Whereas Congress and the president would seek to express the current and deliberate sense of the community, the judiciary would have the task of reminding the others of the permanent sense of the community as expressed in the written Constitution. The result would be responsible government. And responsibility in government means two things: *responsiveness* to the current political inclinations of the people, balanced by an *accountability* to their permanent interests.

68 *Ibid.*, 528, 529; No. 49, p. 340.
69 *Ibid.*, No. 78, pp. 529, 528.

The end sought by the Constitution, the security of civil and political liberty, demanded a structure of government that was at once capable and vigorous, yet limited and stable. The underlying tenet of the framers' science of politics was, as Edmund Randolph expressed it, that "there is no quarrel between government and liberty. The war is between government and licentiousness, faction, turbulence, and other violations of the rules of society [meant] to preserve liberty."[70]

One of the primary ways the Constitution was to secure its great ends was by *not* relying upon "a frequent recurrence to first principles." Simply put, recurrence to first principles "does not substitute for a well-constituted and effective government. In some cases, it may interfere." Herbert Storing pointed out why this is so:

> Does a constant emphasis on unalienable natural rights foster good citizenship or a sense of community? Does a constant emphasis on popular sovereignty foster responsible government? Does a constant emphasis on a right to abolish government foster the kind of popular support that any government needs? The Federalists did not doubt that these first principles are true, that they may be resorted to, that they provide the ultimate source and justification of government. The problem is that these principles, while true, can also endanger government. Even rational and well constituted governments need and deserve a presumption of legitimacy and permanency.[71]

A frequent recurrence to fundamental principles would keep the public passions in continual turmoil and would deprive the government of the necessary popular prejudice in its favor. By replacing a concern for *fundamental* principles with a concern for *constitutional* principles, the framers believed that the public would tend to be involved in debates of more manageable proportions. By drawing all the opinions, passions, and interests into the Constitution and forcing them through its various institutional filters, the framers thought the result would be a consensus of the legitimate majority of the community. Such constitutionally formed majority *public* opinion would be at once deeper than the transient *popular* opinion and less divisive than opinions over fundamental principles. This deliberative rule by a qualitative majority was the republican idea of justice and the great object of the Constitution. And it is in this context that the powers and the limits of all the institutions of the government must be understood.

---

70 Elliot (ed.), *Debates in the Several State Conventions*, III, 37.
71 Storing, "The Constitution and the Bill of Rights," 277.

THREE
THE PECULIAR SECURITY OF
A WRITTEN CONSTITUTION

Although there is a good deal of truth to John Adams' famous pronouncement that the American Revolution occurred in the hearts and minds of the people long before the first revolutionary shot was fired, it is important to keep in mind that *politically* America began with the Declaration of Independence. And the Constitution of 1787, which outlines the forms and creates the powers of government, is but the concrete institutional expression of the political sentiments espoused eleven years earlier in the Declaration. The dry, often administrative language of the Constitution is directed at giving effect to the political theory of the Declaration. In this sense, the Constitution completes what the Declaration began: The great American experiment to establish a government through "reflection and choice" rather than through the ravages of "accident and force." The Constitution seeks to make that government legitimate by resting it upon the consent of the governed.

In his *Jubilee of the Constitution*, John Quincy Adams reminded his audience of the principled basis of American constitutionalism:

> This was the platform upon which the Constitution of the United States had been erected. Its VIRTUES, its republican character, consisted in its conformity to the principles proclaimed in the Declaration of Independence, and as its administration must necessarily be always pliable to the fluctuating varieties of public opinion; its stability and duration by a like overruling and irresistable necessity, was to depend upon the stability and duration in the hearts and minds of the people of that *virtue*, or in other words, of those principles proclaimed in the Declaration of Independence, and embodied in the Constitution of the United States.[1]

Those principles of the Declaration—those abstract truths "applicable to all men and all times," as Abraham Lincoln put it—that prompted the creation of the Constitution were considered by the

---

1 As quoted in Ralph Lerner, "The Supreme Court as Republican Schoolmaster," in Philip B. Kurland (ed.), *The Supreme Court Review: 1967* (Chicago, 1968), 178.

founding generation (in 1776 as well as in 1787) to be a matter of nature and not of convention. "We hold these truths to be self-evident," they proclaimed in the Declaration,

> that all Men are created equal, that they are endowed by their Creator with certain unalienable Rights, that among these are Life, Liberty, and the pursuit of Happiness. — That to secure these Rights, Governments are instituted among Men, deriving their just Powers from the Consent of the Governed. — That whenever any Form of Government becomes destructive of these ends, it is the Right of the People to alter or to abolish it, and to institute new Government, laying its foundation on such principles and organizing its powers in such form, as to them shall seem most likely to effect their Safety and Happiness.

Yet even in the flood of revolutionary fervor, Jefferson and his countrymen were never swept away by their own rhetoric. Following that justly famous catalog of natural rights, the Americans saw fit to append a sober caveat: "Prudence, indeed, will dictate that Governments long established should not be changed for light and transient causes."[2]

The founding generation understood that in order to achieve their noble goal of a nation "conceived in Liberty," it was essential that the idea of the rule of law be venerated among the people. And in order for such veneration to occur, it was absolutely necessary that the Constitution be understood as a *permanent* body of law. Although natural law might demand the creation of institutions of government, those institutions were not necessarily to be guided in the conduct of day-to-day business by recurrence to those natural law principles, marred as such daily recurrence would be by disputes over interpretation.

Nor was the Constitution to be understood as having incorporated the unwritten English common law. The sources of right and justice that characterized the British constitution were undoubtedly influences on the thinking of the American constitutionalists; but once the Constitution was drafted, the explicit influence of those sources ceased. To have incorporated the common law into the Constitution, James Madison pointed out to George Washington, would have been to bring "over from G[reat] B[ritain] a thousand heterogeneous and anti-republican doctrines, and even the *ecclesiastical hierarchy* itself, for that is a part of the common law." To have accepted the common law

2 Abraham Lincoln to Henry L. Pierce and Others, April 6, 1859, in Ray Basler (ed.), *The Collected Works of Abraham Lincoln* (7 vols; New Brunswick, N.J., 1953), III, 376.

would have been to create a "digest of laws instead of a Constitution." The rejection of the common law was, in effect, the rejection of any notion of an unwritten constitution. The *written* Constitution was intended to replace the common law and hence the English higher-law tradition as the fundamental law in America.[3]

The reliance on unwritten law during the revolutionary period must be understood within this context. The written American constitutions of 1781 (the Articles of Confederation) and 1787 reveal the lack of confidence the Americans had in unwritten constitutions. The unwritten English constitution provided a greater latitude to the revolutionary appeals to fundamental law than a written constitution would have allowed. Under an unwritten constitution, one view of tradition could be pitted against another; a written constitution defined the terms of the debate more strictly, because all debate under a written constitution must originate at the literal level.

The preservation of liberty, in the view of the framers, depended upon a faithful adherence to a written constitution. The assumption that the common law or higher law hovers over the republic ready to be summoned down at will is an explicit rejection of the desirability of an emphatically limited government. To preserve liberty, the framers deemed it necessary to preserve the literal provisions of the Constitution inviolate. To have done otherwise and invoked the spirit of natural law in constitutional interpretation would have rendered the Constitution contingent upon the fluctuating and uncertain opinions of the judges and thereby diminished the principles embodied in the presumably paramount provisions of the document. To have admitted this higher-law background of the common law as granting legal or constitutional obligations would have been to confer on the judiciary "a discretion little short of a legislative power." It was for this reason that John Marshall could unqualifiedly observe in *Marbury* v. *Madison* that a written constitution was deemed by the founding generation to be "the greatest improvement on political institutions" and that Jefferson would declare "the possession of a written Constitution" to be

---

3 See "The Constitution and the Common Law in the Early Republic," Chap. III of Gary L. McDowell, *Equity and the Constitution: The Supreme Court, Equitable Relief, and Public Policy* (Chicago, 1982) 51–69. For an opposing view see Thomas C. Grey, "Do We Have an Unwritten Constitution?", *Stanford Law Review*, XXVII (1975), 703; Grey, "Origins of the Unwritten Constitution: Fundamental Law in American Revolutionary Thought," *Stanford Law Review*, XXX (1978), 843.

America's "peculiar security."[4] The theoretical musings of the founding generation, as well as their own harsh political experience, demanded nothing less.

When the delegates to the Constitutional Convention began to gather in Philadelphia in May, 1787, the political road they had traveled had not been smooth. With a rhetorical flourish they had declared their independence from England, with a ragtag army had won that independence, and had, along the way, created the first national constitution, the Articles of Confederation. In the fervor of the Revolution, some had confidently supposed that the Americans were a breed apart from their English brethren and would never be susceptible to the political corruption that had poisoned England. Their confidence soon was shaken.

In their enthusiasm, the founders had shrunk from constitutional arrangements that might have reeked of executive tyranny. They had sought to create their politics based on inviolable republican faith in the people. Their goal was legislative predominance, but they achieved legislative tyranny. The lesson was harsh: Democratic Americans were as susceptible to corruption as aristocratic Englishmen. The problem of politics is deep; it is the problem of human nature.

The experiences at both the state and national levels under the Articles of Confederation taught the Americans a sobering lesson in political science: "Nothing is more certain than the indispensable necessity of Government, and it is equally undeniable that whatever and however it is instituted, the people must cede to it some of their natural rights, in order to vest it with requisite powers."[5] The practical problem was to give the government power sufficient to control the governed, but also to construct that power so as to render it safe for republican liberty. The framers saw as their task the establishment of good government; this required a constitution based not upon the transient circumstances of society but upon the permanent attributes of mankind.

The framers sought to establish a constitution "for future generations, and not merely for the circumstances of the moment"; they

---

4 Thomas Jefferson to Wilson C. Nicholas, September 7, 1803, in A. Lipscomb (ed.), *The Writings of Thomas Jefferson* (20 vols.; Washington, D.C., 1905), X, 419.
5 Jacob E. Cooke (ed.), *The Federalist* (Middletown, Conn., 1961) No. 2, p. 8, hereinafter cited as *The Federalist*.

hoped they could frame a document that would "last forever" or at the very least would "last for ages." Their basic intention, taking into account the strengths and weaknesses of human nature, was to create a government that could be safely administered by men over men. The end sought was a safe balance between governmental power and individual liberty.[6]

To achieve their object, the framers sought to unravel some of the mysteries of human nature. And if they could not explain all causes, they could at least take account of effects. They endeavored to be sharp-eyed realists who, through an examination of man's political history, would be able to distinguish a few fundamental truths about the nature of man. They were committed students of the Enlightenment. As Hamilton asked, "Have we not already seen enough of the fallacy and extravagance of those idle theories which have amused us with promises of an exemption from the imperfections, weaknesses and evils incident to society in every shape? Is it not time to awake from the deceitful dream of a golden age, and to adopt as a practical maxim for the direction of our own political conduct, that we, as well as the other inhabitants of the globe, are yet remote from the happy empire of perfect wisdom and perfect virtue?"[7]

The framers were empirical political scientists who found after a hard look at the "uniform course of events" and the "accumulated experience of the ages" that experience was the "least fallible guide of human opinions." The lessons of experience were clear. Although man may not be angelic, neither is he simply beastly. Human nature is mixed. Beyond a "degree of depravity in mankind" that renders him "ambitious, vindictive and rapacious" there lurks a degree of virtue sufficient for self-government. Although man is so flawed as to demand governance, he nonetheless is capable of doing the job himself. Through the careful construction and judicious arrangement of institutions, man is able to take account of his nature and to "supply the defect of better motives."[8]

The task of the framers was complicated by the end they sought: political liberty through republican government. For the defects in human nature that needed governing would be magnified in those who

6 Max Farrand (ed.), *The Records of the Federal Convention of 1787* (4 vols.; New Haven, Conn., 1936) II, 125 (James Wilson), I, 422, 462 (James Madison). See also *The Federalist*, Nos. 1, 10, 37–39, 47–51, 63.

7 *The Federalist*, No. 6, p. 35.

8 *Ibid.*, 28, 32; No. 55, p. 378; No. 6, p. 28; No. 55, p. 378; No. 51, p. 349.

ruled. It was the unfortunate lot of mankind that reason was not infallible. Further, there exists a reciprocal influence between man's opinions and his passions, so that it is very likely that in the natural course of politics a "torrent of angry and malignant passions" will be let loose over nearly every issue of public policy. Law, in the sense of ordinary legislation, is the most common expression of the dominant passions in the political community. Given that such passions ought to be "controuled and regulated by the government" rather than being allowed to "controul and regulate the government," the rule of legislation was seen as insufficient to create a just regime.[9] There had to be more — there had to be a law more fundamental than ordinary legislation, a law paramount to the normal flow of congressional enactments, a law against which legislation as well as all the actions of the government generally could be measured. It was in this spirit that the Constitution was created. The permanence of the Constitution did not derive from the common-law tradition of natural justice but from its reference to the permanent attributes of mankind.

The Constitution was intended to be "paramount," "fundamental," and "lasting" in order to achieve a steady and just administration of the laws. By drawing unto itself that "veneration which time bestows on everything," the Constitution would contribute to necessary political stability. Certainly the framers knew that they had not written the last word in republican constitutions; they knew the necessity of allowing for future amendments. But they also understood that the process of changing the fundamental law not only had to rest with the people but also had to be cumbersome enough not to be used for "light and transient causes" lest the Constitution be transformed into a mere digest of laws. It would have been dangerous to have rendered the Constitution "too mutable," prone as the people are to be moved by passion or impulse. The Constitution was left to posterity to "improve and perpetuate"; the improvement of the Constitution, where necessary to meet the unforeseen exigencies of the future, was left to the people and not to their deputies alone, be they congressmen, presidents, or judges.[10]

The founding generation knew something about politics that we have to a great degree lost sight of. They understood the salutary effects of public prejudice in behalf of the nation. A dedication to the funda-

9 *Ibid.*, No. 1, p. 5; No. 49, p. 343.
10 *Ibid.*, No. 49, p. 340; No. 43, p. 296; No. 71, p. 482; No. 14, p. 89.

mental law and the polity it creates is essential. "If it be true," James Madison argued, "that all governments rest on opinion . . . when the examples which fortify opinion are *antient* as well as *numerous*, they are known to have a double effect. In a nation of philosophers, this consideration ought to be disregarded. A reverence for the laws would be sufficiently inculcated by the voice of an enlightened reason. But a nation of philosophers is as little to be expected as the philosophical race of kings wished for by Plato. And in every other nation, the most rational government will not find it a superfluous advantage to have the prejudices of the community on its side."[11] This popular prejudice —a "noble prejudice"—is essential to the maintenance of a constitution that creates a limited government. For limited government depends upon a *permanent* body of fundamental law.

Beyond their concern for remedying the defects of human nature, the framers looked to history for other guides as well. In particular, they sought to understand the institutional reasons for the general failure of republican governments in the past. However exalted were the histories of Athens and Rome, their institutional instability was infamous. They generally were kept in "a state of perpetual vibration between the extremes of tyranny and anarchy," between too much power and too little. The secret to success, the framers thought, lay in a properly constructed system of institutions wherein power and liberty could be held in safe balance.[12]

The purpose of the Constitution was to create political power that would be sufficient to the exigencies of the nation, yet would be controlled. The framers (both Federalists and anti-Federalists) were in complete agreement that "power is of an encroaching nature." Any constitution, to be safe, must contain provisions for its own control. The primary control lay in the fact of a written constitution that delegated "few and defined" powers to the government. But such a "parchment barrier" was insufficient. The most solid foundation for the maintenance of a limited constitution was to be found in the political arrangements it created: the separation of the powers of government.[13]

A striking feature of the Constitution is its silence. It does not *speak* of the separation of powers; it simply separates them. As Madison

11 *Ibid.*, No. 49, p. 340.
12 *Ibid.*, No. 9, p. 50; No. 37.
13 *Ibid.*, No. 48, p. 332; No. 45, p. 313.

argued, "the defect must be supplied by so contriving the interior structure of the government, as that its several constituent parts may, in their mutual relations, be the means of keeping each other in their proper places."[14] The Constitution achieves in deed what it omits in word. The separate powers of government each have the same foundation. Each department — the executive, the legislative, and the judicial — draws its power independently from the Constitution itself. Only in this way can they truly be equal and coordinate branches with the *constitutional* means to resist the encroachments of the others.

It is for this reason that the Constitution was held by the framers to be paramount and permanent. Stable government demands that the source of all power be permanent. There can then be no doubt, confusion, or arbitrariness. There will always exist a standard distinct from the government itself that will provide a measure of the legitimacy of all the actions of the government.

The Constitution was seen by the framers as the embodiment of the consent of the governed, reflecting fundamental notions of politics and of what is right and what is wrong. The Constitution is the political creed of the American people. Anything inconsistent with the principles of the document — its rules and rights — is inconsistent with the consent of the people and hence illegitimate.

The framers understood only too well the political vices that flowed from "mutable government." The problem of mutable legislation under the Articles of Confederation had been critical; a constitution that would be "too mutable" would be fatal. The only legitimate means of altering the fundamental law, the formal process of amendment, would not only deter frequent tampering but would draw unto any amendment the same popular consent that had originally been given the Constitution. In no instance would it be acceptable for any branch of the government to alter the meaning of the fundamental law.

It was precisely the permanence of the Constitution that would make it flexible. By painting in broad strokes, the framers were able to produce a constitution instead of a digest of laws. For the Constitution had to be broad enough to comprehend the "various crises of human affairs that the future would bring." In the deepest sense, the Constitution was an attempt to "reconcile permanence and change."[15]

14 *Ibid.*, No. 51, 347–48.
15 Paul Eidelberg, *The Philosophy of the American Constitution* (New York, 1968), 224.

The "great outlines" of the Constitution itself were carefully drawn so that the details of government — and all the change that might imply — could be handled through the ordinary course of legislation, through law that need not in any way be considered permanent. The founders thought they had secured a proper balance between what they saw as the necessity of permanence and the inevitability of change by creating a flexible government that would change with changing circumstances through the instrumentality of statutory law drafted within the broad and permanent outlines of the Constitution.

In *McCulloch* v. *Maryland*, Chief Justice John Marshall spoke to this critical balance. In speaking of the necessary and proper clause as part of a "constitution intended to endure for the ages, and, consequently, to be adapted to the various crises of human affairs," Marshall was pointing to the fact that although the Constitution establishes certain *ends*, it is through ordinary legislation that the *means* of achieving those ends are to be effected.[16] The necessary and proper clause was intended to allow Congress by law to adapt the means so better to achieve the great ends of the Constitution. The law changes; the Constitution does not. In order to adapt the Constitution to the various changing circumstances that time would inevitably bring, the latitude for enacting legislation had to be generous. For example, the commerce power of the Constitution is as applicable to the modern intricacies of AT&T and IBM as it was to nineteenth-century steamboats. The commerce power is a permanent power; what changes are the laws from one age to another deemed necessary to achieve the end for which the power was created — commercial regulation and development. In sum, "while the Constitution is absolutely permanent in *essence*, it is only relatively permanent in *fact*." To preserve the Constitution as permanent law it is necessary "to render what is permanent in essence permanent in fact."[17] And it is this necessary reconciliation of the permanent with the transitory that lies at the core of the judicial power within the Constitution.

The Court's role as the balancer of the past with the present, of permanence with change, is inherently problematical. Justice Robert Jack-

---

16   See Gerald Gunther (ed.), *John Marshall's Defense of McCulloch v. Maryland* (Stanford, Calif., 1969).
17   Eidelberg, *The Philosophy of the American Constitution*, 240-41.

son, recognizing that "thin is the line that separates law and politics," explained that the

> political function which the Supreme Court, more or less effectively, may be called upon to perform comes to this: In a society in which rapid changes tend to upset all equilibrium, the Court, without exceeding its own limited powers, must strive to maintain the great system of balances upon which our free government is based. . . . Chief of these balances are: first, between the Executive and Congress; second, between the central government and the states; third, between state and state; fourth, between authority, be it state or national, and the liberty of the citizen, or between the rule of the majority and the rights of the individual.[18]

The problem of judicial power is the problem of discretion. An appeal to the discretion of the Court, as John Marshall said, "is a motion, not to its *inclination*, but to its *judgment*." But although such judgment is to be characterized and guided by "sound legal principles," the line between inclination (or will) and judgment is at best a blurred one. In truth the judicial function occupies "some middle ground between a technician's deductions from general rules and a legislator's pure reason prescribing such general rules," for judicial power, by definition, is directed toward resolution of disputes or controversies over legal and constitutional meaning. Such disputes and controversies very often "spring from political motives, for the object of politics is always to obtain power."[19] And the resolution of disputes over the meaning of statutes or the Constitution will inevitably have ramifications in the distribution of political power.

The controversies that come before the Court for resolution require more than mere judgment; they require interpretation, which is often as much a matter of exercising the will as it is exercising judgment. For however careful the lawgiver may be, be he a founder or a legislator, there is the problem of "indeterminate language," or what John Hart Ely has termed "open-ended provisions." Disputes in the judicial forum appeal to a judicial discretion that must be guided by a "consideration of the experiences and statements of the framers which indicated the original will, or by reference to some relevant subsequent events and currents of opinion deemed controlling." But whatever the method, one

18 Robert H. Jackson, *The Supreme Court in the American System of Government* (Cambridge, Mass., 1955), 31, 61.

19 Marshall quoted in Robert K. Faulkner, *The Jurisprudence of John Marshall* (Princeton, 1961), 67; Lerner, "The Supreme Court as Republican Schoolmaster," 165; Jackson, *The Supreme Court in the American System of Government*, 56.

fact is certain: The judicial role is undeniably political because "all constitutional interpretations have political consequences."[20]

The indeterminacy of some constitutional language renders the interpretation and application of the Constitution—the highest judicial function—a massive problem.[21] Sound constitutional interpretation must begin with examination of what the document says. Most often, the provisions of the text are clear and unambiguous. There are, however, those areas that do lack clarity and demand that the Court look elsewhere for the meaning of the Constitution. The first place to look is to what the founders' intentions were. Since we still live under basically the same document, we have an obligation to understand what it was intended to do and what it was *not* intended to do. Yet, although there is a hefty collection of writings such as *The Federalist* and James Madison's "Notes on the Federal Convention," it is not always possible to divine the framers' intentions.

To supplement the fundamental mode of interpretation—the literal import of the document and the original intention behind it—the Court often must be creative. It may be best to approach a case on the basis of precedent or *stare decisis*; or to resort to logical reasoning (for example, as John Marshall did in *Marbury* v. *Madison*); or perhaps even resort to the construction of constitutional doctrines (for example, "clear and present danger"), which may be a combination of precedent, logic, and constitutional language. But whatever the method, it is essential that the Court never lose sight of the Constitution. It must first seek to understand the intentions of the framers, "not because they were demigods and not because we are obligated to yield to their will or authority and to embrace their judgment uncritically . . . [but] because they did, after all, establish the constitutional order within which we live, and as long as that order remains in force, we need to know as much about the Constitution as possible including what purposes it was designed to achieve and what evils it was intended to avert." Joseph Story said it best:

> In construing the Constitution of the United States, we are in the first instance to consider, what are its nature and objects, its scope and design, as

20 John Hart Ely, *Democracy and Distrust: A Theory of Judicial Review* (Cambridge, Mass., 1980); Jackson, *The Supreme Court in the American System of Government*, 56.

21 The following section is drawn from my introduction to Gary L. McDowell (ed.), *Taking the Constitution Seriously: Essays on the Constitution and Constitutional Law* (Dubuque, Iowa, 1981), 1–4.

apparent from the structure of the instrument, viewed as a whole and also viewed in its component parts. Where its words are plain, clear and determinate they require no interpretation. . . . Where the words admit of two senses, each of which is conformable to general usage, that sense is to be adopted, which without departing from the literal import of the words, best harmonizes with the nature and objects, the scope and design of the instrument.[22]

And in attempting to determine the true sense of the words of the document, the Court is best bound by the chains of history. "I entirely concur in the propriety of resorting to the sense in which the Constitution was accepted and ratified by the nation," James Madison confessed to Henry Lee in 1824. "In that sense alone," he continued,

> it is the legitimate Constitution. And if that be not the guide in expounding it, there can be no security for a consistent and stable, more than for a faithful exercise of its powers. If the meaning of the text be sought in the changeable meaning of the words composing it, it is evident that the shape and attributes of the government must partake of the changes to which the words and phrases of all living languages are constantly subject. What a metamorphosis would be produced in the code of law if all its phraseology were to be taken in its modern sense![23]

But such a metamorphosis is largely what has come to pass for constitutional interpretation. There has been a substantial loss of appreciation for the virtues of a permanent constitution. The idea of a permanent constitution has been replaced by the idea of a living constitution, a constitution whose substantive meaning depends more upon time and circumstance than upon clearly discernible political principles. This notion of a living constitution has encouraged the belief that the Constitution is merely an "old bottle" into which the courts are able—and obligated—to "pour new wine." This belief, in turn, has led to a startling conclusion: "It is naive to assert that the Supreme Court is limited by the Constitution."[24]

The Court has heeded the jurisprudential lessons of this perspective very well. For quite some time now the Court has embraced and articulated the belief that we do indeed live under a living rather than a

22 Ralph A. Rossum and G. Alan Tarr, *American Constitutional Law and Interpretation* (New York, 1983), 3; Joseph Story, *Commentaries on the Constitution of the United States* (3rd ed.; 2 vols; 1858), Sec. 405.

23 James Madison to Henry Lee, June 25, 1824, in Gaillard Hunt (ed.), *The Writings of James Madison* (9 vols.; New York, 1900–1910), IX, 191.

24 John P. Roche, "Judicial Self-Restraint," *American Political Science Review*, XLIX (1955), 762.

permanent constitution, that our basic law is moving not fixed. A necessary distinction between the Constitution and constitutional law has been blurred. The prevailing sentiment is that any serious regard for the document is nothing more than an "antiquarian historicism" that purports to "freeze" the meaning of the Constitution. To thus freeze the meaning of the Constitution, so the orthodoxy goes, is to sacrifice social progress for "legal subtleties." The litany usually ends like this: "Judicial decisions should be gauged by their results and not by . . . their coincidence with a set of allegedly consistent doctrinal principles."[25]

The advocates of the ideology of a living constitution generally reject the notion of original intention and permanent meaning on the grounds not only that the Court should not follow original intent but that it cannot. Whereas the first is at best an indefensible position, the latter is an utter sham. To argue that judges and justices should not be guided by original intention is, as Justice Hugo Black once dissented, to reject completely the idea of a written constitution. After all, a written constitution of explicit rules is aimed at providing a basis for keeping all discretion — including judicial discretion — bound down and hemmed in. Those who argue for judges to base their opinions on evolving notions of social morality ultimately are arguing for nothing more than judicial responsiveness not to rules and powers rooted in a broadly based and legitimate public opinion but to that fleeting popular opinion that happens to be "in vogue in circles to which the court responds."[26] To argue, as is usually done, that such an approach to constitutional adjudication is a "principled process" is to defend a process that at the moment better serves certain interests in question. For example, those who now defend the current prescriptive activism as the Court doing justice would be unlikely to defend the institution and its processes should the ideological presumptions change. To defend judicial activism the proponents in every age have had to shy away from asking the hard institutional question of whether such an exercise of judicial power would be defensible if put in service of the other side. In the end, such defenses of judicial excursions into the realm of public policy are nothing more than manifestations of the old whose-

25 Leonard Levy, *Judgments* (Chicago, 1972), 17; Paul L. Murphy, *The Constitution in Crisis Times* (New York, 1972), 45; Arthur S. Miller and Ronald F. Howell, "The Myth of Neutrality in Constitutional Adjudication," *University of Chicago Law Review*, XXVII (1960), 661, 690–91.
26 Thomas Sowell, *Knowledge and Decisions* (New York, 1980), 296.

ox-is-being-gored logic; it is more a matter of passion than of principle.

The other argument, that the courts *cannot* follow original intention, is ludicrous. Because the whole point of a written constitution was to provide a tangible guide for the exercise of political power, this argument quickly reveals itself to be nothing more than a not-so-clever cover for the argument that the courts should not follow original intent. The argument here is generally based on what Thomas Sowell has called the "precisional fallacy": Because certain provisions of the Constitution lack precision, they cannot be binding. But, as Sowell shows, this "practice of asserting the necessity of a degree of precision exceeding that required for deciding the issue at hand" is disingenuous. "Ultimately there is no degree of precision — in words or numbers — that cannot be considered inadequate by simply demanding a *higher* degree of precision. If someone measures the distance from the Washington Monument to the Eiffel Tower accurately to a tenth of a mile, this can be rejected as imprecise simply by requiring it in inches, and if in inches, requiring it in millimeters, and so on *ad infinitum*. . . . However fascinating these where-do-you-draw-the-line questions may be, they frequently have no bearing at all on the issue at hand."[27]

"In the law," Sowell continues,

> the question is not *precisely* what "due process" or other constitutional terms mean in all conceivable cases, but whether it *precludes* certain meanings in a given case. No one knows *precisely* the original meaning or boundaries of the constitutional ban on "cruel and unusual punishment" — but it is nevertheless clear from history that it was never intended to outlaw capital punishment. Therefore its "vagueness" is not *carte blanche* to substitute any standard that Supreme Court justices happen to like. In the same vein, Chief Justice Earl Warren's remark in *Brown* v. *Board of Education* about the "inconclusive nature" of the Fourteenth Amendment's history "with respect to segregated schools" confused the crucial point that there was *no* evidence that the writers of the Amendment intended to outlaw any kind of segregation, and much evidence that social policy issues were outside the scope of the Amendment. Because we do not know *precisely* what the boundaries of the Fourteenth Amendment are does not mean that we cannot know certain things about those boundaries. A border dispute between Greece and Yugoslavia does not prevent us from knowing that Athens is in one country and Belgrade in another. Decisiveness is not precision.

Given a certain lack of precision in some constitutional language, so the argument expands, it is only reasonable that none of the language

27 *Ibid.*, 292.

be considered precise. Because of alleged imprecision, then, it is demanded that the Court blow away the fog of archaic obscurity by reinterpreting constitutional provisions in light of the present in order to keep the document "adjusted to the advancing needs of time."[28] This tendency to keep the Constitution abreast of the times by judicial interpretation is displayed most clearly in one of the most controversial decisions of the Warren Court, *Griswold* v. *Connecticut*.

Griswold v. *Connecticut* came to the Supreme Court after a state appeals court and the Connecticut Supreme Court of Errors affirmed the convictions of the director and the medical director of the Planned Parenthood League of Connecticut. The plaintiffs had been convicted and fined under a Connecticut law that made giving information or instruction on birth control devices to married persons a criminal offense. The Supreme Court reversed their convictions and struck down the state law as violative of the Constitution. But in order to find constitutional grounds for its decision, the Court, led by Justice Douglas, had to search carefully in the nooks and crannies of the document; the law had to fall, the Court decided, because it violated a constitutional right to privacy, a right nowhere mentioned in the Constitution.

The logic of the Court's opinion rested on what Douglas called the "peripheral rights" of the Constitution, rights that issued from "specific" constitutional rights. As Douglas put it, the "specific guarantees in the Bill of Rights have penumbras, formed by emanations from those guarantees that help give them life and substance." For the case at hand, Douglas argued, such intimacies of marital life as birth control are constitutionally protected against state intervention by a general right to privacy that grows out of certain other explicitly protected rights. Douglas then endeavored to bolster his newly discovered constitutional right by marshaling all the constitutional evidence he could find.

> Various guarantees [in the Bill of Rights] create zones of privacy. The right of association contained in the penumbra of the First Amendment is one. . . . The Third Amendment, in its prohibition against the quartering of soldiers "in any house" in time of peace without the consent of the owner is another facet of that privacy. The Fourth Amendment explicitly affirms the "right of the people to be secure in their persons, houses, papers, and effects, against unreasonable searches and seizures." The Fifth Amendment in its Self-Incrimination Clause enables the citizen to create a zone of pri-

28 *Ibid.*, 292, 293, n. 344.

vacy which the government may not force him to surrender to his detriment. The Ninth Amendment provides: "The enumeration in the Constitution, of certain rights, shall not be construed to deny or disparage others retained by the people."

The present case, Douglas concluded, "concerns a relationship lying within the zone of privacy created by [these] several fundamental constitutional guarantees." But it was even sturdier than that. The right to marital privacy was "a right of privacy older than the Bill of Rights" itself.[29]

To bolster Douglas' argument, Justice Arthur Goldberg in his concurring opinion sought to emphasize the crucial role of the Ninth Amendment in allowing the Court to find this new constitutional right. The language and history of the Ninth Amendment, he wrote, show that the framers of the amendment (and James Madison in particular) believed that there were "additional fundamental rights . . . which exist alongside those rights specifically mentioned in the first eight constitutional amendments."[30] Thus, to a majority of the Court, there lurks outside the Constitution a constellation of fundamental (and, one is left to assume, *natural*) rights that constitutes, to borrow Justice Holmes's felicitous phrase, "a brooding omnipresence" ready to be summoned down and invoked by judicial authority. There is only one problem: That is not what the Ninth Amendment meant.

The Ninth Amendment must be understood in light of two facts the majority of the Court chose to overlook in *Griswold*. First, the Bill of Rights was aimed at the national government, not the states. It has only been through a judicial fiction that the Bill of Rights was "incorporated" into the Fourteenth Amendment and made applicable to the states. Therefore, the Ninth Amendment must be viewed as saying *only*, as James Madison told his colleagues in the First Congress, that any rights not enumerated were *not* "intended to be assigned into the hands of the General Government" and thus be rendered "consequently insecure." The Ninth Amendment, as Justice Hugo Black pointed out in his scathing dissent to *Griswold*, "was passed, not to broaden the powers of [the] Court on any other department of the 'General Government' but . . . to assure the people that the Constitution in all its provisions was intended to limit the Federal Government to the powers granted expressly or by necessary implication." What the Court was

29 *Griswold* v. *Connecticut*, 381 U.S. 479, 483, 484, 486.
30 *Ibid.*, 488.

doing, Justice Potter Stewart said, was turning "somersaults with history." To suggest that the Ninth Amendment somehow empowered the federal government—and especially the Court—to move against the domestic policies of the states "would have caused James Madison no little wonder," to say nothing of the anti-Federalists whose fear of the consolidating tendencies of the Constitution was what led to the Bill of Rights in the first place.[31]

The second fact ignored by the Court is that the language of the Ninth Amendment—"the enumeration in the Constitution of certain rights, shall not be construed to deny or disparage others retained by the people"—in no way extends constitutional protection to those rights. Only those rights enumerated can logically be said to enjoy constitutional protection; those not enumerated are protected only in the sense that the Constitution created a government of limited and delegated powers. By singling out certain rights—the protection against unreasonable searches and seizures, for example—the framers sought to provide these particular rights with explicit constitutional protection. However, from such an enumeration in a constitution meant to be limited and express it is not to be inferred that those rights not mentioned have the same status. Those rights not enumerated were left to the people and the states to be given legal (as distinguished from constitutional) protection as they might see fit. The framers said what they meant and meant what they said.

In his dissent, Justice Black attacked the heart of the majority opinion. "I get no where in this case," he confessed, "by talk about a constitutional 'right to privacy' as an emanation from one or more constitutional provisions. I like my privacy as well as the next one, but I am nevertheless compelled to admit that government has a right to invade it unless protected by some specific constitutional provision." To suggest that the Court, through the due process clause, the Ninth Amendment, or emanations from other rights, had the power to strike down legislation that a majority of the justices might find "irrational, unreasonable or offensive" is to resurrect the notion that judicial power is guided by natural law rather than by the Constitution. "Use of any such broad, unbounded judicial authority," Black argued, "would make [the Court] a day-to-day constitutional convention."[32]

Even when legislation is as "uncommonly silly" as the Connecticut

31 *Ibid.*, 520, 529, 530.
32 *Ibid.*, 510, 511, 520.

birth control law, it is not the place of the Court to strike it down for such subjective reasons. Black exposed the theoretical kinship of the two great periods of judicial activism. "The Due Process Clause with an 'arbitrary and capricious' or 'shocking to the conscience' formula was liberally used by this Court to strike down economic legislation in the early decades of this century, threatening, many people thought, the tranquillity and stability of the Nation. . . . That formula, based on subjective considerations of 'natural justice' is no less dangerous when used to enforce this Court's views about personal rights than those about economic rights." Judicial reliance on any "mysterious and uncertain natural law concept" as a justification for judicial review undermines not only the idea of a written constitution but the place of the judiciary in the political order as well. The Constitution creates other branches of the government more politically responsive to the changing moods of popular opinion (bolstered by a formal process of amendment) in order to meet the "advancing needs of time." The Court's job is to make sure that in reflecting those changing moods the more politically responsive branches do not go too far.[33]

The judiciary, like the other branches of government, is always prone to a kind of institutional self-righteousness that leads to attempts to "do" justice. As Sowell states, "Those in higher, more powerful, and more remote institutions face the constant temptation to prescribe results rather than define the boundaries of other institutions' discretion. Nothing is easier than to confuse broader powers with deeper insight."[34] This fact lies at the heart of the Constitution's separation of powers.

The Constitution creates a healthy tension between the branches by giving each just enough partial agency in the affairs of the others so that the government will restrain itself. Such written, explicit rules and limits are intended to "encumber the state . . . so that the state may not encumber the citizen."[35] Although the Court typically pays more lip service than the other branches to a doctrine of self-restraint, any firm reliance on self-restraint in the Court (just as in Congress or the

---

33 *Ibid.*, 522. Prophetically, the right of privacy created in *Griswold* proved to be the foundation of the Court's decision regarding abortion in *Roe* v. *Wade* (1973).
34 Sowell, *Knowledge and Decisions*, 302.
35 *Ibid.*, 303.

president) is foolhardy. Like any other governmental institution, the Court cannot be trusted with substantive powers without power being lodged in the coordinate branches to provide procedural shackles. Just as the Constitution created an independent judiciary in part to protect us from the Congress, so it created Congress in part to protect us from the Court. The framers were too wary of political zeal to leave republican safety and political liberty to the good intentions of any one branch.

FOUR

CONGRESS, THE CONSTITUTION AND THE COURTS

When the delegates to the Constitutional Convention began to discuss the defects of the Articles of Confederation, they focused their attention on the problems of legislative power in a republican form of government. The legislative power at the national level had been too weak to meet the most basic exigencies of any government worthy of the name. The framers saw their task as shoring up the national authority by giving it enough power to truly govern. But the recent experiences with legislative power in the several states loomed large and cast an unavoidable shadow over any effort to increase the powers of the national government. Characterized by instability, injustice, and confusion, the state legislative councils had proved to be rather politically shabby places where the public good was generally lost in the "conflicts of rival parties" and where public measures were "too often decided, not according to the rules of justice and the rights of the minor party; but by the superior force of an interested and over-bearing majority." Thus, the states' experiences demanded that the delegates, in their enthusiasm to create a truly national government, avoid introducing the same "unsteadiness and injustice" into the new national legislature that had "tainted" the public administrations of the states.[1]

The problem of legislative power was greater than merely finding institutional cures for instability and confusion, however. State experience had confirmed sound theory: "power is of an encroaching nature." Recognizing that the "legislative department is everywhere extending the sphere of its activity and drawing all power into its impetuous vortex," the framers had to look to limiting national legislative power at the same moment they were endeavoring to increase it. It was against the "enterprising ambition" of the legislature that the founders' attention also had to be directed, in order to create a legisla-

---

1   Jacob E. Cooke (ed.), *The Federalist* (Middletown, Conn., 1961), No. 10, p. 57, hereinafter cited as *The Federalist*. On the state experiences see Gordon S. Wood, *The Creation of the American Republic, 1776-1787* (Chapel Hill, N.C., 1969); and Willi Paul Adams, *The First American Constitutions* (Chapel Hill, N.C., 1980).

ture sufficiently energetic to govern and yet adequately restrained from overwhelming the other departments and concentrating all powers in its own hands. A simple "parchment barrier" of constitutional language would not do. What was necessary, the framers concluded, was to supply the defect "by so contriving the interior structure of the government, as that its several constituent parts may, by their mutual relations, be the means of keeping each other in their proper places." Yet a simple institutional separation was insufficient. In all republican systems of government the legislative power would necessarily predominate, and it would not be possible "to give each department an equal power of defence" against the awesome power of the legislature.[2]

The remedy for this "inconveniency" was twofold. First, the legislative branch had to be weakened through bicameralism (so that each house would be a check on the other); second the coordinate branches (and, in Madison's argument, especially the executive) had to be fortified. Such a scheme of separated powers with each department deriving its authority equally from the same source — the Constitution and, hence, the people — lay at the heart of the framers' design of a government at once capable of controlling the governed and obliged to control itself. This scheme allowed them to think of their proposed government as a popular if not a simply democratic one, for the control of both the governed and the governors was derived from society itself and did not come from an authoritative will independent of society (such as in a monarchy). Their greatest claim was "a Republican remedy for the diseases most incident to Republican Government." In addition to fortifying the executive with powers of appointment, veto, and a general constitutional independence, the founders looked also to creating a judiciary sufficiently powerful and independent that the courts could confidently be expected to serve as "the bulwarks of a limited constitution against legislative encroachments."[3]

The dilemma the convention had to resolve was best summed up by James Wilson of Pennsylvania. "Bad Governts.," he reminded his colleagues, "are of two sorts. 1. that which does too little. 2. that which does too much: that which fails through weakness; and that which destroys thro' oppression." In their quest to establish good government, the delegates had to wrestle constantly with the two issues — state

---

2 *The Federalist*, No. 48, p. 333; No. 51, p. 347.
3 *Ibid.*, No. 10, p. 65; No. 78, p. 526.

power and national power—that tended to tear them apart. They were all well aware of the tragedy wrought by the "turbulence and follies of democracy"; but they were equally aware that the basis of any "remedy . . . must be the republican principle."[4] And their task was made all the more difficult by the mere presence of the states as political entities with at least a historical claim to sovereignty.

Any remedy for the inconveniences of democracy had to take into account the proud independence of the several states. And this was no small problem given that such a remedy had to address the "evils . . . which prevail within the States individually as well as those which affect them collectively." To provide "more effectually for the security of private rights, and the steady dispensation of Justice," it was necessary to knock down the high confederal walls that accident had built between the states and to allow for some sort of national "negative on the will of the particular States" to act as a check on their internal "pernicious machinations." A vulgar politics within the states during the confederal period had produced a good deal of public misery, James Madison argued, in the form of "1. the multiplicity of laws passed by the several States. 2. the mutability of their laws. 3. the injustice of them. 4. the impotence of them." The proposed cure for these ill effects of "popular intemperance" was the creation of a national legislature with the power to "legislate in all cases to which the separate States are incompetent, or in which the harmony of the United States may be interrupted by the exercise of individual legislation." But a national government blessed with a "compleat and *compulsive* operation" and centered in a national legislature demanded "an effective Judiciary establishment commensurate to the legislative authority." For "if the Legislative authority be not restrained, there can be neither liberty nor stability." The most important question that confronted the convention, as Roger Sherman pointed out, was not "what rights naturally belong to men; but how they may be most equally & effectually guarded in society." The relative and generally quiet unanimity of the convention on the nature and extent of judicial power reflected the general understanding that "a government is not a government without courts."[5]

---

4 Max Farrand (ed.), *The Records of the Federal Convention of 1787* (4 vols.; New Haven, Conn., 1936), I, 48, 19.

5 *Ibid.*, I, 318-19, 360, 21, 34, 124, 254, 450; Paul M. Bator *et al.* (eds.), *The Federal Courts and the Federal System* (2nd ed.; Mineola, N.Y., 1973), 6.

Besides the need to control the Congress, another weighty reason lay behind the general agreement over the necessity of courts. That reason was that laws, however just, are meaningless if not backed by some sort of sanctions. To a good number of the delegates the problem with the Articles of Confederation was that under them the United States had provided "the extraordinary spectacle of a government destitute even of the shadow of constitutional power to enforce the execution of its own laws." The want of a national judicial power in the Articles was seen as a crowning defect of the confederation. "Laws," Publius declared, "are a dead letter without courts to expound and define their true meaning and operation." And in a national government that would embrace the states in a subordinate role, it was essential that there be "one court paramount to the rest — possessing a general superintendance, and authorized to settle and declare in the last resort, an uniform rule of civil justice."[6]

These general sentiments issued in several basic premises that came to characterize the proceedings of the convention with regard to the creation of a national judiciary. First, it was agreed that any national judicial power had to operate on both individual citizens and the states. Second, the courts and the judges (like the president) had to be as politically "independent as the lot of humanity will admit." As James Wilson pointed out toward the end of the convention, "The judges would be in a bad situation if made to depend on every gust of faction which might prevail in the [other] two branches of our Govt."[7] Third, the power of the courts should be "judicial only" (however, the consensus included the power to rule on the constitutionality of legislative and executive acts and actions) and should be vested constitutionally in one supreme court and beyond that in any inferior courts as Congress might see fit to establish. Fourth, federal jurisdiction should be limited to certain clearly specified classes of cases. Fifth, the Supreme Court should be vested with original jurisdiction in particular cases that would present a clear national problem or in which the states could not be expected to be impartial, and appellate jurisdiction should be subject to "such Regulations as the Congress shall make."

One of the most important debates over the judiciary centered on

---

6 *The Federalist*, No. 21, p. 130; No. 22, pp. 143, 144.
7 Farrand (ed.), *Records of the Federal Convention*, II, 429.

the question of instituting inferior national courts. The proposals ran from the predictably nationalistic suggestion for mandatory establishment to the predictably confederalist suggestion that lower jurisdiction be left completely to the already existing state judiciaries. In the end a compromise was reached that left "a discretion to the Legislature to establish or not establish them."[8]

A second important argument arose over whether the national courts should be given any extrajudicial functions. A rather popular plan (and one championed until the end by Madison and Wilson) was to include the Supreme Court with the president in a Council of Revision with the power to determine the constitutional validity of legislation. The proposal was defeated each time and in each form that it emerged. A proposal by Oliver Ellsworth to make the chief justice a member of the president's Privy Council was also defeated, as was Charles Pinckney's plan to allow the judges power to render advisory opinions. In the end the logic of Nathaniel Gorham triumphed. "Judges," he warned, "are not to be presumed to possess any peculiar knowledge of the mere policy of public measures."[9]

An independent judiciary (along with an independent and energetic executive and an indirectly elected Senate) was intended as a means of tempering the democratic passions that would tend to characterize the public councils. It was part of an effort to combine the "requisite stability and energy in Government, with the inviolable attention due to liberty, and to the Republican form." Such a combination was considered to be the essence of good government. The judiciary, like the Senate, was looked upon as a "necessary fence" against the dangers posed by the "fickleness and passion" of the most representative body. Also, like the Senate, the Court was expected to be composed of a "portion of enlightened citizens, whose limited number, and firmness might seasonably interpose agst. impetuous counsels." Good republican government (as opposed to simple democratic government) called for political bodies "sufficiently respectable" for their "wisdom & virtue" with the constitutional power to throw their weight when necessary into the scale of those oppressed by any "unjust and partial laws"

8 *Ibid.*, I, 125.
9 *Ibid.*, I, 21, 97–104, 108–10, 138–40; II, 73–80, 298, 328–29, 340–41, 73.

passed by "interested co-alitions."[10] Republican liberty, it was believed, demanded more than simple representation of the aggregate interests of the community.

In fulfilling their constitutional duties, the courts were expected to look beyond the aggregate interests of the community that might come to be expressed in public law to the permanent interests of the community that were expressed in the Constitution. The judges of the federal judiciary were to be the "faithful guardians" of the Constitution. Their constitutional obligation was to look beyond the nonfundamental laws that would issue from the legislature and to measure them —whenever a conflict should arise—against the fundamental law of the Constitution. In those instances of an "irreconcileable variance" between the statute and the Constitution, "the constitution ought to be preferred to the statute, the intention of the people to the intention of their agents." By regulating their decisions by the fundamental law, an independent judiciary—"one of the most valuable of modern improvements in the practice of government"—would be an "excellent barrier to the encroachments and oppressions of the representative body." Such an arrangement was "peculiarly essential" in order to secure the "steady, upright, and impartial administration of the laws" under an emphatically limited written constitution.[11]

The judiciary was designed to serve as an "intermediate body between the people and the legislature in order . . . to keep the latter within the limits assigned to their authority." Since a written constitution with a specification of particular powers on its face "excludes all pretension to a general legislative authority," courts were deemed the appropriate institutions to enforce those certain specified exceptions to the legislative authority. As Publius explained it, "Limitations of this kind can be preserved in practice no other way than through the medium of the courts of justice." For without the power to declare acts contrary to the "manifest tenor" of the Constitution void, "all the reservations of particular rights or privileges would amount to nothing."[12]

This power of judicial review was considered by thoughtful critics of the new constitutional plan to be a dangerous embellishment on the republican principle—or perhaps a complete abandonment of it. To

10 *The Federalist*, No. 37, p. 233; Farrand (ed.), *Records of the Federal Convention*, I, 422, 423.
11 *The Federalist*, No. 78, p. 522.
12 *Ibid.*, 525; No. 83, p. 560; No. 78, p. 524.

allow the courts to declare acts of Congress void, argued the anti-Federalist Brutus, was to imply that members of the judicial branch — being unelected and tenured for life — were superior to those of the legislative branch. This was hardly the logic of sound republican government. Brutus' concern was a phantom, countered Publius; such a worry was at best the result of a misconception of the power of judicial review. The power of constitutional review, Publius suggested, "only supposes that the power of the people is superior to both [the judiciary and the legislature]; and where the will of the legislature declared in its statutes, stands in opposition to that of the people declared in the constitution, the judges ought to be governed by the latter, rather than the former."[13]

In addition to the "general theory of a limited constitution" that necessitated that some power of constitutional review of governmental actions be vested somewhere, the "natural feebleness" of the judiciary made it the most appropriate institution to wield such a potentially dangerous power. Publius' famous defense of locating the power in the judiciary merits repeating.

> Whoever attentively considers the different departments of power must perceive, that in a government where they are separated from each other, the judiciary, from the nature of its functions, will always be the least dangerous to the political rights of the constitution; because it will be least in a capacity to annoy or injure them. The executive not only dispenses the honors, but holds the sword of the community. The Legislature not only commands the purse, but prescribes the rules by which the duties and rights of every citizen are to be regulated. The judiciary on the contrary has no influence over either the strength or the wealth of the society, and can take no active resolution whatever. It may truly be said to have neither FORCE nor WILL but merely judgment; and must ultimately depend upon the aid of the executive arm even for the efficacy of its judgments.[14]

The institutional independence of the judiciary was seen as necessary to reduce the fear that the "pestilential breath of faction" would "poison the fountains of justice" in any declaration of unconstitutionality. The courts had to be viewed as standing above the partisan disputes of everyday politics. But such political isolation did not, to the framers' way of thinking, render the courts apolitical institutions. The very nature of their work would force them daily into the whirl and the suck of politics. And it was never assumed that men possessed

13 *Ibid.*, No. 78, p. 525.
14 *Ibid.*, 522–23.

of sufficient character to warrant appointment to the courts would be men bereft of political opinions about the issues that would come before them for resolution. Although it was believed that the "great engines of judicial despotism" were primarily arbitrary impeachments, prosecutions, convictions, and punishments in criminal proceedings, it had to be conceded that there was "not a syllable" in the Constitution that *"directly"* empowered the courts to construe laws according to the spirit rather than the letter of the Constitution. Neither was there a syllable that forbade it. Thus, it was possible that a court might deliberately misconstrue or contravene the will of the legislature, being "disposed to exercise WILL instead of JUDGMENT," and substitute "their pleasure for that of the legislature." Should the judiciary presume to impose its political will rather than merely exercise its judgment in the cases that might come before it, there was a constitutional remedy for such "deliberate usurpations": impeachment.[15]

Impeachment, however, was a recognized redress of considerable magnitude. Impeachments were understood to be "of a nature which may with peculiar propriety be denominated POLITICAL"; they were nothing less than a "NATIONAL INQUEST into the conduct of public men." Because of the gravity of impeachment, it would not always be an appropriate means of politically redressing abuses in the exercise of judicial power. For that reason the Constitution provided that both the appellate jurisdiction of the Supreme Court and the institution and jurisdiction of inferior courts were "left to the discretion of the legislature." The national legislature was given "ample authority" to "obviate or remove" any "inconveniencies" arising from the exercise of judicial power (except to "reverse a determination once made"). Indeed, to "avoid an arbitrary discretion in the courts," Publius acknowledged, "it is indispensable that they should be bound down by strict rules and precedents, which serve to define and point out their duty in every particular case that comes before them." Through a general superintendence of the business of the federal judiciary, the legislature can modify the judicial process whenever it thinks it advisable and in any way it believes will "best answer the ends of public justice and security."[16]

The work of hammering out the details of judicial power was remark-

---

15 *Ibid.*, No. 81, pp. 544, 543, 545; No. 78, p. 526.
16 *Ibid.*, No. 65, pp. 439, 440; No. 82, p. 557; No. 81, p. 545; No. 80, p. 541; No. 78, p. 529; No. 81, p. 552.

ably brief and came rather late in the convention. On July 24, the delegates agreed to submit to the Committee of Detail the resolutions they had approved up to that time. The resolutions concerning the judiciary were brief: "That the Jurisdiction of the national Judiciary shall extend to Cases arising under the Laws passed by the general Legislature, and to such other Questions as involve the national Peace and Harmony . . . [and] That the national Legislature be empowered to appoint inferior Tribunals."[17] With no more to work with than this, the committee (chaired by John Rutledge and including Edmund Randolph, James Wilson, Oliver Ellsworth, and Nathaniel Gorham) buried itself, between July 26 and August 6 while the convention adjourned, in its assigned task to report a constitution "conformable" to the sentiments of the convention. The committee shaped the judicial resolutions into a form close to what was ultimately included in the Constitution.

The committee endeavored to flesh out the sentiments of the proposals in as much detail as it could. After outlining the original jurisdiction of the Supreme Court, which still included trying cases of impeachment, the committee's report sketched the powers of the national legislature pertaining to the superintendence of the national judiciary. "In all other Cases beforementioned [the jurisdiction of the Supreme Court] shall be appellate, with such Exceptions and under such Regulations as the Legislature shall make." Concerning inferior courts that might be established, the committee wrote: "The Legislature may assign any part of the Jurisdiction above mentd . . . in the Manner and under such Limitations which it shall think proper to such other inferior Courts as it shall constitute from Time to Time."[18] Later, when the Constitution was polished by the Committee of Style, the provisions relating to the judiciary for a plenary power of Congress over Supreme Court appellate jurisdiction and over the entire jurisdiction of any inferior courts Congress might create seem to have been readily acceptable.

As a delegate to the Virginia Ratifying Convention, John Marshall explained without apparent objection that under the Constitution "Congress is empowered to make exceptions to the appellate jurisdiction, as to law and fact, of the Supreme Court. These exceptions certainly go as far as the legislature may think proper for the interest and

17 Farrand (ed.), *Records of the Federal Convention*, II, 132–33.
18 *Ibid.*, II, 173.

the liberty of the people." In 1796, when the first case that raised a question as to the extent of congressional power over the jurisdiction of the Court came before the Supreme Court, *Wiscart* v. *Dauchy*, Chief Justice Oliver Ellsworth (a former member of the Committee of Detail) affirmed what had been the sense of the convention. The appellate jurisdiction of the Supreme Court, he proclaimed, is "qualified; inasmuch as it is given 'with such exceptions, and under such regulations, as Congress shall make.' . . . If Congress has provided no rule to regulate our proceedings, we cannot exercise an appellate jurisdiction; and if the rule is provided, we cannot depart from it."[19]

On the basis of the Constitution, Congress is given two means of exercising some control over the federal judiciary. First, Congress is empowered to make "exceptions" to the appellate jurisdiction of the Supreme Court of certain classes of cases as it sees fit; second, it is empowered to make such "regulations" for the exercise of whatever jurisdiction is granted as Congress thinks best serves the objects of the Constitution. Further, at the level of the inferior courts, Congress has the authority to create them or not; to give them complete federal jurisdiction or just a portion of it; and to regulate the exercise of whatever jurisdiction is given through the formulation of rules and procedures.[20] Such congressional control over the business of the national judiciary was thought both possible and prudent because in the federal scheme of the Constitution the state courts, bound as they are to uphold the Constitution as the supreme law of the land, "are the primary guarantors of constitutional rights, and in many cases they may be the ultimate ones."[21] Lest such a reliance on the states seem shocking, it should be recalled that it was not until 1875 that the lower federal courts had any general jurisdiction in cases arising under the Constitution or the laws of the United States; nor was it until 1891 that criminal cases were appealable to the Supreme Court of the United States.

From the earliest years of the Republic, the Supreme Court has consistently upheld this understanding of the power of Congress over the

19 Jonathan Elliot (ed.), *Debates in the Several State Conventions on the Adoption of the Federal Constitution* (2nd ed.; 5 vols.; Philadelphia, 1866), III, 560; *Wiscart* v. *Dauchy*, 3 Dallas 321, 327 (1796).
20 See *Sheldon* v. *Sill*, 8 Howard 440 (1850).
21 Herbert Wechsler, "The Courts and the Constitution," *Columbia Law Review*, LXV (1965), 1001, 1006. See also Henry Hart's famous dialogue on the question of federal court jurisdiction, "The Power of Congress to Limit the Jurisdiction of Federal Courts: An Exercise in Dialectic," *Harvard Law Review*, LXVI (1953), 1362.

federal judiciary. After *Wiscart*, in 1805, Chief Justice John Marshall had occasion to repeat the view he had expressed in the Virginia Ratifying Convention in 1788. In *United States* v. *More*, he noted that the Supreme Court had no criminal appellate jurisdiction because none had been granted by Congress. The affirmative description of the Court's powers had to be understood, under the Constitution, "as a regulation . . . prohibiting the exercise of other powers than those described." In 1810 he emphasized yet again that "an affirmative description has been understood to imply a negative in the exercise of such appellate power as is not comprehended within it." Marshall stated further: "The appellate powers of the court are not given by the judicial act. They are given by the constitution. But they are limited and regulated by the judicial act, and by such other acts as have been passed on the subject. When the first legislature of the Union proceeded to carry the third article of the constitution into effect, they must be understood as intending to execute the power they possessed by making exceptions to the appellate jurisdiction of the supreme court." Marshall's successor to the helm of the highest court, Roger B. Taney, was of the same mind. "By the Constitution of the United States," he affirmed, "the Supreme Court possesses not appellate power in any case, unless conferred upon it by act of Congress; nor can it, when conferred, be exercised in any other form, or by any other mode of proceeding than that which the law prescribes."[22]

In the most famous instance of the Court having to address the question of the limits of congressional power over its jurisdiction, *Ex parte McCardle,* the Court, under Chief Justice Salmon Chase, affirmed the traditional view. In McCardle's case, Congress, feeling that the Court might use the case as a vehicle for overturning much of the Reconstruction program in the South after the Civil War, withdrew that portion of the Habeas Corpus Act of 1867 under which William McCardle had brought his action. The act provided for appeals to the Supreme Court from judgments of a circuit court; the repealing legislation denied that course of habeas corpus action (though it left other avenues for habeas corpus relief open) as well as "the exercise of any such jurisdiction" by the Supreme Court "on appeals which have been or may hereafter be taken." The result was that the Court, after having heard arguments in the McCardle case, conceded that it could not

22 *United States* v. *More*, 3 Cranch 159, 172 (1805); *Durousseau* v. *United States*, 6 Cranch 307, 313 (1810); *Barry* v. *Mercein*, 5 Howard 103, 119 (1847).

proceed, that the power Congress had exercised in repealing the Court's jurisdiction was constitutionally legitimate. The judicial power could not extend to areas that Congress saw fit to exclude from the Court's jurisdiction. "We are not at liberty to inquire into the motives of the legislature," said the Court. "We can only examine into its power under the Constitution; and the power to make exceptions to the appellate jurisdiction of this court is given by express words . . . [W]ithout jurisdiction the court cannot proceed at all in any case. Jurisdiction is the power to declare the law, and when it ceases to exist, the only function remaining to the court is that of announcing the fact and dismissing the case. And this is not less clear upon authority than upon principle."[23] Although the Court did endeavor in the later cases of *Ex parte Yerger* (1869) and *United States* v. *Klein* (1872) to emphasize the limited scope of the McCardle case, holding that Congress had not denied the Supreme Court's complete jurisdiction over habeas corpus nor could Congress use its exceptions power to further an unconstitutional end, it still conceded that the legislature "undoubtedly" has a complete power over the jurisdiction of the federal courts.

This line of judicial thinking did not end with the *Klein* case; nor has it since changed. In 1881, in *The "Francis Wright"* case, Chief Justice Morrison Waite emphasized again the constitutional relationship between Congress and the courts. He wrote, "What [appellate powers of the Supreme Court] shall be, and to what extent they shall be exercised, are, and always have been, proper subjects of legislative control. Authority to limit the jurisdiction necessarily carries with it authority to limit the use of the jurisdiction. Not only may whole classes be kept out of the jurisdiction altogether, but particular classes of questions may be subjected to re-examination and review, while others are not."[24]

Midway through the twentieth century, the Court again defended this unambiguous line of constitutional authority. "Congress," Justice Wiley Rutledge wrote in *Yakus* v. *United States* (1945), "has plenary power to confer or withhold appellate jurisdiction." Four years later Justice Frankfurter saw fit to reaffirm the judicial commitment to this point. Writing in *National Mutual Insurance Co.* v. *Tidewater Transfer* (1949), Frankfurter argued: "Congress need not establish inferior courts: Congress need not grant the full scope of jurisdiction which it

23   *Ex parte McCardle*, 7 Wallace 506, 513–14 (1868).
24   *The "Francis Wright,"* 105 U.S. 381, 386 (1881).

is empowered to vest in them; Congress need not give this Court any appellate power; it may withdraw appellate jurisdiction once conferred and it may do so even when a case is *sub judice*."[25]

As recently as 1968, Justice Douglas in *Flast* v. *Cohen* argued that "As respects our appellate jurisdiction, Congress may largely fashion it as Congress desires by reason of the express provisions of Section 2, Article III" of the Constitution. And, with regard to the lower courts, in 1973 the Supreme Court summarized their constitutional status this way:

Article III describes the judicial power as extending to all cases, among others, arising under the laws of the United States; but, aside from this Court, the power is vested "in such inferior Courts as the Congress may from time to time ordain and establish." The decision with respect to inferior federal courts, as well as the task of defining their jurisdiction, was left to the discretion of Congress. That body was not constitutionally required to create inferior Art. III courts to hear and decide cases within the judicial power of the United States, including those criminal cases arising under the laws of the United States. Nor, if inferior federal courts were created, was it required to invest them with all the jurisdiction it was authorized to bestow under Art. III. "The judicial power of the United States . . . is (except in enumerated instances, applicable exclusively to this court) dependent for its distribution and organization, and for the modes of its exercise, entirely upon the action of Congress, who possess the sole power of creating the tribunals (inferior to the Supreme Court) . . . and of investing them with jurisdiction either limited, concurrent, or exclusive, and of withholding jurisdiction from them in the exact degrees and character which to Congress may seem proper for the public good." *Cary* v. *Curtis*, 3 Howard 236, 245 (1845). Congress plainly understood this, for until 1875 Congress refrained from providing the lower federal courts with general federal-question jurisdiction. Until that time, the state courts provided the only forum for vindicating many important federal claims. Even then, with exceptions, the state courts remained the sole forum for the trial of federal cases not involving the required jurisdictional amount, and for the most part retained concurrent jurisdiction of federal claims properly within the jurisdiction of the lower federal courts.[26]

Only relatively recently have serious questions been raised as to the

25 *Yakus* v. *United States*, 321 U.S. 414, 472–73 (1945); *National Mutual Insurance Co.* v. *Tidewater Transfer* 337 U.S. 582, 655 (1949).

26 *Flast* v. *Cohen*, 392 U.S. 83, 109 (1968); *Palmore* v. *United States*, 411 U.S. 389, 400–402 (1973). See also *Rhode Island* v. *Massachusetts*, 12 Peters 657, 721–22 (1838); *Sheldon* v. *Sill*, 8 Howard 440 (1850); *Case of the Sewing Machine Companies*, 18 Wallace 553, 577–78 (1874); *Kline* v. *Burke Construction Co.*, 260 U.S. 226, 233–34 (1922); *Turner* v. *Bank of North America*, 4 Dallas 8 (1799); and *United States* v. *Hudson*, 7 Cranch 32 (1812).

scope of congressional power to tamper with the appellate jurisdiction of the Supreme Court and the general jurisdiction of the inferior federal courts. In most cases, however, the critics of a broad congressional power to regulate the courts seem prone to confuse what the Constitution authorizes with what, in their view, "sound constitutional statesmanship admonishes." The debate over congressional power to curb the courts is often as much a matter of dispute over unsettled policy issues as it is a principled argument over constitutional power. The area is truly an "embattled terrain" where the various proponents do rhetorical battle. Gerald Gunther has examined why this issue is again heating up politically. "The central and expanding role of the Court in our modern polity," he points out, "helps explain the recurrent outrage expressed in the media and in academia in response to proposed congressional assertions of power over jurisdiction."[27]

The various defenders of an absolute separation of powers between Congress and the courts go to great lengths to prove their points. The oldest extant theory is also, in a curious sense, the most moderate. Leonard Ratner has argued for years that the power of Congress over appellate jurisdiction of the Court stops at the point where congressional regulations and exceptions would impair the "essential constitutional functions of the Court." Those functions are rather simple: "to maintain the supremacy and uniformity of federal law." A plenary congressional "exceptions" power, he argues, echoing an argument first put forth by Henry Hart, "is not consistent with the constitutional plan."[28]

There is a certain compelling logic to Ratner's account, but there is little in the way of compelling law or convincing history to support it. Textually, "there is simply no 'essential functions' limit on the face of the exceptions clause." Nor does it seem that such a limit was part of the framers' thinking. As Gunther has written, "Even more damaging to the case for an unreachable 'essential' Court role of assuring supremacy and uniformity is congressional practice, beginning in the earliest period, when there was considerable overlap among delegates to the

27 Gerald Gunther, "Congressional Power to Curtail Federal Court Jurisdiction: An Opinionated Guide to the Ongoing Debate," *Stanford Law Review*, XXXVI (1984), 895, 898, 900, 906.

28 Leonard Ratner, "Congressional Power Over the Appellate Jurisdiction of the Supreme Court," *University of Pennsylvania Law Review*, CIX (1960), 157; Ratner, "Majoritarian Constraints on Judicial Review: Congressional Control of Supreme Court Jurisdiction," *Villanova Law Review*, XXVII (1982), 929, 957. See Hart, "The Power of Congress to Limit the Jurisdiction of Federal Courts," 1362.

Constitutional Convention and members of the First Congress. The Judiciary Act of 1789 did *not* grant to the Court all the potential article III appellate jurisdiction even in constitutional cases, necessary to assure that the Supreme Court would be the ultimate provider of both supremacy and uniformity."[29]

The "essential functions" argument falters especially at the level of constitutional principle. The scheme of separation of powers constructed by the Constitution was never intended to provide "total insulation of the judicial branch any more than it does for the other branches."[30] The necessary institutional tensions and checks and balances so essential to the internal constitutional limits on the government would be lost if any one branch of the government, including the judiciary, were to be given such favored treatment.

The advocates of the "essential functions" theory have been more persistent than persuasive. Neither Congress nor the Court has ever taken that view seriously. No doubt this lack of political success accounts at least in part for the recent burst of other more innovative theories in this area. But these new theories tend to go so far beyond the Constitution that they are seen by most scholarly experts to be as tortured as they no doubt seem to the general public and the various representatives the public sends to office.

One of the most unusual ideas — because so blatant — touches upon the question of whether there must be a lower federal court where federal claims can be raised. This idea has arisen because the second popular effort of curbing the courts is to strip jurisdiction of certain classes of cases from the lower courts altogether, leaving only state courts as the primary forum for the resolution of such disputes. Fearing this prospect perhaps even more than exceptions to Supreme Court appellate jurisdiction, Theodore Eisenberg is unflinchingly provocative. "It can now be asserted," he argues, that the existence of lower federal courts "in some form is constitutionally required."[31] The defect of this position is obvious; this theory flies even more directly in the face of history and judicial precedent and theory (not to mention the text of the Constitution) than any other. Never has Congress — especially the First Congress — thought such to be true; never has a

29 Gunther, "Congressional Power to Curtail Federal Court Jurisdiction," 903, 906–907.

30 *Ibid.*, 907.

31 Theodore Eisenberg, "Congressional Authority to Restrict Lower Federal Jurisdiction," *Yale Law Journal*, LXXXIII (1974), 498, 513.

court ever alluded to such logic; never could the clear language and unmistakable intent of the Constitution be so misconstrued. The text of the Constitution cannot be thought to be altered only because circumstances have changed. This argument is akin to one that would hold that because mortality rates have improved since 1787 the clear age requirements for Congress and the president can now be raised accordingly. The violence such an argument, if taken seriously, would do to the idea of a written constitution is incalculable.

A less far-reaching theory holds simply that Article III of the Constitution requires that there must be *some* federal judicial forum for adjudicating federal constitutional claims. That forum may either be the Supreme Court *or* a lower federal court. The obverse of this is that Congress may not bar federal court review of state court determinations of federal constitutional rights by the Supreme Court and by lower courts. One critic of this theory dubs it "a 'floating' essential functions thesis."[32]

At the bottom of all the concern over court-stripping proposals in Congress is a largely unarticulated fear of federalism. The core of this concern is the belief that state courts are inevitably prone to abuse or ignore federal constitutional claims. But just as changed circumstances are not sufficient to rewrite the Constitution independent of formal amendment, neither are current doubts about state governance sufficient to read the federal features out of the Constitution. Henry Hart long ago pointed out that in "the scheme of the Constitution [the state courts] are the primary guarantors of constitutional rights, and in many cases they may be the ultimate ones."[33]

The demand for uniformity in the adjudication of federal claims is not enough to prohibit Congress from lodging certain classes of cases in the hands of the state courts. As Martin Redish has pointed out, "Unless we are able to find objective criteria, grounded in the Constitution, by which to declare state courts technically inadequate forums for the adjudication of constitutional rights, we cannot—as a consti-

32 Lawrence Sager, "Foreword: Constitutional Limitations on Congress' Authority to Regulate the Jurisdiction of the Federal Courts," *Harvard Law Review*, XCV (1981), 17, 61–68. The criticism is from Martin Redish, "Constitutional Limitations on Congressional Power to Control Federal Jurisdiction: A Reaction to Professor Sager," *Northwestern University Law Review*, LXXVII (1983), 143, 145.

33 Hart, "The Power of Congress to Limit the Jurisdiction of the Federal Courts," 1401.

tutional matter, at least — reject the long-accepted history recognizing the competence of state courts to perform this function."[34] This federal feature is, like the power of Congress to make exceptions to the appellate jurisdiction of the Supreme Court, one of the very least ambiguous features of the Constitution.

Thus, in light of the records of the Constitutional Convention, the debates in the several state ratifying conventions, the arguments of *The Federalist*, and the entire history of judicial resolutions of such questions, from Oliver Ellsworth to Byron White, it is clear that Congress has, and was intended to have, the "power by enactment of a statute to strike at what it deems judicial excess by delimitations of the jurisdiction of the lower courts and of the Supreme Court's appellate jurisdiction."[35] When Congress undertakes to exercise its exceptions and regulations power, the question is not one of constitutional legitimacy but of political prudence.

Political prudence lies at the core of statesmanship; it is judgment informed of principle made in light of reality. In American politics, Tocqueville said, it is essential that statesmen "know how to understand the spirit of the age, to confront those obstacles that can be overcome, and to steer out of the current when the tide threatens to carry them away, and with them the sovereignty of the Union and obedience to its laws."[36] Prudence, then, is the attempt to reconcile the demands of the transitory popular opinion that characterizes everyday life in the body politic with the demands of the more permanent public opinion that undergirds the entire enterprise; it is tempering the mere knowledge of the aggregate interests of the community with a certain wisdom concerning the community's permanent interests.

The institutional arrangements of the Constitution were designed to extract the deliberate sense of the community by checking every "sudden breese of passion" or "transient impulse" that might corrupt popular opinion. The aim, in shunning a reliance on public mood in favor of a reliance on the public mind, was to tilt the system in such a way

34 Redish, "Constitutional Limitations on Congressional Power to Control Federal Jurisdiction," 166.

35 Wechsler, "The Courts and the Constitution," 1005.

36 Alexis de Tocqueville, *Democracy in America*, trans. G. Lawrence, ed. J. P. Mayer (New York, 1966), 151.

that public laws would be sensible. The hope was for a system wherein the reason rather than the passions of the people prevailed.[37]

The Constitution, as a whole as well as in its constituent parts, is directed at generating the prudence the framers thought to be necessary to good government. No simple reliance on enlightened statesmen being at the helm would be sufficient. "A reliance on pure patriotism," Hamilton told the convention, "had been the source of many . . . errors." Rather, the Constitution attempted through interior devices to supply the defect of better motives.[38] Yet, the framers did offer an explicit guide to the politics that would develop under the Constitution, for the language of the Constitution vests a constitutional obligation in the various departments to be prudent in the conduct of public affairs. The key to the Constitution's concern for political prudence is the necessary and proper clause.

By granting to Congress the power to "make all Laws which shall be necessary and proper for carrying into Execution" the powers of the Constitution, the framers achieved two broad objectives. First, it gave Congress a moral guide as well as a flexibility to meet whatever exigencies time might bring about; second, it provided a standard by which the coordinate branches might judge legislation. The words *necessary and proper* establish a constitutional standard of political wisdom for the conduct of public affairs.

This political wisdom or prudence derives from two considerations that should go into the drafting of any sound law: necessity and propriety. The standard of necessity forces public officials to defend a proposal as a means that will best or most effectively achieve the ends of the constitutional provision under which the proposal is undertaken. The standard of propriety encourages that the means chosen be consistent with the rest of the Constitution, with "a fair construction of the whole instrument." Necessity and propriety were intended as guides to the legislature to exercise its "best judgment" in selecting the means to "carry into execution the constitutional powers of the government." The demands of constitutional government require both flexibility and fixed standards. If the end sought by the legislation is

37 See Bessette, "Deliberative Democracy: The Majority Principle in Republican Government," in Robert A. Goldwin and William A. Schambra (eds.), *How Democratic is the Constitution?* (Washington, D.C., 1980); and *The Federalist*, No. 49, p. 343.

38 Farrand (ed.), *Records of the Federal Convention*, I, 376; *The Federalist*, No. 51, pp. 347, 349.

legitimate, if it is within the scope of the Constitution, then "all means which are appropriate, which are plainly adapted to that end, which are not prohibited, but which consist with the letter and spirit of the constitution, are constitutional."[39]

John Marshall's famous explication of the necessary and proper clause in *McCulloch* v. *Maryland* exposed its principled logic. "The subject," the chief justice wrote, "is the execution of those great powers on which the welfare of a nation essentially depends."

> It must have been the intention of those who gave these powers, to insure, as far as human prudence could insure, their beneficial execution. This could not be done by confining the choice of means to such narrow limits as not to leave it in the power of Congress to adopt any which might be appropriate, and which were conducive to the end. This provision is made in a constitution intended to endure for ages to come, and, consequently, to be adapted to the various *crises* of human affairs. To have prescribed the means by which government should, in all future time, execute its powers, would have been to change entirely, the character of the instrument, and give it the properties of a legal code. It would have been an unwise attempt to provide, by immutable rules, for exigencies which, if forseen at all, must have been seen dimly, and which can be best provided for as they occur. To have declared that the best means shall not be used, but those alone without which the power given would be nugatory, would have been to deprive the legislature of the capacity to avail itself of experience, to exercise its reason, and to accommodate its legislation to circumstances.[40]

Beyond being a broad guide, the standards of necessity and propriety also serve as more precise standards on which one house of Congress may base its refusal to give effect to the designs of the other; as principled bases for a presidential veto of legislation; and, in the last resort, as standards for judicial review. In the case of attempts to enhance or restrict any powers of the government, each party to the legislation is constitutionally obligated to consider whether the proposal is necessary and proper. That is, will it achieve the end for which it is intended? And, does it achieve that end without violating any provision of the Constitution?

There are enough obstacles to any legislation to ensure that by the time a law is enacted, the opinions that originally prompted it have been sufficiently enlarged and refined so that the law will rest solidly on a broad base of popular consensus. This mechanical safety applies

39 Gerald Gunther (ed.), *John Marshall's Defense of McCulloch v. Maryland* (Stanford, Calif., 1969), 28, 38-39.
40 *Ibid.*, 34.

with no less effect to efforts to adjust the administration of certain judicial powers. There are, and there must be remembered to be, "political limits on the Supreme Court's authority to bind the other branches and the states by its interpretation of the Constitution."[41] And when public protest over what are perceived to be abuses of judicial power is sufficiently broad and deep to result in a "national consensus shared by both the President and Congress," and when the proposed legislation does not violate a constitutional provision (such as the due process of law clause) or deny any other constitutional power (for example, the original jurisdiction of the Supreme Court), it is a valid exercise of political power.

John Marshall, writing pseudonymously as "A Friend of the Constitution" in defense of his opinion in *McCulloch* v. *Maryland*, explained the constitutional relationship between Congress and the courts. The power explicitly given to Congress in Article I of the Constitution to constitute tribunals inferior to the Supreme Court, he argued, implies that any "act constituting these tribunals, defining their jurisdiction, regulating their proceedings, &c, is not an incident to the power but the means of executing it.—The legislature may multiply or diminish these tribunals, may vary their jurisdiction at will." When a court takes it upon itself to function more as the "originator of controlling norms than as the interpreter of norms derived from acts of Congress," it is altogether fitting—that is, necessary and proper and thus politically prudent—for Congress and the president to give greater definition to the forms and limits of judicial power, or at least to try to do so.[42]

41 Wechsler, "The Courts and the Constitution," 1009.
42 Gunther (ed.), *John Marshall's Defense of McCulloch v. Maryland*, 173; Wechsler, "The Courts and the Constitution," 1002, 1009, 1014.

FIVE

RESPONSES TO JUDICIAL ACTIVISM

There is a level of principle to which the Congress and the president must appeal in any endeavor to evaluate judicial power and in any attempt to give greater definition to the forms and limits of that power. At that level two political principles that lie at the heart of American constitutionalism give greater substance to the notions of the necessity and propriety of curbing the courts. Any effort to curb the courts that aspires to be a principled rather than merely a partisan response to perceived judicial excesses must be defended in light of the principles of federalism and separation of powers. Together these doctrines provide a constitutional standard against which the exercise of judicial power can be measured.

In the logic of the Constitution, the doctrines of separation of powers and federalism are the primary means of checking the powers of the national government. These two principles—modified as they were by the delegates to the Constitutional Convention—provide a "double security" to the rights of the people against the power of the government. "In the compound republic of America," Publius explained, "the power surrendered by the people, is first divided between two distinct governments, and then the portion allotted to each, subdivided among distinct and separate departments. . . . The different governments will controul each other; at the same time that each will be controuled by itself."[1]

In weighing alleged improprieties of judicial power, the president and Congress must raise two fundamental questions. First, is the judiciary exercising its powers in such a way as to violate the doctrine of separation of powers? Second, is the judiciary exercising its powers without what Justice Stone called a "scrupulous regard for the rightful independence of the states"? The president and Congress have an obligation not only to defend themselves against judicial encroachments but to defend the states as well. It was for this reason that the framers

[1]   Jacob E. Cooke (ed.), *The Federalist* (Middletown, Conn., 1961), No. 51, p. 351, hereinafter cited as *The Federalist*.

reached their compromise on the nature and extent of the federal judicial power. By allowing Congress the power to regulate and to make exceptions to the appellate power of the Supreme Court, the Constitution leaves open the possibility that certain classes of cases can be left to the highest court of the states for final review. And, by allowing Congress plenary power over the creation and structure of any inferior courts, the Constitution also leaves open the possibility that the state judiciaries may indeed be the first (and perhaps the only) defense against infringements of constitutional rights.[2] It is thus left up to political discretion to determine just how far federal jurisdiction shall extend, how it is to be parceled out between the national government and the states, and how judicial power is to be exercised within the jurisdiction that is granted to the federal courts.

Legislation dealing with the federal judiciary has always been "a very empiric response to very definite needs." The focus of such responses has tended to be on the problems arising from the general institutional tensions posed by the federal balance of the Constitution. The political passions and attachments spawned by our "incomplete national government," as Tocqueville described it, have generated an inevitable give-and-take struggle between a national government designed to be supreme and the several states who persist in claims — however truncated by the language of the Constitution — to sovereignty. The fact that we are at once a federation and a continent (a nation of states, to be precise) has resulted in a continuous controversy over the nature and extent of national power in general and the national judicial power in particular. "How to distribute judicial power between state and national courts, how to make a system of national courts workable over so vast and diversified a country, have been far-reaching political issues since 1789."[3] But the controversy has been intensified by two historical facts: the Civil War and the Great Depression. Each event called into question the very legitimacy of the nation and led to an increase in sentiment and power on the national side of the federal scale.[4] Although court-curbing has had a long history, the most sig-

---

2 See Felix Frankfurter and James Landis, *The Business of the Supreme Court* (New York, 1928), 4.

3 *Ibid.*, 13, 217; Alexis de Tocqueville, *Democracy in America*, trans. G. Lawrence, ed. J. P. Mayer (New York, 1966), 143.

4 See the introduction to Morton J. Frisch and Richard G. Stevens (eds.), *American Political Thought: The Philosophic Dimension of American Statesmanship* (New York, 1971): "As we see in retrospect, there have been . . . great crises in the life of our country. They are the critical moments in the fulfillment of the words and phrases of the Declaration of Independence" (p. 8).

nificant sustained movements have occurred after the Civil War and the ratification of the Civil War amendments, and after the advent of the New Deal.

From the beginning of the republic, the federal judiciary was the object of a good bit of political wrath and personal invective. The passage of the Judiciary Act of 1789 (and the related Process Acts of 1789 and 1792) occasioned hard-fought rhetorical battles in the halls of Congress. The bill was alternately praised as an "astutely contrived" piece of legislative wisdom and scorned as a "vile bill." The first judiciary acts foreshadowed the controversial role the judiciary was to occupy in the American political order.

Throughout the Jeffersonian-Federalist skirmishes over the passage and repeal of the Judiciary Act of 1801, the impeachment of Justice Samuel Chase in 1804 (and the rumored pending impeachment of John Marshall should he persist in declaring congressional acts unconstitutional as he had done in *Marbury* v. *Madison*), the public outrage over Chief Justice Marshall's opinion in *McCulloch* v. *Maryland* (and his subsequent public though pseudonymous defense of that opinion in the press), and Justice Story's opinion in *Prigg* v. *Pennsylvania* (1842), the Marshall and Taney courts were "pretty much continuously in trouble with Congress, the Executive, or the States."[5] But after Chief Justice Taney's opinion in the case of *Dred Scott* v. *Sandford* (1857), the efforts to curb the courts were characterized by an enthusiasm and creativity that surpassed even the most ardent Jeffersonians and Jacksonians.

Since the middle of the nineteenth century there have been frequent efforts to curtail the powers of the federal judiciary. They fall into four distinct eras. The first period ran from the *Dred Scott* decision to *Chicago, Milwaukee, and St. Paul Ry. Co.* v. *Minnesota* (1890); the second period, the era of substantive due process, lasted from 1890 through 1937; the third period, 1938 to 1954, was characterized by a concern for efficiency in judicial administration; and the final era, the era of the new activism, began in 1954 with *Brown* v. *Board of Education of Topeka, Kansas*. The first three periods generally found a conservative judiciary confronted by a more liberal public and Congress; the present period has reversed that order. Yet, each period displays

5 Ann Stuart Diamond, "Containing the Least Dangerous Branch: From Founding to Civil War" (Paper presented at a conference entitled "Judicial Power in the United States: What are the Appropriate Constraints?" held at the American Enterprise Institute, Washington, D.C., October 1-2, 1981), 5.

similar concerns and approaches: efforts to redefine the jurisdiction of the courts and especially the appellate jurisdiction of the Supreme Court; attacks on the independence of the judicial branch; and efforts to manipulate the organization and personnel of the judiciary.

1857–1890

Probably no case ever decided by the Supreme Court has incurred as much wrath, both contemporarily and historically, as *Dred Scott*. The opinion lives in legend as a judicially "self-inflicted wound." But what was most striking about the contemporary response to *Dred Scott* was that the popular outcry was, for the most part, limited to the decision and did not extend to the Court as an institution. In Congress a solid majority "rebuffed repeated attempts to punish the Court or curtail its powers" because of the case.[6]

Although the most radical politicians were eager to rail at their colleagues that *Dred Scott* was an instance of "judicial usurpation" that was "more odious and intolerable than any other among the manifold practices of tyranny," and some even demanded the abolition of the Supreme Court, most members of Congress remained more sober. Publicly the decision was debated spiritedly. The press hotly criticized both Taney and his opinion; the decision and the reasoning of the several opinions were carefully and thoughtfully examined in such leading publications of the day as the *Law Reporter* and the *North American Review*; Thomas Hart Benton offered an extensive analysis of the case in *An Historical and Legal Examination of . . . the Dred Scott Case*; and Samuel Nott in the introduction to the fifth edition of *Slavery and the Remedy* offered a defense of Taney's effort.[7]

Several states passed resolutions denouncing the opinion and refusing to consider themselves bound by the dicta of the decision. Louisiana sent its resolution to Congress; Massachusetts sent its to the president, to the governors of the other states, and to each representative and senator.

Undoubtedly the most famous effect of the opinion was to spawn the debates in 1858 between Abraham Lincoln and Stephen A. Douglas as

6 Stanley I. Kutler, *Judicial Power and Reconstruction Politics* (Chicago, 1968), 163.

7 See Carl B. Swisher, *The Taney Period, 1836–1864* (New York, 1974), 592–652. Vol. V of Paul A. Freund (ed.), *History of the Supreme Court of the United States*, 6 vols.

they battled for the Senate seat that Douglas eventually won. But even the debates focused on the decision and not on the Court as an institution. When Lincoln spoke so eloquently against *Dred Scott*, he urged legal measures to overturn the ruling. On the whole, the critics of *Dred Scott* continued to appreciate the necessary role of an independent judiciary.

In the confusion of Lincoln's election to the presidency and the rapid disintegration of domestic affairs by secession and war, the reactions to *Dred Scott* were overwhelmed. Lincoln's policy of reversing the decision would not be brought to fruition until the adoption of the Thirteenth, Fourteenth, and Fifteenth amendments to the Constitution. As president, Lincoln's policies toward the judiciary were directed at procedural and organizational matters not directly related to curbing the courts as such (although one might detect at least a shred of *Dred Scott* politics involved in the expansion of the number of Supreme Court justices to ten, which seems to have provided Lincoln with a firmer hand on the Court with four appointees).[8] But after Taney handed down *Ex parte Merryman* and Justice David Davis *Ex parte Milligan*, it seemed clear that the Court had put itself on a collision course with the more political branches of the government.

Although there are important substantive legal differences between such cases as *Ex parte Merryman* (1861), *Ex parte Milligan* (1867), *Ex parte Garland* (1867), and *Cummings* v. *Missouri* (1867), politically they are of a piece. Together they demonstrate the willingness of the judiciary to attempt to resist the tide of majority opinion as reflected in presidential and congressional actions; they show the least democratic of our institutions resisting the more democratic on what the former viewed as constitutional principle. As Charles Fairman put it, *Milligan* especially signaled a "breach of comity between the Court and Congress."[9]

The public outcry against both *Merryman* and *Milligan* was similar in intensity to the outcry over *Dred Scott*. But more than *Dred Scott*, *Merryman* and *Milligan* drew opprobrium upon the Court as an insti-

8   In 1865 Congress reduced the number of justices to seven to prevent President Andrew Johnson from making any appointments. In 1869, Congress raised the number to nine only a month after Ulysses Grant was elected.

9   Charles Fairman, *Reconstruction and Reunion, 1864–1888 (Part One)* (New York, 1974), 182–252. Vol. VI of Freund (ed.), *History of the Supreme Court of the United States.*

tution. After *Merryman*, the New York *Tribune* pontificated that "of all the tyrannies that affect mankind, that of the judiciary is the most insidious, the most intolerable, the most dangerous." In viewing *Milligan*, one editor decried the "ugly squint" he detected in the eye of a Court willing to thwart the "solemn purpose of the People." Even the staid *American Law Review*, while applauding *Milligan* as espousing a "solid principle of law," admonished the Court to be more sensitive to the political realities, advising that when a case becomes more political the judges should make every effort not to exceed their "proper limit."[10]

Not content with a hope for judicial self-restraint, Congress undertook to pass the Indemnity Act of 1867 in response to what Representative James Wilson of Iowa called the "judicial impertinence" of Davis' dicta in *Milligan* that went beyond the question at issue — presidential power — to suggest that Congress could never authorize a trial by military commission. The act declared that "certain proclamations of the President and acts done in pursuance thereof, including approval of proceedings and acts of military commissions" were valid. Although the bill overwhelmingly passed both houses, President Johnson never signed it, and it was never taken up again. In spite of Thaddeus Stevens' insistence that *Milligan* was "far more dangerous" than *Dred Scott*, the congressional response was generally "quite limited, indirect, and ultimately fruitless."[11]

When the Court handed down decisions on the test oath cases, *Ex parte Garland* (invalidating a federal loyalty oath) and *Cummings* v. *Missouri* (invalidating a state loyalty oath), congressional outrage heightened and the responses to the judiciary became more pointed. Representative Thomas Williams of Pennsylvania immediately introduced a bill (which subsequently died) requiring the Court's unanimity to invalidate a federal statute. Representative George S. Boutwell of Massachusetts urged passage of a bill that provided for the exclusion from the federal bar all those guilty of a felony or of "engaging in or encouraging a rebellion." Boutwell's effort passed the House but died in the Senate.

It was becoming increasingly clear to more members of Congress that the Court was a serious threat to Reconstruction. When Republican Congressman John Bingham (perhaps best known as one of the primary architects of the Fourteenth Amendment) grumbled that the

10 *Ibid.*, 218, 224–25.
11 Kutler, *Judicial Power and Reconstruction Politics*, 68.

Court had "dared to descend from its high place in the discussion and decision of purely judicial questions to the settlement of political questions," which in his opinion it had no more right to do than "the Court of St. Petersburg," he found an attentive audience. Again, bills were introduced to require either a two-thirds or three-fourths majority or even the unanimity of the Court before "the validity of any statute or of any authority exercised by the United States could be denied."[12] Senator Lyman Trumbull sought to have the entire package of Reconstruction legislation declared by Congress to be inherently political and beyond the reach of the courts (a questionable tactic, to say the least).

Although *Milligan*, *Garland*, and *Cummings* alarmed many of the Republicans, the overall effect of the cases was hardly unifying. Efforts to curb the courts were scattered and ineffectual. There simply was "no immediate, concrete reprisal," for the party never lost a basic respect for the idea of an independent judiciary.[13] The harshest critics of the courts could not muster a consensus. Further, just when the Court appeared to be bent on thwarting Congress' efforts to reconstruct the South, it handed down decisions in *Mississippi* v. *Johnson* (1867), refusing to enjoin presidential enforcement of the Reconstruction Acts, and *Georgia* v. *Stanton* (1868), extending that refusal to lower executive officers. Such matters, the Court argued, constituted a nonjusticiable "political question." But then, a week after ruling on *Georgia* v. *Stanton*, the Court announced its intention to take jurisdiction of *Ex parte McCardle*. Congress finally made a move, but rather stealthily.

Fearing the Court would use *McCardle* as a vehicle for invalidating the Reconstruction Acts *in toto*, the opponents of the Court attached an amendment to another unobjectionable judiciary bill. The Democrats were caught dozing, and the bill, with its soon-to-be controversial amendment, sailed into law. The amendment repealed the portion of the Habeas Corpus Act of February 5, 1867, under which William McCardle had brought his action. The act had provided for appeals to the Supreme Court from judgments of a circuit court; the repealing legislation denied that course of action as well as "the exercise of any such jurisdiction" by the Supreme Court "on appeals which have been or may hereafter be taken." The result was that the Court, after having heard arguments in *McCardle*, conceded that it could not proceed, that

12   *Ibid.*, 75–76.
13   *Ibid.*, 73.

the power Congress had exercised in repealing the Court's jurisdiction was constitutionally legitimate. The judicial power could not extend to areas that Congress saw fit to exclude from the Court's jurisdiction.

McCardle was not as sweeping a removal of habeas corpus jurisdiction as is frequently assumed. It affected only that jurisdiction that had been granted by the 1867 legislation. In *Ex parte Yerger* (1869) the Court emphasized the limited scope of *McCardle* and the fact that it was not willing to allow Congress the power to deny its total jurisdiction over habeas corpus. As in *McCardle*, a bill was promptly introduced in the Senate to remove the Court's jurisdiction in all cases involving the Reconstruction Acts and all writs of habeas corpus; another was introduced to prohibit Supreme Court review of *any* federal act. A compromise between Yerger's lawyers and the attorney general removed the case to a civilian court, and the petition for the writ was withdrawn. No congressional action against the Court proceeded. In the wake of *Yerger*, congressional motions toward curbing the Court received short consideration. Senator Charles Drake's proposal to abolish the "hoary error" of judicial review was pointedly rebuked by Republicans as well as Democrats and died in committee.

Two years later the Court returned to the question of congressional power over its jurisdiction. In *United States* v. *Klein* (1872) Chief Justice Salmon Chase held, following his opinion in *McCardle*, that although Congress had such a power it could not be used toward furthering an unconstitutional end. By the exception in question in *Klein*, Congress had sought to impair the executive power to pardon and to make the Court "instrumental to that end." Such jurisdictional exceptions were beyond the legitimate scope of Congress's power, Chase insisted.[14]

Far from being intimidated by *McCardle*, the Supreme Court for the remainder of the nineteenth century actively restricted the powers of Congress without receiving much criticism, either publicly or congressionally. In cases such as *United States* v. *Dewitt* (1870), *Hepburn* v. *Griswold* (1870), and *Collector* v. *Day* (1871), Chief Justice Chase led his Court through the densest parts of the political thicket of postbellum American politics. Beyond the usual partisan grumbling that accompanies any decision, the reaction to the uses of judicial power was "tepid."[15] Instead of seeking to restrict judicial power, Congress

14 Fairman, *Reconstruction and Reunion*, 843–46.
15 Kutler, *Judicial Power and Reconstruction Politics*, 123.

actually sought to extend it. The Jurisdiction and Removal Act of 1875 is perhaps the best indication of how much and how quickly the antijudicial sentiment in Congress had subsided.

The postbellum fervor of nationalism, Felix Frankfurter and James Landis observed, "was triumphant; in national administration was sought its vindication." They explained, "In the Act of March 3, 1875, Congress gave the federal courts the vast range of power which had lain dormant in the Constitution since 1789. These courts ceased to be restricted tribunals of fair dealing between citizens of different states and became the primary and powerful reliances for vindicating every right given by the Constitution, the laws, and treaties of the United States. Thereafter, any suit asserting such a right could be begun in the federal courts; any such action begun in a state court could be removed to the federal courts for disposition."[16] The consequences of this legislation would be vast; its utility would continue through the civil rights movement of the twentieth century.

Between 1873 in the *Slaughterhouse Cases* and 1908 in *Adair* v. *United States*, a new trend began to develop in constitutional law. The Court wrestled with the question of whether the due process clause of the Fourteenth Amendment had a substantive content or if it was merely a procedural guarantee. By 1890, when the Court declared a Minnesota rail rate statute in violation of the Fourteenth Amendment, it was clear that a majority of the Court was willing to look at the substance of legislation in determining whether or not it violated due process of law.[17] In *Reagan* v. *Farmers' Loan and Trust* (1894) and *Smyth* v. *Ames* (1898), the Court removed whatever doubt remained. In 1908, the Court decided that the meaning of the due process clause of the Fifth Amendment meant precisely what the clause in the Fourteenth Amendment meant and broadened the concept of substantive due process to limit congressional legislative power as well as the legislative powers of the states. The stage was set for another, even more vitriolic confrontation between the Court and Congress, the president, and the public.

1890–1937

The era of substantive due process was a time of vigorous *proscriptive*

16 Frankfurter and Landis, *The Business of the Supreme Court*, 65.
17 *Chicago, Milwaukee & St. Paul Ry. Co.* v. *Minnesota*, 134 U.S. 418 (1890).

judicial activity. Between 1898 and 1937 the Supreme Court issued some 50 decisions invalidating acts of Congress and about 400 invalidating state laws (as compared to 12 and 125 respectively for the period 1874-1889). It seemed as though no progressive social or economic legislation was constitutionally permissible. For example, in a series of cases between 1897 and 1906, the Court consistently thwarted the regulatory efforts of the Interstate Commerce Commission (out of 16 cases appealed to the Supreme Court the Commission lost in all but one instance). In 1895, the Court declared federal income tax unconstitutional, and in *United States* v. *E. C. Knight Co.*, it effectively gutted the Sherman Antitrust Act. By 1896, the reform impulse in Congress began to wane; however, it did not die. In 1901, with the ascendancy of Theodore Roosevelt to the presidency, a new wave of liberal reform began to sweep the country.

Judicially, it was a mixed time. The period from 1901 to 1920 found the Court recognizing the use of the commerce power as a source of national police power in *Champion* v. *Ames* (1903); upholding the use of an excise tax as an instrument of social control in *McCray* v. *United States* (1904); and validating such progressive legislation as the Pure Food and Drug Act in *Hipolite Egg* v. *United States* (1911).

Beginning in 1902, President Roosevelt, aided by his attorney general, Philander C. Knox, began to move against several business combinations that seemed immune to prosecution under the logic of *United States* v. *E. C. Knight*. The first and perhaps the most important victory was in 1904 with the decision of the Court in *Northern Securities Co.* v. *United States*. The Court, in a bitterly divided five-to-four decision, held that under the Sherman Antitrust Act, the Northern Securities Company was an unlawful combination in restraint of trade. The opinion by Justice John Marshall Harlan considerably broadened the definition of "commerce" that had been restricted by the Court in *Knight*. The effect was to resuscitate the Sherman Act to such a degree that during the rest of Roosevelt's time in the White House his administration initiated more than forty prosecutions under the act, many of which ended successfully. In *Swift & Co.* v. *United States* (1905), the Court fashioned the "stream of commerce" doctrine that quickly became a standard legal concept allowing the expansion of the commerce power to such a degree that after 1937 the distinction between "commerce" and "manufacturing" would be completely broken down.

But what the Court gave with one hand it took back with the other.

During this same period the Court handed down *Lochner* v. *New York* (1905), *Adair* v. *United States* (1908), and *Hammer* v. *Dagenhart* (1918). And despite the apparent liberalism of the decisions in such cases as *Champion*, *McCray*, and *Hipolite*, the resistance of the Court to social progress shown in the *Lochner*, *Adair*, and *Hammer* decisions raised the political hackles of the Progressives and the Populists. In terms of antijudicial sentiment the period was one of the most vehement as well as one of the most creative.

The Progressives' response to the judiciary was felt on both the national and the state levels. The most popular reaction to what the liberals saw as judicial meddling was the advocacy of a recall of judges and judicial opinions. The dispute was deeply ideological. Members of the Progressive-Populist coalition sought to transform what was considered to be an archaic oligarchic institution into a more modern and democratic one. They sought to curtail the independence of the Court and render it more subservient to what they argued was the dominant mood of the country. Theodore Roosevelt (who was editor of *Outlook* from 1909 to 1914) led the attack for increased democracy, but even he conceded that in questions of constitutionality the opinions of the Supreme Court should stand. However, between 1881 and 1920 thirty-one constitutional amendments were proposed in Congress providing for the popular election of the lower-level federal judges. A good many people agreed with Robert M. La Follette's characterization of these judges as "petty tyrants and arrogant despots." Congress also trotted out some other old favorites, which never seem to work, such as requiring a two-thirds majority of the Court in order to declare congressional acts unconstitutional, and a provision allowing Congress by a two-thirds vote to repass any statute declared invalid by the courts. Congress did succeed in overruling *Pollock* v. *Farmers' Loan and Trust* (1895) when it passed the Sixteenth Amendment in 1913. Most of the Progressive-Populist demands were resisted by President William Howard Taft as being against sound democratic government. To subject the judiciary to "momentary gusts of passion," Taft argued, echoing the sentiments of *The Federalist*, would be a tragic mistake.

The scholarly response to Roosevelt's advocacy of the recall was in some ways even more extreme. Writing in the *Harvard Law Review* in 1913, John Palfrey advocated an alternative. It seemed to Palfrey that a reasonable remedy for judicial excesses in the area of social legislation would be the establishment of a tribunal "composed of experts trained in matters of government and sociology," the function of which would be "in part judicial and in part legislative." Palfrey explained: "To this new body the courts may refer the question whether an act passed by the legislature for a proper purpose is arbitrary in its effect upon individual rights. The decision of the new body, certified to the court, will furnish the basis of decision for the particular case, and, if against the law, will suspend it for a certain length of time, or in any event until further action by the legislature."[18]

The twenties were characterized by a more subdued exercise of judicial power. Although the Court did decide such cases as *Bailey* v. *Drexel Furniture* (1920), *Adkins* v. *Children's Hospital* (1923), and *Wolff Packing Co.* v. *Kansas Court of Industrial Relations* (1923) — voiding child labor, minimum wage, and public utilities laws, respectively — it also upheld several pieces of regulatory legislation such as provisions of the Transportation Act of 1920, the Packers and Stockyards Act of 1921, and the National Motor Vehicle Theft Act of 1919. Even the Clayton and Sherman acts fared better at the hands of the Court. On the whole, the twenties were a time when there were "two streams of thought upon the issue of national power. Sometimes the Court found itself in one, sometimes in the other. Its selection did not appear to be dictated so much by any logical constitutional principle as by the social and economic implications of the case at hand." It was a relatively quiet time as far as court-curbing efforts went. For example, the number of amendments proposed to alter the Constitution to allow for popular election of federal judges fell to four between 1920 and 1931 (during the tenure of the Taft Court) compared to six such efforts in 1907 and 1912 alone. And the 1924 Progressive party presidential candidate, Robert M. La Follette, found little public enthusiasm for his proposed constitutional amendment "providing that Congress may by enacting a statute make it effective over a judicial veto."[19] As America edged its way into the thirties, however, it became clear that the relative quiet of the twenties was only the calm before the storm.

In the first years of Franklin Roosevelt's New Deal, the judicial sen-

18 John G. Palfrey, "The Constitution and the Courts," *Harvard Law Review*, XXVI (1913), 507, 526.
19 Alfred H. Kelly and Winfred A. Harbison, *The American Constitution* (5th ed.; New York, 1976), 655; La Follette quoted in *Guide to the U.S. Supreme Court* (Washington, D.C., 1979), 693.

timents that had gurgled to the surface in such cases as *Hammer*, *Bailey*, *Adkins*, and *Wolff* were now brought to a full boil. Between March 4, 1933, when Roosevelt took office, and the end of 1936, the Court had on twelve occasions, including the cases of *Schecter Poultry Corp.* v. *United States, United States* v. *Butler*, and *Carter* v. *Carter Coal Co.*, effectively blocked the president's legislative program aimed at economic recovery. In response to the Court's firm stand, the president undertook to "pack" the Court. Whether or not his increasingly unpopular plan had any effect on the Court's change of heart is at least debatable.[20] But shortly thereafter the Court did change its position and in *West Coast Hotel* v. *Parrish* (1937) demonstrated a new-found willingness to accept nearly any piece of economic or social legislation without a fuss.

Besides Roosevelt's plan, there were also congressional efforts at court curbing during the decade. In 1932, Congress passed the Norris-La Guardia Act, which restricted within rather narrow bounds the power of the federal courts to issue injunctions (either interlocutory or permanent) in labor disputes and provided that the so-called yellow dog contract would not be enforceable in any court of the United States and would not "afford any basis for the granting of legal or equitable relief by any such court." Two years later Congress struck again. The Johnson Act of 1934 deprived the district courts of the jurisdiction to enjoin either "the operation of, or compliance with, any order of a state administrative agency or local rate-making body fixing rates for a public utility in certain circumstances" including whenever "a plain, speedy and efficient remedy may be had in the courts of [a] state."

In 1937, Congress moved against the federal courts twice. In the Tax Injunction Act, Congress forbade an injunction against "the assessment, levy, or collection of any tax under state law" as long as "a plain, speedy and efficient remedy may be had in the courts of such a state." An act of August 24, 1937, went even further. It specifically commanded the courts of the United States to notify the attorney general whenever the constitutionality of any act of Congress was involved in a case to which the United States is not a party, and it secured the right of the attorney general to intervene. It further provided that any

20   See William E. Leuchtenburg, "The Origins of Franklin D. Roosevelt's 'Court-Packing' Plan," in Philip B. Kurland (ed.), *The Supreme Court Review: 1966* (Chicago, 1967), 347–400; and Henry J. Abraham, *Justices and Presidents* (New York, 1974), 195–232.

interlocutory or permanent injunctions that would suspend the operation of congressional acts on grounds of unconstitutionality would be heard in district courts by three judges, one of whom would be required to be a circuit judge. And in these cases, five days notice to the attorney general would be required; a direct appeal to the Supreme Court was guaranteed.

By the time Justice Stone wrote his opinion in *United States* v. *Carolene Products* (1937) with the famous footnote promising increased judicial scrutiny when violations of the constitutional rights of discrete and insular minorities were alleged, the Court was already moving away from its long tradition of interfering with legislation affecting proprietarian interests. But it would be 1954 before the full implications of Stone's footnote would be drawn out and a new stage in the history of court-curbing efforts would begin. Between 1938 and 1954, however, some actions by Congress did touch upon the exercise of judicial power. The actions were taken in the area of procedure and administration; the general concern was to increase the efficiency and certainty of the judicial process. In a limited way, these actions were attempts at court curbing, although they were far less flamboyant than court packing or jurisdiction tampering. Paradoxically, in the end, some of these measures would contribute to even greater arbitrariness in the exercise of judicial power.

1938–1954

The period from 1938 to 1954 was characterized by a concern for efficiency in every branch of the government. Concerns for efficient judicial administration were but one manifestation of the broader impulse. Although at first glance the concerns over judicial procedure and administration may seem to have no immediate connection with concerns over judicial activism, the roots of the procedural and administrative reforms were firmly planted in the concerns over activism of an older generation that saw procedural arrangements as one of the most efficacious ways to curb the courts. There is another reason this period of institutional reform is significant in any attempt to understand court-curbing efforts in American history. Many of the procedural reforms of the period would contribute a good deal to the extreme *prescriptive* activism of the post-1954 era.

Writing in 1928, Felix Frankfurter and James Landis pointed out that the "mechanism of law — what courts are to deal with which causes and subject to what conditions — cannot be dissociated from the ends that the law subserves. . . . After all, procedure is instrumental; it is the means of effectuating policy." The impact of procedure on substance is formidable. Indeed, Frankfurter and Landis were convinced (and were convincing) that the "practical workings" of the Court are "determined by the extent of appellate jurisdiction allotted to it by Congress, the issues open on review, the range of jurisdiction of the inferior courts, and the available disposition of business, as by the learning and outlook of the justices, the quality and training of the bar."[21] Frankfurter and Landis skillfully distilled one of the underlying premises of American constitutionalism: That there is an intimate connection between procedure and substance, that the institutional arrangements of a polity have a direct bearing on its substantive actions. It was this understanding that encouraged the reformers of the time.

One of the principal accomplishments of the period was the adoption of the Rules of Civil Procedure of 1938, which merged actions of law with actions in equity in the federal judiciary. Although the idea of merging the procedures was not new (such mergers in state systems had occurred since 1848, when New York adopted the controversial Field Code of civil procedure), it was a striking reform at the federal level. The main impetus of David Dudley Field and the codification movement in securing such a merger was to render the administration of the law more certain, uniform, and objective. By clearing out the dead underbrush of common-law pleadings, Field and his followers sought to make the processes of the law more "intelligible to lawyer and layman alike." In particular, the object was to reduce the gross subjectivity of judicial discretion.

Such an effort was hardly new in American politics. Judicial discretion had always rubbed the republican sensibilities of most Americans the wrong way. As early as 1756, John Dickinson found the exercise of judicial power in Pennsylvania to be "a confused mixture of private passions and popular error [with] every court assum[ing] the power of legislation." On the eve of the Revolution, one New Yorker complained that too often the issues of a legal cause tended to depend "not so much on the right of a client, as on the breath of the Judge." Long before Field triumphed in New York, there had been a series of at-

21 Frankfurter and Landis, *The Business of the Supreme Court*, 2, 86.

tempts during the Jeffersonian and Jacksonian periods to reduce the mystical qualities of the law to simple rules, "legible to every reader," as Thomas Jefferson put it. Thus, the effort to simplify the processes of American law in the thirties was merely the culmination of a long struggle to trim judicial "excrescences."[22]

The reform impulse of the thirties had another objective however. Although the merger of law and equity was rooted in a traditional distrust of judicial power, the twentieth-century reformers were also motivated by the principles of legal realism and sought to bring the law and its procedures into line with modern sentiment in order to make the law a more efficient instrument of social reform and political change. And this meant, in the twenties, thirties, and forties, a great expansion of the public role of the courts.[23] With the passage of the Declaratory Judgments Act of 1934 and the liberalization of requirements concerning class actions in the 1938 rules, the reformers sought to push the judiciary more fully into the political fray. These reforms coincided perfectly with the Court's professed intention to move toward an increased sensitivity to civil rights and away from the traditional concern over proprietarian rights. Bolstered by the Judges Bill of 1925 allowing the Supreme Court its certiorari procedure whereby it would determine which cases it would hear, the Court was procedurally ready to flex its political muscle. All of these reforms embraced the animating sentiments of the Progressive era.

The concern for the modernization of federal procedure, however, was but one strand of reform that developed from the earlier tradition. There was also, in the twenties, thirties, and forties, a strong movement to reform the administrative organization of the judiciary. Although efficiency was the reason most often cited for reforming the administrative structures, there were deeper issues at stake. As Peter Fish has shown, the Administrative Office Act of 1939 "clearly constituted the judges' response to broad political attacks on the courts."[24]

In short, influential federal judges, including the chief justice of the United States, "allied with a dynamic President of the American Bar Association" in an effort "to insulate the federal courts from forays by

22 See Gary L. McDowell, *Equity and the Constitution: The Supreme Court, Equitable Relief, and Public Policy* (Chicago, 1982), 51–69.

23 See William Kristol, "The American Judicial Power and the American Regime" (Ph.D. dissertation, Harvard University, 1979), 40–118.

24 Peter G. Fish, *The Politics of Federal Judicial Administration* (Princeton, 1973), 20, 427, 428.

the political branches of the government." The Administrative Office Act was in part the judiciary's substitute for Roosevelt's court-packing plan of 1937. Such administrative reform "afforded a safe course. It gave visible evidence of the courts' recognition of popular opinion. At the same time, such reform would leave intact and untouched the substantive heart of the judicial decision-making process."[25]

The forties and early fifties were a time of judicial restraint and relative political calm regarding the role of the courts. Although the Court did begin its concerted effort to "incorporate" the Bill of Rights into the Fourteenth Amendment, and did seek more vigorously to protect certain rights of dissident minorities, there was no serious effort to curtail judicial power. When Congress did move to juggle jurisdictional lines in the Emergency Price Control Act of 1942, the Court, in *Lockerty* v. *Phillips* (1943) and *Yakus* v. *United States* (1944), upheld the scheme. Between 1939 and 1954 only two court-curbing bills were introduced in Congress, standing in sharp contrast to the thirty-seven that had been introduced between 1935 and 1937 and the fifty-three that would be introduced between 1955 and 1957.[26] It was an unusually quiet time.

1954–1986

Charles Warren once remarked that "nothing is more striking in the history of the Court than the manner in which the hopes of those who expected a judge to follow the political views of the President appointing him are disappointed." Confirming Warren's judgment, Harry Truman confessed that "whenever you put a man on the Supreme Court he ceases to be your friend." Certainly few presidents were more surprised by their appointees than was President Eisenhower by Earl Warren. Eisenhower allegedly once remarked that appointing Warren was "the biggest damn fool mistake" he had made during his presidency.[27]

Since the thirties, the Court under both Chief Justice Stone and Chief Justice Fred Vinson had been moving toward taking an expanded judi-

25 Peter G. Fish, "Crises, Politics, and Federal Judicial Reform: The Administrative Office Act of 1939," *Journal of Politics* XXXII (August, 1970) 625, 626; Fish, *The Politics of Federal Judicial Administration*, 428–29.

26 Stuart Nagel, "Court-Curbing Periods in American History," *Vanderbilt Law Review*, XVIII (1965), 925.

27 Charles Warren, *The Supreme Court in United States History* (3 vols.; Boston, 1924), II, 22; Truman quoted in Henry J. Abraham, *The Judicial Process* (4th ed.; New York, 1980), 80; Eisenhower quoted in Walter Murphy and C. Herman Pritchett (eds.), *Courts, Judges, and Politics* (3rd ed.; New York, 1979), 155.

cial role in civil liberties. But it was not until Warren took the helm that the full implications of Stone's logic in the *Carolene Products* footnote were completely drawn out. Since 1954, the federal judiciary, with the Supreme Court leading the way, aided by a more flexible procedure in equity and looser requirements for class actions and standing, has been more *prescriptively* active than at any other time in the nation's history. Not only does the contemporary judiciary decree what the government may not do, but it has taken it upon itself increasingly to decree what the government must do to achieve what a majority of the Court holds to be the good life under the Constitution. The new activism differs radically from the old activism in being far more positive in its assertion.

Yet, even though the new activism is markedly more prescriptive than the old activism, the old and the new are united on a deeper level. Like the old activism, the new issues from a judicial reliance on the so-called Rule of Reason. The negative activism of the Court against the Progressives and the New Dealers and the positive activism of the Warren and Burger Courts (and especially of lower federal judges such as Arthur Garrity and Frank Battisti) have more to do with the individual notions of justice embraced by the justices and judges than with the Constitution. In both instances a concern for social justice has replaced a concern for constitutionality.

The prescriptive activism of recent years has grown as a result of the procedural reforms introduced in the thirties coupled with Congress' general willingness to delegate its constitutional prerogatives over the procedure and practices of the judiciary to the judiciary itself. The result is courts largely unbound by the procedural niceties that traditionally served as a source of restraint on the expressions of the judicial will. Without such procedural fences the judges have been left (to borrow the memorable language of James Kent) to "roam at large in the trackless field of their own imagination." Bolstered by substantial academic support, it is no wonder that federal judges decree the things they do.[28]

28 See Owen Fiss, *The Civil Rights Injunction* (Bloomington, Ind., 1978); Fiss, "The Forms of Justice," *Harvard Law Review*, XCIII (1979), 1; Abram Chayes, "The Role of the Judge in Public Law Litigation," *Harvard Law Review*, XC (1976), 1281; Chayes, "Public Law Litigation in the Burger Court" *Harvard Law Review*, XCVI (1982), 4. For a clear judicial example, see the decree of Judge Frank Battisti in *United States* v. *City of Parma*, 504 F. Supp. 913 (1980). Another example is that of Judge Arthur Garrity. In 1981, Garrity ruled that budget cuts made by the city of Boston that require athletic teams to pay a fee for the use of Park and Recreation Department fields

Since 1954 there has been a steady stream of political challenges to the presumed authority of the federal courts. The attacks have ranged from efforts to limit the institutional independence of the courts to efforts to reverse particular decisions of the courts either by legislation or by constitutional amendment. The efforts have run the gamut from the very unlikely, such as the campaign to impeach Earl Warren, to the very likely, such as the 1982 Helms-Johnston bill to curb the power of the federal government to take legal actions that might result in busing as a remedy for segregation.

ATTACKS ON INSTITUTIONAL INDEPENDENCE

The warning shot against judicial independence was fired in 1954 when a constitutional amendment was proposed in the Senate to "fortify the independence of the Supreme Court." The particulars of the measure would have set the number of Supreme Court justices at nine; it would have rendered the justices ineligible for either the presidency or the vice-presidency; and it would have prohibited any federal judge from serving past the age of seventy-five. Like most of the measures concerning the courts since 1954, the proposal died. In 1957, Senator James O. Eastland and Representative Thomas G. Abernathy proposed to amend the Constitution in order to limit the tenure of federal judges to four-year terms. This, too, died rather quickly.

Congress frequently returns to the question of judicial independence, holding hearings and debating at some length the issues of judicial tenure, removal from office, and professional ethics. In 1970, for example, no fewer than twenty-seven bills were pending in Congress relating to such issues as the disclosure of judges' personal finances and investments; definitions of "good behavior" as used in the Constitution; plans for removal for disabilities; standards for conflict of interest situations; and whether a judicial commission could be created with the power to impose sanctions on federal judges including removal by means other than impeachment. During the 1970 hearings before

---

and that abolished student fares and discounts on Boston's mass transit system constituted "a very grievous impeding of the court's desegregation orders." Garrity made it clear that he believed it was his duty to "use his authority to try to modify or overturn at least some" of the budgetary actions (Boston *Globe*, September 11, 1981, Sec. A, p. 23). See Nathan Glazer, *Affirmative Discrimination* (New York, 1975), for an account of how federal judges can transform political principles as they involve themselves in the fashioning of public policies. See also Elizabeth A Marek, "Education by Decree," *New Perspectives*, XVII (Summer, 1985), 36.

the Subcommittee on Improvements in Judicial Machinery of the Senate Judiciary Committee, William H. Rehnquist, then a spokesman for the Justice Department, told Senator Sam Ervin's committee that he believed a commission with the power of removal would be "constitutionally permissible." A good many others had their doubts.[29]

In 1978, the Senate approved a measure to create a commission of twelve federal judges to hear complaints against other federal judges and to prosecute the most serious offenses before a proposed Court on Judicial Conduct and Disability. The new court would have been empowered to order involuntary removal, retirement, censure, or dismissal. In the case of a justice of the Supreme Court, the court would recommend impeachment to the House of Representatives. The House failed to act on the proposal, leaving it to die in the Senate. Similar efforts were made again in the next session, and finally the House and Senate agreed to a version of the 1978 bill. In 1980, President Carter signed the measure (but without any provision allowing removal by means other than impeachment) into law.

Most recently, Senator Joseph Biden introduced a bill that would establish a ten-year term for federal judges rather than life tenure. Even more elaborate was Senator John East's Judicial Reform Bill. Introduced in 1982, this legislation would have severely restricted the possibility of federal judges rendering far-reaching opinions. By restricting the equity procedures of federal courts along with other procedural restructuring, the Judicial Reform Bill struck at the heart of the new, looser judicial procedures. Like most other efforts, however, this proposal, only slightly defended by its sponsor, withered and eventually died. However, the East bill may have foreshadowed the way judicial activism may ultimately prove to be curbed. On the whole, efforts that are aimed at institutional independence are far fewer in number and far less frequently developed than efforts designed to overrule or limit the applicability of particular decisions or lines of decisions.

ATTACKS ON PARTICULAR DECISIONS

Sedition and Un-American Activities
In its early years the Warren Court sought to proscribe both state and

29 U.S. Congress, Senate Committee on the Judiciary, *The Independence of Federal Judges. Hearings Before the Subcommittee on the Separation of Powers*, 91st Cong., 2nd Sess., 330. For an example of doubt on this, see Philip B. Kurland, "The Constitution and the Tenure of Federal Judges: Some Notes from History," *University of Chicago Law Review*, XXXVI (1969), 665.

national legislative efforts to deal with the threat of communism. The stance of the Court was directly at odds with the cold-war mood of the country generally and Congress in particular. A clash was inevitable.

In July, 1958, a measure was introduced in the House affirming that federal laws were to be construed as intending to invalidate state laws *only* if Congress had stated specifically that it wished to preempt a field of legislation between state and federal law. This bill further proposed that federal laws should not be construed as indicating a congressional intention to bar states from passing laws punishing sedition against the federal government. These same concerns were also addressed by measures being discussed in the Senate.

Perhaps the most famous and surely the most controversial of the congressional efforts at court-curbing in the fifties was the Jenner-Butler Bill. Although it was eventually tabled, it generated a heated public and academic debate. Its critics saw its breadth as posing a grave threat to the First Amendment; its defenders believed it was nothing less than absolutely necessary for the preservation of the American way of life. The thrust of the bill was to remove Supreme Court appellate jurisdiction in certain antisedition cases; to make each house of Congress the final judge of whether the questions asked by its investigative committees were "pertinent"; to restrict "pertinency" as a defense against contempt of Congress charges; and to liberalize certain provisions of the Smith Act of 1940 that had been restricted by the Court. In particular, it provided that the Smith Act would be enforceable against advocacy of abstract doctrine as well as against practical incitement to action, and it expanded the meaning of the term *organize* as used in the act to include such continuing efforts as recruitment and the teaching of classes by allegedly subversive groups. In sum, the bill sought to reverse some of the most controversial decisions of the Supreme Court such as *Watkins* v. *United States* (1957).

The failure of the Jenner-Butler Bill was close enough not to deter the critics of the Court. In 1957, following the urging of the Eisenhower administration, Congress enacted legislation that restricted, though it did not overrule, the Court's decision in the case of *Jencks* v. *United States* (1957), which decreed that the government had to provide a defendant with documents necessary to his defense. In 1958 the House succeeded in passing a bill aimed at overruling the decision in *Yates* v. *United States* (1958), which ruled that the Smith Act did not outlaw mere advocacy of the violent overthrow of the United States. This legislation contained only the part of the Jenner-Butler Bill relating to the meaning of *organize*. The Senate, in 1958, took no action on the bill; then in 1959, a Senate subcommittee approved the bill but the full committee never considered it.

Reapportionment

Congress also moved to pull the Court out of the "political thicket" it thought it had wrongly wandered into in the apportionment cases of *Baker* v. *Carr* (1962), *Gray* v. *Sanders* (1963), *Wesberry* v. *Sanders* (1964), and *Reynolds* v. *Sims* (1964). In typical fashion, a constitutional amendment was introduced in 1964 by Representative William M. McCullough of Ohio. Coming on the heels of *Reynolds* (and the companion case of *Lucas* v. *Forty-Fourth General Assembly of Colorado*) it provided that "nothing in the Constitution of the United States shall prohibit a state, having a bicameral legislature, from apportioning the membership of one house of the legislature on factors other than population if the citizens of the state shall have the opportunity to vote upon the apportionment." McCullough's amendment failed but the sentiment and similar language found their way into amendments offered by Senator Everett Dirksen in 1965 and 1966. In each instance the amendments secured a simple majority but failed (by only seven votes each time) to achieve the necessary two-thirds majority.

A statutory effort by Representative William M. Tuck also failed. Tuck's proposal was simply to deny to any federal court all jurisdiction in any apportionment case. Other efforts since 1966 have occasionally appeared in Congress, but none with any mark of success.

The most recent attention paid to the issue of apportionment was an idea toyed with by Senator Orrin Hatch. Hatch, along with Senator Thad Cochran, considered introducing a constitutional amendment that would limit the basis of apportionment to citizens or citizens and *legal* aliens. The senators believed that a mere census count would reward those districts and states with large numbers of *illegal* aliens and penalize those without. The scheme was an effort to introduce a qualitative measure into the apportionment process rather than to leave it merely at the level of quantitative standard. Perhaps because the political ire raised by the original reapportionment cases has died down considerably, the measure faded away.

School Prayer

In 1962 when the Court, in *Engel* v. *Vitale*, moved to prohibit prayer in public schools, it was hit by a torrent of angry public protest. When it went even further in *Abington School District* v. *Schempp* the following year and prohibited Bible reading in the classroom, political opposition began to solidify and to focus on constitutional amendments specifically framed to reverse the decisions. During the Eighty-eighth Congress, no fewer than 150 resolutions for such amendments were introduced. A massive mail campaign was orchestrated by those opposed to the Court's decisions, and the idea of an amendment was endorsed by the Policy Committee of the Republican party and later adopted as a plank in the party's national platform. But there were serious objections by the major religious groups to oppose such tampering with what they considered to be the politically necessary metaphoric wall of separation between church and state. Ultimately, the enthusiasm of 1964 dwindled and no amendment was reported back out of committee.

In 1967, Senator Dirksen made another stab at amending the *Engel* and *Schempp* decisions out of American constitutional law. This effort, the first since 1964, fell nine votes short of the two-thirds requirement. In 1971, another amendment strikingly similar to Dirksen's 1967 effort also fell short, this time by twenty-nine votes. In 1976 the Senate overwhelmingly rejected a proposal by Senator Hugh Scott that would have removed all cases involving public schools including, but not limited to, school prayer.

More recently, the Senate adopted an amendment to a formerly uncontroversial judiciary bill that would deprive any federal court of the jurisdiction to hear a case or an appeal involving a challenge to the constitutionality of a state statute that allowed voluntary prayer in public schools. Under this plan, proposed by Senator Jesse Helms, such prayer cases would be restricted to the state courts; and, with the appellate jurisdiction of the Supreme Court denied, the highest state court would be the court of final authority. Although the *Engel* and *Schempp* decisions would not be overruled per se, there would be no opportunity for future litigation on the issue to be reviewed by a federal court. The amendment never emerged from committee, but Helms and his followers proved persistent. A similar amendment came to a floor vote in the Ninety-ninth Congress. The Helms proposal was decisively defeated in August, 1985; such court-stripping measures seem, with this defeat, to have been clearly rejected as a way to circumvent the Supreme Court rulings prohibiting school prayer.

In 1983, President Ronald Reagan's longtime campaign in behalf of restoring traditional family values to American life was also made manifest in a proposed constitutional amendment that would allow for voluntary silent school prayer. Although in reality more a proposal in behalf of the principle of federalism than a defense of any notion that there is a substantive demand that prayers be offered in the classroom, this proposal—the first occasion for the issue of school prayer itself to make it to the floor of the Senate—was also defeated.

But the Court has continued to entertain suits that seek at least in part to reverse the strict prohibitions subsequently drawn out of the *Engel* and *Schempp* cases. In the 1984 term, for example, the case of *Wallace* v. *Jaffree* went before the Court. The issue was whether Alabama's moment-of-silence legislation violated the ban on school prayer. The Court held that, in general, such a moment of silence did not violate the ban on school prayer, but Alabama's law, in particular, did so violate the ban. Although these sorts of efforts are not congressionally sponsored inroads into judicial power, such efforts to convince the Court to rethink and then abandon, or at least refine, its earlier controversial decisions are related to more overt efforts to curb the courts. The possibility that an administration may join such suits by filing *amicus curiae* briefs makes this yet another avenue whereby the political views of the nation can be brought to bear on the judicial process.

Criminal Justice

The efforts of the Warren Court to secure the rights of the accused constituted its most far-reaching revision of existing constitutional law. In cases such as *Mallory* v. *United States* (1957), *Miranda* v. *Arizona* (1967), and *United States* v. *Wade* (1967), the Court radically transformed the procedure and thereby the substance of criminal law in the United States. A good many people, gripped by a law-and-order mood, stood bewildered. But they did not remain so for long. The political response against the Court was one of the most successful efforts ever at reversing judicial opinions. The provisions of the Crime Control Act of 1968—aimed directly at reversing or at least seriously limiting the *Mallory*, *Miranda*, and *Wade* decisions—made substantial inroads into what many perceived to be the excessive leniency of an overly liberal Court. Five years later in a more subtle way, Congress would again seek to exert a degree of influence over the judicial process.

In 1973, Congress exercised its constitutional prerogative to participate actively in the reform of the federal rules of evidence. Traditionally, Congress, in criminal as well as in civil procedures, delegates such power over judicial practices and procedures to the judiciary itself. Although the 1973 effort was not a court-curbing plan as such, it does demonstrate Congress' constitutional power—and occasional political willingness—to take a hand in the fashioning of the procedural niceties that govern the judicial branch. It demonstrates one way, far less drastic than making jurisdictional exceptions or drafting constitutional amendments, by which Congress can legitimately exert some measure of control over the courts.

On other criminal law fronts, in 1974 the Senate moved to reinstate the death penalty for certain offenses, but the House failed to act. In 1975, the Criminal Justice Reform Act was introduced in an effort to expand and reinvigorate existing criminal law in what critics saw as a threat to civil liberties. It died at the end of the session. Other moves regarding criminal law reform have been afoot in each Congress, such as the possibility of withdrawing federal court jurisdiction over death penalty cases, although, as always, such plans are very much subject to change.

The Criminal Justice Reform Act of 1984 was successful, however. Its provisions have done much to strengthen the prosecutorial efforts of the government and its powers to seek stiff punishments. Various components of the criminal justice system—capital punishment, habeas corpus, the exclusionary rule—remain standard subjects for deliberation by the various committees of Congress. And the characterization of the *Miranda* case as "infamous" by Attorney General Edwin Meese III, which let loose a flurry of public debate, foreshadows continued political battles against the past decisions of the Court that have transformed the procedures of the criminal justice system at both the state and national levels.

Race

In no decision since *Dred Scott* has the Court incurred such sustained political wrath as in *Brown* v. *Board of Education of Topeka, Kansas* (1954) and its progeny. From the initial "massive resistance" of the South to the more recent outbursts of violence in the urban North, the desegregation decisions have continued to disrupt American politics. But after some carefully planned and hard-fought legislative battles, Congress did fall in behind the Court's judgment in *Brown* (and those later decisions that extended the principle in *Brown* to public facilities other than schools) by passing civil rights legislation and the Twenty-fourth Amendment. The most recent congressional resistance in the area of desegregation has been directed not at the principle of *Brown* but at the various remedies the courts have chosen for implementing that principle.

In particular, the decision of the Court in *Swann v. Charlotte-Mecklenburg Board of Education* (1971) approving court-ordered busing to achieve desegregation has been the object of increasingly popular efforts to curb such remedial powers. *Swann* is but the most visible example of what Abram Chayes has called the "triumph of equity" in public-law litigation. Unrestrained by the old and cumbersome procedures, the historic equitable remedial powers of the federal courts have become something of their wild card. One need only recall Chief Justice Burger's dicta in *Swann* to catch a glimpse of how undefined equity has become. After paying a bit of lip service to the traditional restraints on equitable relief, the chief justice confessed that he found that in seeking "to define the scope of remedial power or the limits on remedial power of the courts . . . words are poor instruments to convey the sense of basic fairness inherent in equity." He concluded that "substance, not semantics, must govern." With such guidance by our highest court, it is little wonder that the city of Parma, Ohio, now finds itself obligated to advertise in minority publications in order to recruit more minorities to move within its borders. Such decrees have become one of the most widely disliked manifestations of the judicial power.[30]

The hostility toward busing and the related desegregation decrees is not simply a white phenomenon. Although a large majority of white families oppose such measures, a good percentage of black families are similarly unsupportive.[31] In fact, the differences between civil rights leaders and ordinary black citizens on this question is quite dramatic. A 1985 study showed that 77 percent of the civil rights leaders support such measures and that 77 percent of the black population oppose them. The persistence of antibusing measures in Congress is

30 Chayes, "The Role of the Judge in Public Law Litigation," 1292; *Swann v. Charlotte-Mecklenburg Board of Education*, 402 U.S. 1, 31; *United States v. City of Parma*, 504 F. Supp. 913 (1980).

31 U.S. Congress, Senate Committee on the Judiciary, *The Fourteenth Amendment and School Busing. Hearings Before the Subcommittee on the Constitution*, 97th Cong., 1st Sess., 136–209. See especially the testimony of Nathan Glazer. See also Linda S. Lichter, "Who Speaks for Black America?" *Public Opinion*, VIII (August–September, 1985), 41.

attributable to a broadly based consensus, cutting across racial lines, that this remedy is no remedy at all; in fact, to many, the remedy may be worse than the disease.

The first serious efforts to restrict the scope of the busing remedy announced in *Swann* came in 1972 when President Richard Nixon submitted two bills to Congress. The first, the Student Transportation Moratorium Act of 1972, would have had the effect of freezing the situation until Congress had ample opportunity to consider a long-range solution to the problem of continuing segregation in public schools. The second proposal, the Equal Educational Opportunities Act of 1972, was Nixon's plan for such a solution. The president's plans were presented as justified under Section 5 of the Fourteenth Amendment, which grants Congress the power to enforce the provisions of the amendment. Because the proposals did "not attempt to overturn the relationship between the legislature and the judiciary" and because they dealt with specific remedies in a rather limited way, Professor (now Judge) Robert Bork believed that if enacted they would have been constitutional.[32] Other scholars were not so sure. But the proposals were never adopted and the potential constitutional battles were never fought.

The next serious effort at curbing the remedy came in 1975 when Representative Marjorie S. Holt proposed an amendment to limit the power of the Department of Health, Education, and Welfare in forcing school districts to adopt busing plans to desegregate their schools. The antibusing language was strengthened in appropriations legislation for the department in 1977 and 1978. The problem with the effort was that it was misdirected, for most busing was—and is—not the result of that or any other agency; it is the result of the courts. The Holt legislation did not touch the powers of the courts.

In a more direct attempt, amendments to legislation extending the Elementary and Secondary Education Act of 1965 were offered by Representatives Marvin Esch and John Ashbrook and Senators Dan Gurney, Robert P. Griffin, Mike Mansfield, and Birch Bayh. These amendments provided for strict limits on the powers of the courts to decree busing as a remedy for segregation. But they failed. Other proposals by Senators Helms, Biden, and Robert C. Byrd similarly failed.

In 1976, President Gerald Ford presented his antibusing proposal,

32 Robert H. Bork, *Constitutionality of the President's Busing Proposals* (Washington, D.C., 1972).

the School Desegregation Standards and Assistance Act. Like the others, Ford's legislative package sought to limit the scope of the busing remedy by creating standards for using it. For example, busing would be barred as a remedy for de facto segregation. The package, the culmination of eight months of research by the Justice Department, received no action by Congress. Like the Ford proposal, other measures by Senators William V. Roth and Helms also withered away.

In 1978, the Senate again tabled an amendment to the Elementary and Secondary Education Act of 1965 offered by Senators Roth and Biden that would have limited the powers of the courts to order busing. (When Biden's 1976 amendment was reported by the Senate Judiciary Committee in 1977, it was the first time that such an antibusing proposal ever made it out of committee; however, it was never brought to a vote.)

In 1979, a House-passed amendment to the Justice Department authorization bill that sought to restrict the department's use of funds to pursue busing cases was dropped in conference. Repeating his 1973 effort, Senator Helms proposed an amendment to energy legislation that would have prohibited busing during an energy crisis; like the earlier effort, this one failed. Gathering momentum, antibusing forces secured a discharge petition in the House to force a proposed antibusing constitutional amendment out of committee to a floor vote. The amendment was voted down, 216–209.

In November, 1980, Senator Helms returned to the busing issue by proposing another amendment to the fiscal 1982 Justice Department authorization bill. The proposal, which would have barred the department from spending its money for legal actions that would lead either directly or indirectly to court-ordered busing, was strengthened by Senator J. Bennett Johnston's proposals. Johnston's plan would have prevented any federal court from ordering a student bused beyond the school nearest his home as well as authorized the attorney general to file suits in behalf of students who have been subjected to such a judicial remedy. Beginning in June, 1981, opponents of the Helms-Johnston proposal, led by Senator Lowell Weicker, successfully held the issue off by a filibuster. But on September 16, the Senate voted cloture (61–36) and paved the way for passage of the Helms-Johnston amendments (60–39). The House had already passed a piece of legislation similar to the Helms measure but without the stronger Johnston language. Weicker vowed that he and the other opponents of the legis-

lation—which he referred to as a "malodorous meadow muffin"—
would continue the fight on the grounds that such legislation is
unconstitutional.[33]

The Right to Life Controversy

After the Supreme Court's landmark decisions in *Roe* v. *Wade* and *Doe*
v. *Bolton* (1973), the intense public debate over the issue of abortion
and the question of when exactly life begins for the purposes of constitutional protection deepened. The initial responses to *Roe* and *Doe* were
designed to nullify the Court's rulings in a variety of innovative ways.
On the state and local level, many governments moved to restrict
Medicaid funds to "therapeutic" abortions. Some areas prohibited the
use of hospital facilities for abortions, and a variety of legislation was
passed that demanded spouse and parent notification and approval,
that created defined waiting periods, and that formulated regulations
governing the "manner and means" of performing abortions.[34]

At the national level, there have been a long string of proposed constitutional amendments (of both the Right to Life and the Federalism
variety) and numerous legislative proposals directed at curtailing the
use of federal funds being used to finance abortions. No constitutional amendment has as yet found its way out of committee, but the
opponents have been relatively successful in securing the passage of
limiting legislation. The appropriations tactic began in 1974, but it
was not until 1976 with the passage of the Hyde Amendment that the
antiabortion advocates succeeded.

At the time of the debate over the Hyde Amendment more than one
million abortions were being performed annually in the United States.
The Department of Health, Education, and Welfare was paying for
between 250,000 and 300,000 of these each year at a cost of around
forty-five million dollars. The Hyde Amendment was passed only
after a protracted debate in the House and the Senate over its language. The final form provided that no federal funds could be used
for an abortion "except where the life of the mother would be endan-
gered if the fetus was carried to term." In 1977 and 1978 a more liberal
construction was used that limited federal funds to those abortions
deemed "medically necessary." Opponents of abortion insisted that
such language defeated the true purpose of the legislation. After all, it

33 Weicker quoted in the Boston *Globe*, September 17, 1981, Sec. A, p. 1.
34 For a comprehensive survey of the subject see "Special Project: Survey of Abortion Law," *Arizona State Law Journal*, LXVII (1980).

was argued, a woman could undoubtedly find a doctor who would willingly confirm that her abortion was "medically necessary." In 1979 antiabortion groups were able to restore more restrictive language in six appropriations bills to prohibit federal funds being spent for abortions except where it would be necessary to save the life of the mother or in cases of incest or rape.

The most innovative legislative approach to reversing the Court's holding in *Roe* and *Doe* ("that the word 'person' as used in the Fourteenth Amendment does not include the unborn") was the Human Life Statute of 1981.[35] This legislation sought to define when human life begins. Employing the fifth section of the Fourteenth Amendment (authorizing Congress to enforce the amendment by "appropriate legislation"), the measure stated "that for the purposes of enforcing the obligation of the States under the Fourteenth Amendment not to deprive persons of life without due process of law, human life shall be deemed to exist from conception." The bill restricted any federal court from issuing "any restraining order, temporary or permanent injunction, or declaratory judgment in any case involving or arising from any state law or municipal ordinance that (1) protects the rights of human persons between conception and birth, or (2) prohibits, limits or regulates (a) the performance of abortions, or (b) the provision at public expense of funds, facilities, personnel, or other assistance for the performance of abortions." The Human Life Statute was reported by the Senate Judiciary Subcommittee on Separation of Powers to the full committee. However, the proposed statute eventually died.

In 1983 Senator Hatch was successful in taking his proposed Human Life Federalism Amendment to the Senate floor. This was the very first legislative initiative to be actually voted on on the floor. In essence, the measure sought to make the provisions of the Hyde Amendment permanent. In the vote, the proposal was defeated 50–50. Perhaps nothing reflects more accurately than that vote the high level of controversy the issue of abortion has generated in American politics.

The Reagan administration also explicitly addressed what it considered the judicial policy making of *Roe* v. *Wade*. In 1985 the Justice Department filed as *amicus curiae* in *Thornburgh* v. *American College of Obstetricians and Gynecologists*. In a brief prepared by Acting Solicitor General Charles Fried (on leave from his position as a professor of jurisprudence at Harvard Law School), the department asked

35 *Roe* v. *Wade*, 410 U.S. 113, 158.

the Court to reconsider its holding in *Roe* "and on reconsideration [to] abandon it." Although the majority of scholarly opinion thought the brief had little chance of success, the very filing unleashed an outpouring of criticism, led by another *amicus curiae* brief filed on behalf of members of Congress and written by Laurence Tribe. So visible did the Justice Department's brief become that Justice Harry Blackmun, the author of the *Roe* opinion, violated Court tradition to comment publicly on the brief; he said he found it a "truly amazing" argument. Tipping his judicial hand still further, he speculated that the Court would be unpersuaded by Fried's legal arguments.[36]

On June 11, 1986, Blackmun, in handing down the majority opinion in *Thornburgh*, made official what he had intimated in his earlier extrajudicial remarks. Writing for the majority of five, Blackmun affirmed the Court's holding in *Roe*. Taking up the political rhetoric of the prochoice interest groups, Blackmun concluded that laws such as that of Pennsylvania (which required a physician to give a patient seeking an abortion full information concerning abortions after the fetus becomes viable) were designed to intimidate women from exercising their "freedom of choice." Such requirements, Blackmun asserted, were clearly an effort by the state to influence a woman's decision. Such state influence constituted an unconstitutional impairment of privacy rights.[37]

For the first time, the Court ranked abortion as a "fundamental" right. Blackmun went so far as to suggest that "few decisions . . . are . . . more basic to individual dignity and autonomy than a woman's decision . . . to end her pregnancy." So far had Blackmun gone that even Chief Justice Burger, who had joined the majority in *Roe*, chose to dissent.[38]

But the most important dissent came from the pen of Justice Byron White. To his way of thinking, the majority in *Thornburgh*, like the majority in *Roe*, had wandered so far from the Constitution as to be guilty of imposing "its own controversial choices of value upon the people." His wrath against "the warped point of view of the majority" was without apology.[39]

What makes *Thornburgh* interesting and potentially important

36 Nos. 84-495 and 84-1379 (October term, 1985), 2.
37 *Thornburgh* v. *American College of Obstetricians and Gynecologists*, 54 U.S.L.W. 4618 (1986), 4621, 4625.
38 *Ibid.*, 4630.
39 *Ibid.*, 4636.

from the perspective of court-curbing efforts is twofold. First, it was a five-to-four opinion, whereas *Roe* had been decided by a seven-to-two vote and *Maher* v. *Roe* (1977) by a six-to-three vote. The tide of opinion may be changing, however glacierlike it may seem. With the addition of Antonin Scalia to the Court, there may now be a far more likely shift toward a majority against *Roe* than ever before.

The second point of interest lies in another opinion by Justice White. In the case of *Bowers* v. *Hardwick*, White wrote the majority opinion upholding the constitutionality of the state of Georgia's sodomy statute. While acknowledging that the Court in the past had "recognized rights that have little or no textual support in constitutional language," White and the majority refused to extend such protection to "homosexual sodomy," citing the "ancient roots" in the law against such behavior.[40] *Hardwick* was, in brief, a harsh blow against the so-called right of privacy created in *Griswold*. Together with his dissent in *Thornburgh*, White's opinion in *Hardwick* represents the most cogent attack yet on the foundations of the abortion privilege.

The most striking feature of efforts to curb the courts is their marked lack of success. Even those who point with alarm to such close calls as the Jenner-Butler Bill (which failed by only one vote) have to concede that the most important factor is that it did fail. The reason most efforts fail is that they are imprudent. They tend to be excessive in that they go far enough to seriously impair the necessary role of an independent judiciary, which is a risk most officials are simply not willing to take. Such measures are insufficient in that they fail to treat the causes of judicial activism at a level deep enough to make a permanent difference.

Political responses to what are perceived to be excesses of judicial power take one of two forms. The response will either be a policy response against a particular decision or line of decisions or an institutional response against the structure and powers of the courts. In any event, the response may either be partisan or principled. More often than not, it will be partisan.

For any political attempt to adjust or limit judicial power to be successful it is necessary that it be, and that it be perceived to be, a principled rather than a merely partisan response. Only then will the issue

40 *Bowers* v. *Hardwick*, 54 U.S.L.W. 4919 (1986), 4921.

of judicial activism be met on a ground high enough to transcend the more common and generally fruitless debates over judicial liberalism and judicial conservatism. The deepest issue is not whether a particular court is too liberal for some and too conservative for others; the point is whether the courts are exercising their powers capably and legitimately. Together the standards of institutional capacity and constitutional legitimacy are far more helpful in thinking about the nature and extent of judicial power than the ideological stamps of liberal and conservative. Keeping the courts constitutionally legitimate and institutionally capable benefits both the liberal and conservative elements in American politics.

Typically, political responses to judicial activism are aimed at single issues, such as school desegregation, crime, abortion, and prayer in public schools. They are, for the most part, attempts to curtail the jurisdiction of the federal courts in particular areas. Thus we find bills on abortion, bills on school prayer, bills on busing to achieve desegregation, and so forth. It is at best a piecemeal approach to a problem that demands a more thorough solution.

Congressional efforts to deal with judicial activism are troubling in two ways. First, they fail to reach to the heart of the matter. The real problem is not the exercise of judicial power in a particular case (*Roe* v. *Wade*, permitting abortions, for example) but the exercise of judicial power more broadly considered. By addressing judicial activism on the level of particular decisions, Congress treats symptoms at the expense of curing causes. The most important issue ultimately may not be how *Roe* v. *Wade* was decided but how the matter became a cause of action in the first place.

The second troubling aspect of most court-curbing efforts is deeper yet. Efforts that attempt to treat the symptoms of judicial activism by keying on particular decisions imply that the authority of the Court is not binding, that its decisions can be lightly dismissed or ignored. A case in point is the issue of school prayer. One proposal would remove federal court jurisdiction, at both the lower and the Supreme Court levels, to entertain such suits. But the plan would leave standing as good law the controlling Supreme Court decision banning prayer in public schools, *Engel* v. *Vitale*. The effect would be to say that although the decisions remain there will be no way to seek judicial enforcement of them at the national level. This is nothing more than allowing Congress to give the states a "knowing wink and say 'go ahead—they can't touch you now.' " In the end such an arrangement would serve only to undermine the stature of the judiciary in American politics and respect for the rule of law. However much one might think that the Court has exceeded its legitimate authority in deciding certain issues such as school prayer, one should not be so rash in attempting to remedy the situation as to sacrifice the all-important veneration for the institution. "Governments in general," Tocqueville warned, "have only two methods of overcoming the resistance of the governed: their own physical force and the moral force supplied to them by the decisions of the courts."[41]

By turning its attention away from the more politically dramatic proposals for jurisdictional exceptions and focusing on the more mundane business of procedures and practices of the judiciary, Congress can direct its energies where they will be most successful. Through tightening up the judicial process Congress can effect a constitutionally legitimate and politically safe restraint on the exercise of judicial power.

The current spate of judicial intrusiveness is the result of loose procedural arrangements that have allowed, even encouraged, a movement of judicial activity away from deciding concrete cases to pondering abstract principles, and from considering clearly defined particular controversies that admit of judicial decision to questions of broad policy that admit more of political deliberation. By addressing the issue of judicial activism at this level of procedural cause and restructuring the judicial process in such a way as to better regulate how the courts deal with whatever issues lie within their jurisdiction, Congress will be far more efficacious. The most successful remedy for judicial activism will be a procedural remedy.

41 Kenneth Kay, "Limiting Federal Court Jurisdiction: The Unforeseen Impact on Courts and Congress," *Judicature*, LXV (October, 1981), 185, 188; Tocqueville, *Democracy in America*, 139.

SIX

THE FORMS AND LIMITS
OF JUDICIAL POWER

The history of the forms of judicial procedure is a history inseparable
from the quest for efficiency in government; the surge of enthusiasm
for a theory of scientific management during the early part of the
twentieth century did not pass the courts by. With their focus on an
apolitical polity characterized by maximum efficiency in the administration of its duties, the tenets of scientific management began rather
early to seep into the language of the judicial reformers. In 1928 Felix
Frankfurter and James Landis put it bluntly: "Scientific standards of
legislation really demand a comprehensive judicial code, defining the
structure of the entire judicial system and bringing the scope of judicial power of the various parts of the judicial hierarchy within the
ready understanding of the profession and the public."[1] Yet, while
insisting that "questions of federal jurisdiction and procedure are
largely matters of a technical and non-partisan nature," even the most
keen-eyed scientific reformers had to concede that "technical issues of
jurisdiction" would "continue to reveal the interaction of political
forces between States and Nation." After all, federal judges are inevitably "called upon to deal with issues of the liveliest political and
social implications." Despite the inherent tension between the premises of scientific management and the principles of popular government, the bench and the bar persisted in their quest to develop an
American "procedural jurisprudence."[2]

A central theme harped on by those attempting to create a "procedural jurisprudence" was the need to "make procedure subsidiary to
the substantive law" in order to free the judiciary from externally

---

1   Felix Frankfurter and James Landis, *The Business of the Supreme Court* (New
York, 1928), 281. See also Herbert J. Storing, "American Statesmanship: Old and
New," in Robert A. Goldwin (ed.), *Bureaucrats, Policy Analysts, Statesmen: Who
Leads?* (Washington, D.C., 1980), 88–113; and William Kristol, "The American Judicial Power and the American Regime" (Ph.D. dissertation, Harvard University, 1979),
4–8.
2   Frankfurter and Landis, *The Business of the Supreme Court*, 243, 287, 245;
Charles E. Clark, "The Influence of Federal Procedural Reform," *Law and Contemporary Problems*, XIII (Winter, 1948), 144, 163.

imposed constraints so the judges would be better able to "do things." The immediate point was to urge Congress (and the state legislatures, as well) to delegate its "acquired power" over judicial procedure to the judiciary itself. It was argued that, because they embodied "legislative theory, not judicial experience," legislatively fashioned rules and procedures often tended to destroy by their "clumsy abstractness" the very purposes they were meant to serve. It would be far safer politically and far more efficient administratively to lodge the rule-making power in the judges where the rules could "grow out of experience, not out of the ax-grinding desires of particular law-makers." Judges, it seemed to the reformers, would have a more delicate touch than legislators in tampering with the "intricate mechanism" of judicial procedure. Simply put, judges would be more sensitive to the need to subordinate "procedure to its proper place as an aid to the understanding of a case, rather than a series of restrictions on the parties or the court."[3]

The belief that efficient administration (in the scientific management sense) of judicial business is essential to serve justice caught on. The result has been a willingness in Congress to defer to the judgment of judges on matters of judicial administration and procedure. Generally speaking, judiciary legislation has been directed at, and has been most successful in achieving, more efficient methods of limiting what otherwise would be "a heavy stream of petty litigation."[4] Thus relieved of petty matters, the courts have been free to devote most of their attention to matters of greater national interest. But what qualifies for their attention under this loftier banner has been left to the judgment of the courts themselves. The task of the federal courts has become the resolution of issues that they (and the Supreme Court in particular) define as being of sufficient national interest.

The judicial efficiency movement failed to recognize to a sufficient degree that procedural rules are "inextricably interwoven" with substantive law. How a polity is administered has a pervasive influence on what the polity does. There is such an intimate connection between procedure and substance in political life that procedure in part not only shapes substantive issues but affects how those issues are

---

3 Roscoe Pound, "The Rule-Making Power of the Courts," *American Bar Association Journal*, XII (1926), 599, 602, 603; Edson R. Sunderland, "The Exercise of the Rule-Making Power," *American Bar Association Journal*, XII (1926), 548, 550; Clark, "The Influence of Federal Procedural Reform," 154.

4 Frankfurter and Landis, *The Business of the Supreme Court*, 299.

resolved. The concern that judicial rule making would impinge on or affect substantive rights was not empty. With increased power over their own procedures, judges find themselves without much restraint should they be inclined to modify their procedures in order to allow themselves a greater hand in making important decisions of public policy.[5]

The result has been a movement from concrete standards to more abstract standards governing the conduct of judicial business. Requirements for what constitutes standing have been significantly loosened; the traditional demand for a concrete legal interest has been replaced by the more abstract standards of "zones of interest" and injury in fact. In the area of class actions the requirement of a clearly defined class with a strictly defined common legal interest has been nudged aside in favor of more loosely defined classes raising more abstract claims. The intervention procedure has been modified so that nearly any person or group who can articulate an interest in the outcome of the case may intervene in a suit. The procedural device of the consent decree — which "embodies primarily the results of negotiation rather than adjudication" — has come to be used in such a manner as to result in a kind of litigious blackmail of defendants by plaintiffs and a means of ignoring if not violating the legal interests of parties not privy to the decree. Declaratory relief has facilitated a pronounced movement away from concrete standards of what constitutes a case or controversy (claims arising under a contract, for example) to more abstract standards, such as a violation of equal protection by a malapportioned legislative district. And in the area of equitable relief there has been a drastic movement away from a rather narrow understanding of equitable relief as a proper means of vindicating concrete property rights (generally claims dealing with accidents, mistakes, frauds, and trusts) to a more amorphous understanding that equity is somehow competent to vindicate more abstract rights such as equality. This procedural looseness has led to a near total abandonment of the traditional two-party lawsuit and the ascendance of the multi-party public interest lawsuit. In each procedural instance Congress has the power —

5   A. Leo Levin and Anthony G. Amsterdam, "Legislative Control Over Judicial Rulemaking: A Problem in Constitutional Revision," *University of Pennsylvania Law Review*, CVII (1958), 1, 14, 13, 40.

and, one could argue, the political responsibility — to return the judiciary to a more concrete and traditional exercise of its powers.

STANDING

In the area of standing to sue (a concept that Professor Paul Freund has labeled "among the most amorphous in the entire domain of public law") the Court endeavors to establish a threshold test to determine if the particular plaintiff has a sufficient interest in the case to warrant judicial intrusion.[6] That is, is the plaintiff a sufficiently adverse party with a vested legal interest in the outcome of a case or controversy that can be finally resolved by the courts? The doctrine of standing is an effort to distinguish a threshold procedural requirement from the actual merits, or substantive issues, of the case. The debate over whether such a distinction is indeed possible need not detain us here, for the Court in fact *assumes* that such a distinction can be made and has attempted to articulate standards to evaluate claims of standing. It is in the area of those standards that the looseness and ambiguity have developed.

The relaxed procedural restraints generally, and the creation of new causes of action especially, are the results of a transformation at the level of legal theory; the practical effects only reflect its fundamental theoretical flaws. Our legal system has undergone a radical evolution from being based on a contractarian theory of law to being characterized by what one proponent has aptly called a "fiduciary ethic." This has been made possible by the transformation of what is meant by the traditional case or controversy requirement. More accurately, there has not been so much a transformation of that concept as there has been a diminution of it.

Delegates to the Constitutional Convention seem, as Max Farrand has suggested, to have "readily accepted" the necessity of a national judiciary. The "judicious modification" of the federal principle that the Constitution had effected, coupled with the residual sovereignty left to the states, demanded a judicial system that was capable of resolving disputes in a clear and uniform manner. As Hamilton succinctly said, "If there are any such things as political axioms, the propriety of the judicial power of a government being co-extensive with

---

6 Freund quoted in Kristol, "The American Judicial Power and the American Regime," 61.

its legislative, may be ranked among the number. The mere necessity of uniformity in the interpretation of the national laws decides the question. Thirteen independent courts of final jurisdiction over the same causes, arising upon the same laws, is a hydra in government, from which nothing but contradiction and confusion can proceed." Thus the very creation of Article III, which extended the judicial power to the various cases and controversies, was intended at once to expand that power and restrict it. It was expanded to enable the judiciary to reach to causes theretofore unnecessary (given there had not yet been a national government), and it was restricted to certain categories of issues so as not to allow the judges a "roving commission to do good." The original constitutional logic was to limit the necessary judicial power to clearly defined disputes between individuals over legal and constitutional meaning. The power to resolve "abstract legal issues" was understood only as "a necessary by product of the resolution of particular disputes between individuals."[7]

As with many of the provisions of the Constitution, there would come to be disputes over the very meaning of *cases* and *controversies* under Article III. What, precisely, did those apparently clear terms mean? When these questions arose, it fell to the courts themselves to fashion a guide. The historical development of this body of case law is a history of the judicial creation of subordinate standards of what a case or a controversy actually *is* under the terms of the Constitution. "The case or controversy requirement," Lea Brilmayer has explained, "includes more specialized notions of ripeness, mootness, and standing to sue, and prohibits consideration of constitutional issues except as a necessary incident to the resolution of a concrete 'case' or 'controversy.' "[8] Until recently, at least, these judicially created standards were traditionally understood as expressions of judicial self-restraint.

The various doctrines of standing to sue, ripeness, and mootness constitute the strands of judicial interpretation of the case or controversy requirement of the Constitution. Woven together, they constitute the doctrine of justiciability. The question raised is whether a certain dispute admits of judicial resolution; if so, it qualifies as a case or

7 Max Farrand, *The Framing of the Constitution* (New Haven, Conn., 1913), 79; Jacob E. Cooke (ed.) *The Federalist* (Middletown, Conn., 1961), No. 80, p. 535, hereinafter cited as *The Federalist*; Lea Brilmayer, "The Jurisprudence of Article III: Perspectives on the Case or Controversy Requirement," *Harvard Law Review*, XCIII (1979), 297, 300.
8 *Ibid.*, 297.

controversy under the Constitution and falls within the jurisdiction of the federal courts. The doctrine of justiciability is, then, a threshold test to determine whether a plaintiff is a sufficiently adverse party with a vested legal interest in the outcome of a dispute; it further demands that the threat to his rights is both real and immediate, not hypothetical; and it demands that the threat is still current, not past, and that the question raised is still open.

Related to this doctrine of justiciability is the overlapping belief that courts may not properly seek to resolve "political questions," nor should they presume to offer "advisory opinions" on pending legislative or governmental actions. Thus to be a case or controversy under the Constitution an issue must not constitutionally lie with one of the political branches. It must, as James Madison put it, be a question of a "Judiciary Nature." Further, to be a case or controversy, there must be a concrete claim that something *has* happened, that an actual claim is being raised; courts should not offer opinions before an issue has been brought for strict resolution. Thus Congress, for example, cannot ask the Supreme Court whether a certain piece of legislation is constitutional; it has to wait for the Court's determination after someone has claimed in court that the legislation is indeed unconstitutional.

But whatever importance the political question doctrine and the ban on advisory opinions have for defining the constitutional meaning of *cases* and *controversies*, the essence of the justiciability doctrine is formed by the ideas of standing, mootness, and ripeness. And of those three essential doctrinal strands, the central one is the doctrine of standing to sue. But it is important to remember that unlike " 'case or controversy,' which can summon the express terms of Article III, 'standing' is not mentioned in the Constitution or the records of the several conventions. It is a judicial construct pure and simple."[9] And as will be shown later, this is precisely the reason that the case or controversy requirement has come to be so weakened in recent years.

Generally, the doctrine of standing holds that in order to maintain a suit, "The individual must establish the sufficiency of his interest in the controversy, and this involves satisfying the courts on two main points: (1) that his interest is one that is peculiarly personal to him, and not one which he shares with all other citizens generally; and (2)

9   Raoul Berger, "Standing to Sue in Public Actions: Is it a Constitutional Requirement?" *Yale Law Journal*, LXXVIII (1969), 816, 818.

that the interest he is defending is a legally protected interest, or right, which is immediately threatened by government action."[10]

It is not clear when the doctrine of standing crept into constitutional law. Although it is generally agreed that the first clear statement of the doctrine appeared in 1923 in the case of *Frothingham* v. *Mellon*, traces of such a judicially evolving standard appeared far earlier. In 1831, for example, in *Cherokee Nation* v. *Georgia*, Justice Smith Thompson insisted that it is "only where the rights of persons or property are involved, and when such rights can be presented under some judicial form of proceedings that courts of justice can interpose relief." In 1863, the Court held further that a plaintiff could not maintain a case "unless he shows that he has sustained, and is still sustaining individual damage." And in 1911 in *Muskrat* v. *United States*, the Court affirmed this logic by declaring that "the judicial power . . . is the right to determine actual controversies arising between adverse litigants, duly instituted in courts of proper jurisdiction."[11]

Although still not explicitly mentioned in *Frothingham*, it is in that case that the doctrine of standing received its clearest articulation. Rejecting Mrs. Frothingham's claim that as a taxpayer she possessed standing sufficient to sue to enjoin the operation of a congressional statute to which she objected, the Court through Justice George Sutherland's pen held that, although such suits might obtain in state and local courts, "the relation of a taxpayer of the United States to the Federal Government is very different. His interest in the moneys of the Treasury — partly realized from taxation and partly from other sources — is shared with millions of others; is comparatively minute and indeterminable; and the effect upon future taxation, of any payment out of the funds, so remote, fluctuating, and uncertain, that no basis is afforded for an appeal to the preventive powers of a court of equity."[12]

To have standing to sue, Sutherland concluded, the plaintiff "must be able to show not only that the statute is invalid but that he has sustained . . . some direct injury as the result of its enforcement, and not thereby that he suffers in some general way in common with people

10 C. Herman Pritchett, *The American Constitution* (3rd ed.; New York, 1977), 132.

11 *Cherokee Nation* v. *Georgia*, 5 Peters 1, 75 (1831); *Mississippi & Missouri Railroad Co.* v. *Ward*, 67 U.S. 492 (1863); and *Muskrat* v. *United States*, 219 U.S. 346, 361 (1911).

12 *Frothingham* v. *Mellon*, 262 U.S. 447, 487.

generally." As Frankfurter summed it up in 1951, if no "common law right exists and no . . . constitutional or statutory interest has been created, relief is not available judicially."[13]

This doctrine of standing was part of those "passive virtues" Alexander M. Bickel celebrated in 1962 in *The Least Dangerous Branch*. As Bickel viewed it,

> One of the chief faculties of the judiciary, which is lacking in the legislature and which fits the courts for the function of evolving and applying constitutional principles, is that the judgment of courts can come later, after the hopes and prophecies expressed in legislation have been tested in the actual workings of our society; the judgment of courts may be had in concrete cases that exemplify the actual consequences of legislative and executive actions. Thus is the Court enabled to prove its principles as it evolves them. The concepts of "standing" and "case and controversy" tend to ensure this, and there are sound reasons, grounded not only in theory but in the judicial experience of centuries, here and elsewhere, for believing that the hard, confining and yet enlarging context of a real controversy leads to sounder and more enduring judgments.

Following his mentor, Justice Frankfurter, Bickel concluded that had the Court in *Frothingham* adjudicated the constitutional issue, it would have "materially alter[ed] the function of judicial review and seriously undermine[d] any acceptable justification for it."[14]

But that was in 1962. In 1968 the Court would again explicitly turn to the question of taxpayer suits and the issue of private challenges to public actions. In *Flast* v. *Cohen*, the Court undertook to reconsider the issue that, since *Frothingham*, had been "the source of some confusion and the object of considerable criticism." The very doctrine of justiciability, Chief Justice Warren asserted, "is itself a concept of uncertain meaning and scope . . . a blend of constitutional requirements and policy considerations." Indeed, he concluded, it is a doctrine of "uncertain and shifting contours."[15]

The Court, although recognizing that "federal judicial power is limited to those disputes which confine federal courts to a role consistent with a system of separated powers and which are traditionally thought to be capable of resolution through the judicial process," also noted that, despite the holding in *Frothingham*, there was no reason to sus-

13 *Ibid.*, 488; *Joint Anti-Fascist Refugee Committee* v. *McGrath*, 341 U.S. 125, 152 (1951).
14 Alexander M. Bickel, *The Least Dangerous Branch: The Supreme Court at the Bar of Politics* (Indianapolis, 1962), 115, 122.
15 *Flast* v. *Cohen*, 392 U.S. 83, 92, 95, 97 (1968).

pect that taxpayer suits as such were not cognizable in federal courts. Indeed, the Court affirmed that the only difficulty is in "determining the circumstances under which a federal taxpayer will be deemed to have the personal stake and interest that impart the necessary concrete adverseness to such litigation so that standing can be conferred on the taxpayer *qua* taxpayer consistent with the constitutional limitations of Article III."[16]

The chief justice then offered the now-famous "nexus" test: "The nexus demanded of federal taxpayers has two aspects to it. First, the taxpayer must establish a logical link between that status and the type of legislative enactment attacked. . . . Secondly, the taxpayer must establish a nexus between that status and the precise nature of the constitutional infringement alleged. . . . When both nexuses are established, the litigant will have shown a taxpayer's stake in the outcome of the controversy and will be a proper appropriate party to invoke a federal court's jurisdiction."[17]

The chief justice was also quick to point out that the "result in *Frothingham* is consistent with the test of taxpayer standing announced today." Frothingham's claim had been properly dismissed insofar as her suit failed to satisfy the dual nexus text; her case had been a misguided effort "to employ a federal court as a forum in which to air . . . generalized grievances about the conduct of government or the allocation of power in the federal system."[18]

At the heart of the *Flast* decision was the issue of standing for "Hohfeldian," or traditional, plaintiffs versus standing for "non-Hohfeldian," or ideological, plaintiffs. Although he explicitly rejected the idea that "suits brought by non-Hohfeldian plaintiffs are excluded by the 'case or controversy' clause of Article III . . . from the jurisdiction of the federal courts," Justice Harlan in dissent argued that the *Flast* test was no test at all.[19] The question for Harlan was not whether "individual litigants, acting as private attorneys-general, may have standing as 'representatives of the public interest,' " for clearly there were occasions where they could. The deepest issues posed by the majority in *Flast* were ultimately questions of constitutional structure, institutional balance, and the limits of judicial power.

Harlan prophetically wrote: "It seems to me clear that public

16   *Ibid.*, 97, 101.
17   *Ibid.*, 102–103.
18   *Ibid.*, 104, 106.
19   *Ibid.*, 120.

actions, whatever the constitutional provisions on which they are premised, may involve important hazards for the continued effectiveness of the federal judiciary. Although I believe such actions to be within the jurisdiction conferred upon the federal courts by Article III of the Constitution, there surely can be little doubt that they strain the judicial function and press to the limit judicial authority. There is every reason to fear that unrestricted public actions might well alter the allocation of authority among the three branches of the Federal Government."[20]

The traditional understanding of the case or controversy requirement of the Constitution was, as mentioned earlier, that any judicial power to resolve abstract legal and constitutional questions was secondary to the resolution of particular concrete disputes between parties. But, as Harlan feared in *Flast*, this traditional, limited notion has been all but lost. It now seems that the resolution of the more abstract questions is too often understood to be the primary focus of judicial power and the resolution of particular disputes only of secondary importance.

The older notion that there *had* to be a legal interest to establish standing has faded. In its place has come the more liberal (judicially speaking) standard of an "injury in fact." By this standard a previously existing legal right is not requisite for standing; a provable injury to any interest is sufficient. A dominant sentiment is that in the absence of any congressional exceptions to this new doctrine, the standard is merely, as Kenneth Culp Davis has argued that it should be, "a judicial judgment as to whether the interest asserted is, in the circumstances, deserving of judicial protection."[21] As a result, the Court has abandoned the sense of restraint that the legal interest standard demanded and now willingly grants standing for interests that go far beyond what the old legal interest standard would ever have permitted.

This trend is seen most clearly in a 1973 case, *United States* v. *SCRAP*, in which a group of law students claimed they suffered an injury because of certain railroad surcharges permitted under an Interstate Commerce Commission order. They alleged that as a result of the surcharge they " 'suffered economic, recreational, and aesthetic harm directly as a result of the adverse environmental impact of the

---

20 *Ibid.*, 130.
21 Kenneth Culp Davis, "Standing: Taxpayers and Others," *University of Chicago Law Review*, XXXV (1968), 601.

railroad freight structure,' that each of its members was caused to pay more for finished products, that each of its members uses the forests, rivers, mountains, and other natural resources of the area . . . and that these uses have been adversely affected by increased freight rates."[22]

The Court was impressed. Justice Stewart agreed that the effect of the rates allowed would result in the depletion of natural resources and, among other problems, increase the litter in the national parks in the area to such an extent as to constitute a "specific and perceptible harm" to the members of SCRAP, a group whose interests, to the Court's way of thinking, were sufficiently distinct from the interests of the public at large to meet the threshold requirement for standing. Thus, under the new standards of standing, a public interest group claiming what is at best an abstract injury—aesthetic damage to the environment—can press its policy views under the guise of a lawsuit and influence the course of public policy through judicial resolution of the alleged cause of action.

As Justice Lewis Powell would endeavor to remind his brethren in the 1974 standing case of *United States* v. *Richardson*, the "relaxation of standing requirements is directly related to the expansion of judicial power." But the expansion has been accompanied by a transformation of judicial power as well. For the looser standards for standing have allowed the exercise of judicial power to move from the "determination of cases and controversies to explicit judicial guardianship of the public interest."[23]

It is clear from judicial history that if there is to be a meaningful and stable standard for standing it will have to come from outside the Court itself. Constitutionally, under the grant of power by the necessary and proper clause, Congress has the authority to impose minimum standards for what constitutes a case or controversy for purposes of having access to the judicial process. The Constitution grants Congress the power "to make all Laws which shall be necessary and proper for carrying into Execution the foregoing Powers, and all other Powers vested by this Constitution in the Government of the United States, or in any Department or Officer thereof." Through statute, Congress can give greater and more stable definition to the threshold standard of standing. Having exercised such a power in the

22 *United States* v. *SCRAP*, 412 U.S. 669, 678 (1973).
23 *United States* v. *Richardson*, 418 U.S. 166, 188 (1974); Kristol, "The American Judicial Power and the American Regime," 111.

Administrative Procedures Act (1966), Congress can legitimately replace the loose "injury in fact" standard with a version of the more concrete "legal interest" standard.

CLASS ACTIONS

The legal device of a class-action suit greatly emphasizes the "legislative" quality of the judicial decision-making process. Its purpose is judicial efficiency, to bring together separate parties with a common claim where "one or more sue or defend for the benefit of the whole." The point is to reduce multiple litigation, thus conserving judicial time and effort. Its effect is to present the Court with an opportunity to render judgments affecting whole classes of people. It is important, then, that what constitutes a class be carefully and clearly defined.

Through various reforms, the class-action suit has become one of the most common devices whereby the judiciary imposes its politics on the country. And, with a loosening of the standards of what constitutes a class, the result has been, as Donald Horowitz has pointed out, that the individual adverse litigant, "though still necessary," has faded a "bit into the background."[24] Broad decrees fashioned and effectuated for broadly defined classes of people (for example, a particular race or gender) are in essence judicially created social policies.

In the beginning, the class-action suit demanded that the class be clearly defined and the claim be concrete as well as common. Before the promulgation of the Rules of Civil Procedures of 1938, class-action suits were guided by a strict community of interest (or joint rights) doctrine. That is, all members of the class had to stand in the same relationship to the opposing party and raise the same claim. For example, a well-defined class with a community of interest would be all those who purchased an Oldsmobile only to discover that each automobile had been outfitted with a Chevrolet engine. Each individual claim is identical; each plaintiff stands in the same relationship to the defendant. By bringing all the plaintiffs together an obvious multiplicity of suits can be avoided. Such a situation was the original object of the class-action suit.

With the rise of legal realism, however, the concrete standard of a community of interest came to be viewed as hopelessly out of phase with the new "more pragmatic, more empirical" jurisprudence of the

24 Donald Horowitz, *The Courts and Social Policy* (Washington, D.C., 1977), 7.

times. The Rules of Civil Procedure of 1938 loosened this strict community of interest standard to include suits where there are "several rights" and a "common question of law or fact affecting the several rights," in addition to suits involving the traditional "joint rights." As the *Harvard Law Review* reported in its survey of the development of class actions, this distinction between joint and several rights in the 1938 rules was "a source of confusion almost from its date of promulgation." The result was that in 1966 the original 1938 class-action rule was amended, as the Supreme Court interpreted it, in order to replace "the old categories with a functional approach to class action."[25]

Under this new "functional approach," Justice Abe Fortas explained, "the focus shifts from the abstract character of the right asserted to the explicit analysis of the suitability of the particular claim to the resolution in class action." What this actually means is that the concrete standard of a strict community of interest has been abandoned in favor of the more abstract standard of simply a "matter in controversy." The individual adverse litigants are not as important to sustaining the action as are the broader policy implications of the issue. The *Harvard Law Review* explained the rationale this way: "First, to the extent that they open courts to claims not ordinarily litigated, class actions enable courts to expose policies underlying causes of action in circumstances where those policies might not otherwise be effectuated. Second, to the extent that they enable the courts to see the full implications of recognizing rights and remedies, class action procedures assist the courts in judging precisely what outcomes of litigation would best serve the policies underlying causes of action."[26]

As in other procedural areas, and as is amply supported by both the original 1938 rule and its 1966 amendment, Congress has the legitimate authority to restructure the practices and procedures governing the class-action suit in the federal courts. A return to the older, concrete standard of a strict community of interest and a movement away from the abstract functional approach are the places to begin. Further, by ending the present practice of allowing a class-action suit to continue even after the named plaintiff's claim has been satisfied, Congress could guide the Court back to its primary purpose—the resolution of cases or controversies between particular adverse liti-

25 *Snyder* v. *Harris*, 394 U.S. 335 (1969).
26 *Ibid.*, 350–53; "Developments in the Law: Class Actions," *Harvard Law Review*, LXXXIX (1976), 1344, 1353.

gants—and away from what is, by any other name, social policy making. By establishing that mere race or gender or ethnic group is insufficient to satisfy a community-of-interest requirement, Congress can pull the judiciary out of the sociological mire and back on the firmer ground of protecting the rights of individuals.

INTERVENTION

In the traditional civil lawsuit, characterized as a "private controversy between plaintiff and defendant," the joinder of parties was strongly limited by the maxims of common law. As the proponents of judicial efficiency gained a larger audience, their arguments in behalf of greater flexibility and informality in allowing interested parties to join a suit to ensure better representation of issues pushed the "focus of the lawsuit from legal theory to factual context—the 'transaction of occurrence' from which the action arose." With this shift, interested "outsiders" (that is, those not the actual parties to a suit) ceased to be viewed as "undesired meddlers."[27]

With the Adoption of Rule 24 of the Rules of Civil Procedure, intervention was pulled out of the common law closet and given far greater prominence and vitality in the federal courts. The original rule was loosened substantially with amendments to the rules that were adopted in 1966. As amended, the rule now allows "intervention of right" whenever a party "claims an interest relating to the property of transaction which is the subject of the action and he is so situated that the disposition of the action may as a practical matter impair or impede his ability to protect that interest." The rule also now allows "permissive intervention" (intervention at the discretion of the court) whenever an "applicant's claim or defense and the main action have a question of law or fact in common." The amended version of the rule was intended to amplify as well as restate existing practice. The result was to inject "some elasticity" into the procedure of intervention; the question that continues to trouble courts is, how much? The injection of "some elasticity" has meant the injection of a good bit of confusion.[28]

27 David L. Shapiro, "Some Thoughts on Intervention Before Courts, Agencies, and Arbitrators," *Harvard Law Review*, LXXXI (1968), 721; Abram Chayes, "The Role of the Judge in Public Law Litigation," *Harvard Law Review*, LXXXIX (1976), 1281, 1289, 1290.

28 *Cascade Natural Gas Corp* v. *El Paso Natural Gas Co.*, 386 U.S. 129, 134 (1967).

In its pronouncement on the nature and scope of the intervention procedure, the Supreme Court, in *Cascade Natural Gas Corp.* v. *El Paso Natural Gas Co.*, "expanded the right to intervene beyond the dreams, or nightmares," of those who drafted the 1966 amendment to Rule 24. The impact of *Cascade* was, in the words of the dissenters, Justices Stewart and Harlan, to allow "general and indefinite interests" that do not even resemble a "direct and concrete stake" in the litigation to intervene. The problem of *Cascade* was that it posited as a standard of "adequate representation" a loose and institutionally disruptive rule. The standard, Stewart and Harlan argued, came down to saying that "if, after existing parties have settled a case or pursued litigation to the end, some volunteer comes along who disagrees with the parties' assessment of their respective interests, intervention must be granted to that volunteer as of right." To Stewart and Harlan, the scheme would increasingly draw judges into the fray of the adversarial process as active participants and require that they "second-guess the parties in pursuit of their own interests." Such a scheme, they were convinced, was not only "strange" and "unprecedented" but "unwise" and "unworkable." The majority had stumbled into a "jurisprudential quagmire."[29]

The logic of the new juridically liberal attitudes toward intervention is rooted in three empirical facts. First, litigation in an increasingly complex society becomes increasingly complex; second, many scholars and judges believe that in order to deal with increasingly complex litigation, judges must be more than mere passive arbiters in the adversarial process and must make a conscious effort to resolve the issues in dispute by whatever means are at their disposal; third, there is a new and rather pervasive logic of judicial legitimacy that holds that courts are both morally and politically obligated to undertake the structural reform of existing political and social institutions in "responding to, indeed by stirring, the deep and durable demand for justice in our society." These three factors have transformed the way we think about courts and the extent of their powers and the details of their procedures. No longer seen to be apolitical (in the broadest and not merely partisan sense) and constrained to perform functions "purely judicial," courts have come to be viewed, and to be defended, as mini-legislatures.[30]

29 *Ibid.*, 155, 147, 156, 155, 160.
30 Chayes, "The Role of the Judge in Public Law Litigation," 1316, 1312. See also

Because the courts, in the handling of public-law litigation and institutional reform, have demonstrated a willingness to assume a quasi-legislative posture, so the new logic goes, it seems only reasonable that their procedures be accommodated to support their legislative dabblings. Because the courts are already involved in such undertakings as school desegregation and the reform of prisons and mental health facilities, it is only reasonable that they be allowed to adjust and manipulate their procedures in order to "achieve a sensible substantive result." Looser procedural arrangements governing the intervention of interested parties, then, are necessary to allow a court to operate as a more representative institution. Since public-law litigation—the declaration of public rights and the fashioning of public remedies for society at large—naturally affects many diverse and often opposing interests, procedure should not be so narrow as to preclude an adequate representation of those interests (interests conceded to be so "private" in their orientation as to often have as their principal concern delaying or blocking settlement of the actual case). Neither the bench nor the bar seems to realize that certain issues may be more political than judicial in character and hence "wholly unsuited for any form of adjudication."[31]

The expansive concept of "interest" that lies at the heart of contemporary procedures governing intervention is simply too vague to be an adequate restraint on courts willing to enter the political arena. The notion of what constitutes an intervener's interest could be tightened up considerably by resurrecting the more concrete standard of an interest in property alone. Thus, potential interveners would be required to show that their stake in the outcome of the case, although not sufficient to establish the applicant as an adverse litigant in an actual case, would be sufficient to warrant their presentation of issues that might shed greater light on the issues under dispute than could be adequately provided by the actual parties to the suit. Further, lawsuits could be given greater definition so as to truly make them lawsuits

---

Jack B. Weinstein, "Litigation Seeking Changes in Public Behavior and Institutions—Some Views on Participation," *University of California, Davis Law Review*, XIII (1980), 231.

31 Weinstein, "Litigation Seeking Changes in Public Behavior and Institutions," 237; Shapiro, "Some Thoughts on Intervention," 726, n. 110. See also Lon L. Fuller, "The Forms and Limits of Adjudication," *Harvard Law Review*, XCII (1978), 353.

rather than public forums wherein private grievances can be aired. If it were made clear statutorily that the public interest is to be represented by the government of the United States only as an initiator of litigation, an intervener in litigation, or as a litigating *amicus curiae*, and not by admission of various and conflicting interest groups, the lawsuit could be returned to a less explicitly political role.[32]

CONSENT DECREES

Like other procedural reforms, the consent decree originally emerged as a device whereby cases or controversies could be settled amicably without full litigation of the issues. The reasoning was that the result would be a resolution at once more acceptable to the parties in the dispute and less taxing to the already overburdened judicial process. But as in the cases of other such reforms, consent decrees have not proved quite so innocent. Indeed, the decree has come to be celebrated as one of the most "creative approaches" in the modern "quest for social justice in America."[33] That is but another way of saying that, even though it is not a judicial decree in the strict sense, the consent decree allows ideological plaintiffs a judicial forum wherein to pursue their intended transformation of society.

This was not always the way, of course. And consent decrees *do* have much to recommend them as limited devices by which to avoid costly — both socially and financially — protracted litigation. But there is more to recommend how consent decrees were once viewed than how they are now frequently manipulated.

Originally, these voluntarily accepted decrees were understood as being somewhat more limited than ordinary judicial decrees; the argument was that consent decrees, unlike judicial decrees, partook of attributes of a contract. Justice Thurgood Marshall staked out the limits inherent to the consent decree in *United States* v. *Armour & Co.* in 1971. Marshall wrote: "Consent decrees are entered into by parties to a case after careful negotiation has produced agreement on their precise terms. The parties waive their right to litigate the issues in-

32   John Bilyeu Oakley, "The United States as Participant in Public Law Litigation: Recent Developments," *University of California, Davis Law Review*, XIII (1980), 247.

33   Lloyd C. Anderson, "The Approval and Interpretation of Consent Decrees in Civil Rights Class Action Litigation," *University of Illinois Law Review*, XXXV (1983), 579.

volved in the case and thus save themselves the time, expense, and inevitable risk of litigation. Naturally, the agreement reached normally embodies a compromise; in exchange for the saving of cost and elimination of risk, the parties each give up something they might have won had they proceeded with the litigation." He concluded that "the *decree* itself cannot be said to have a purpose; rather, the *parties* have purposes, generally opposed to each other, and the resultant decree embodies as much of those opposing purposes as the respective parties have the bargaining power and skill to achieve. For these reasons, the scope of a consent decree must be discerned within its four corners, and not by reference to what may satisfy the purposes of one of the parties to it." Thus, not too long ago the argument in behalf of such decrees was one of restraint: A consent decree "must be construed as it is written, and not as it might have been written had the plaintiff established his factual claims and legal theories in litigation."[34] But what was once deemed a rather limited device for the resolution of disputes in the judicial process is now deemed a broad instrument of social reform.

The newer view is that, at least in civil-rights litigation, the strict "four corners" rule of *Armour* has been "discarded . . . in favor of a more flexible approach employing extrinsic sources to aid interpretation." No longer is the letter of the decree the point of departure for its subsequent interpretation; now, it is argued, the "spirit of a consent decree [is] the touchstone of interpretation." Civil liberties, the argument goes, are too important for a court to allow them to be "frustrated by an overly narrow construction of the decree."[35]

As civil-rights litigation mushrooms as a result of the apparently boundless energy of what Richard Morgan has aptly dubbed the "rights industry," there is no denying that consent decrees are increasingly complex and ambiguous. As a result, they call for ever more frequent and ever more expansive exercises of judicial interpretation. In the end, the force of the decree lies less in what its letter originally said than in what judges discern its omnipotent spirit to demand. By recourse to extrinsic sources to aid interpretation, therefore, the contemporary consent decree suffers being less a contract between parties than an ideological indictment of the defendant by a plaintiff.[36]

34 *United States* v. *Armour & Co.*, 402 U.S. 673, 681–82 (1971).

35 Anderson, "The Approval and Interpretation of Consent Decrees," 622, 628, 631.

36 Richard E. Morgan, *Disabling America: The 'Rights Industry' in Our Time* (New York, 1984).

This transformation in how consent decrees are best understood rests, at least in part, on the same weak foundation as so many of the other procedural reforms. As one commentator has stated: "A consent decree is a judicial act, and should be treated as such. First, by its very terms it is the equivalent of a judgment. Since the merger of law and equity, the technical distinctions between a 'decree in equity' and a 'judgment in law' have been eased and the terms are used interchangeably. Second, consent decrees providing for structural change, unlike money settlements, are a form of equitable relief." As in the other areas of reform, this loosening of the procedural shackles allows the not-even-slightly invisible judicial hand to remold society to exactly the degree a judge is so inclined. Thus it is no longer so much the procedure of the system as the substance of the claims of the plaintiff that foreshadow how such cases will be resolved. In the case of the consent decree in particular there is little doubt that it has become "one of the hallmarks of modern public law litigation."[37]

The procedural device of the consent decree causes more legal harm than social good in two particular ways. As a general rule, there is nothing to guard against a beleaguered defendant bargaining away the interest of innocent parties not represented in the suit. For example, in a racial discrimination suit, an employer may very well consent to a decree that includes provisions for preferential treatment for one group of employees over another. Should the employer agree to the demands of the plaintiffs for a one-to-one ratio for promotion, one black employee for every white regardless of seniority or other factors, then the interests of the whites (not to mention other racial or ethnic groups that may constitute sizable portions of the work force) are sacrificed to avoid litigation.

This phenomenon is made more critical by the presence of the so-called collateral attack doctrine that prohibits challenges to consent decrees from without; such attacks have been deemed impermissible and dismissed on jurisdictional grounds. Thus those likely to have a stake in the provisions of a consent decree, though not originally parties to it, are denied access to the judicial process. There is a strong argument that such a restriction denies the most basic conception of what "due process of law" means. Indeed, as Justice William Rehnquist, joined by Justice William Brennan, stated in the dissent to *Ash-*

---

37 Anderson, "The Approval and Interpretation of Consent Decrees," 585, 582.

ley v. *City of Jackson* (1983), the court of appeals in question had "erred in holding that a district court cannot entertain suit challenging practices allegedly mandated or permitted by a prior consent decree." Rehnquist pointed out that the plaintiffs' "cause of action did not even accrue until at least a year after the entry of the consent decrees." To dismiss their claim, the dissenters argued, was clearly inconsistent with the basic demands of due process, the belief that "everyone should have his day in court." They concluded that it is "a violation of due process for a judgment to be binding on a litigant who was not a party nor a privy and therefore has never had an opportunity to be heard."[38] The confusion that reigns over the collateral attack doctrine, the rights of intervention, and the resultant unrestricted negotiability of the interests of innocent third parties, is sufficient to cause the rethinking and reform of existing procedural arrangements governing the use of the consent decree.

DECLARATORY RELIEF

A declaratory judgment is, in Henry Abraham's words, a "device that enables courts generally to enter a final judgment between litigants, *in an actual controversy*, defining their respective rights under a statute, contract, will, or other document, *without* attaching to the otherwise binding judgment any consequential or coercive relief." All of this occurs before the intricacies of an actual lawsuit start up. This procedure has been available only since 1934. In 1933 the Supreme Court hinted that such a procedure would, despite a 1928 Supreme Court opinion to the contrary, probably fit comfortably within the limits of the case or controversy requirement of Article III of the Constitution. In 1934, taking the hint to heart, Congress passed the Declaratory Judgment Act; in 1937, true to its word, the Court upheld it.[39] Writing for the Court, Chief Justice Stone held that "the operation of the Declaratory Judgment is procedural only" and conforms to the Constitution by still demanding an actual adversarial dispute between real parties that is "manifestly susceptible of judicial determination. It calls, not for an advisory opinion upon a hypothetical basis, but for an adjudication of present right upon established facts."[40]

38 *Ashley* v. *City of Jackson*, 104 S. Ct. 255, 256, 257 (1983) [quoting *Parklane Hosiery Co.* v. *Shore*, 439 U.S. 322, 327 n. 7 (1979)].

39 Henry J. Abraham, *The Judicial Process* (4th. ed.; New York, 1980), 380. See *Willing* v. *Chicago Auditorium Association*, 277 U.S. 274 (1928); *Nashville, C. and St. L. Ry.* v. *Wallace*, 288 U.S. 249 (1933); *Aetna Life Insurance Co.* v. *Haworth*, 300 U.S. 227 (1937).

40 *Aetna Life Insurance Co.* v. *Haworth*, 300 U.S. 227, 239–43.

The problem is that, despite the Court's confidence, the act has proved to be more than "procedural only," and such judgments do appear to fade into advisory opinions. In conjunction with the other procedural developments in areas of standing, class actions, and equitable relief, the Declaratory Judgment Act has led to the creation of new causes of action and, as David Dickson has shown, "changed both the substantive rights of parties and the jurisdiction of courts."[41] (*Roe* v. *Wade*, the abortion case, was an action for declaratory relief.) The result of the act has been to blur the boundaries of what constitutes an actual case or controversy.

One of the traditional standards for a case or controversy is the notion of "ripeness"; that is, the dispute must not be hypothetical, dead, or moot. A ripe controversy is one that is both clear and present; only then, it is agreed, can a court competently reach a judgment on the merits of the case because only then will the legal issues be clearly exposed. By allowing a resolution of the conflict by declaratory judgment at an early stage of the dispute, before any concrete motions have begun to secure the claim in court, the act serves to denigrate the idea of ripeness as a meaningful standard of whether a conflict is, in fact, a case or controversy.

There is additionally a threshold problem. By attempting to declare certain rights prior to the completion of the adversarial process, which is replete with discovery (the underlying logic of which, it must be remembered, is to draw out all the facts and issues possible), a declaratory judgment is often based on arguments other than those that emanate from the facts of the case at hand. Hence, judgments are often declared more in accordance with the social and political predilections of the court than with the established facts of the case. (In one case an ordinance banning obscene films was upheld *before* the details of the film in question were revealed.)[42] Not unlike the new class action, the declaratory judgment is often based more on the broader implications of the substantive policy issue than on the particular legal claims of the parties. Bolstered by the new, looser class-action requirements and the nearly nonexistent standards for proving standing to sue, the Declaratory Judgment Act has greatly facilitated the rise of public-interest litigation by private parties. The declaratory judgment

41 David L. Dickson, "Declaratory Remedies and Constitutional Change," *Vanderbilt Law Review*, XXIV (1971), 257.
42 *Times Film Corp.* v. *City of Chicago*, 365 U.S. 43 (1966).

has become a device whereby the Court may in effect convert what are essentially political issues into legal ones.

The declaratory judgment has also proved to be much more than a simple declaration. Such a declaration implies enforcement because, as Chief Justice Marshall wrote in *Marbury* v. *Madison*, where there is a right there must be a remedy. Thus, the declaratory judgment has come to be closely tied to equitable relief. Once the rights have been declared, the logic of the legal process demands more, as, for example, the reapportionment cases show. In the area of legislative districting, beginning with *Baker* v. *Carr* (1964), the Supreme Court "departed from the judicial task of applying the Constitution to invalidate existing districts, and assumed the political task of legislating new districts." The results, as Dickson reports, were tragically predictable:

> In the reapportionment cases the Supreme Court, once embarked on requiring district court supervision of redistricting, was driven by the inexorable limits of judicial competence to simplify the issue to 'one man, one vote' in all situations, regardless of interference with a coordinate branch of the government, the amount of litigation provoked, competing considerations, and the will of a majority of the people involved. The Court has felt compelled to give orders to a state legislature regarding the bills it might pass, and to strike down variations of less than four percent because the legislative solution departed from "the mathematical ideal."[43]

This tendency of a judicial idea to expand itself to the limits of its logic (as Benjamin Cardozo put it) is hardly limited to the reapportionment area. It has characterized the areas of school desegregation, low-income housing, and the reform of prisons and mental health facilities. The result is that judges now find themselves administering social services on a more or less daily basis with more or less disastrous results.[44] Experience under the Declaratory Judgment Act suggests that it is time for Congress to reexamine the premises of the act and to take a close look at how it has contributed to a much more politically active judiciary. Through statutory reform a good deal can be done to restrict the use of the declaratory judgment to those occasions when its use is demanded only by considerations of judicial efficiency.

---

43 Dickson, "Declaratory Remedies and Constitutional Change," 288.
44 See Nathan Glazer, "Should Judges Administer Social Services?" *The Public Interest*, L (Winter, 1978), 64–80.

EQUITABLE RELIEF

When the Rules of Civil Procedure of 1938 merged actions in law with actions in equity into one unified civil procedure, a traditional view that equity is a potentially dangerous source of unfettered judicial discretion was ignored. Since Aristotle first articulated the idea of juridical equity, and through its development in the later jurisprudential works of Coke, Hobbes, Blackstone, and Story, it has generally been accepted that although equity is essential to any sound system of law, it is necessary that equity be hemmed in by principles and bound down by precedent lest it degenerate into arbitrary discretion.[45]

In the American Constitution, the judicial power was created so as to extend to all cases in law and equity. The failure of the Constitution to distinguish procedurally the two great spheres of law and equity did not go unnoticed. Keen-eyed anti-Federalist critics of the Constitution such as Brutus and the Federal Farmer, wary of all the particulars of the Constitution anyway, immediately jumped on the problem posed by the blurred jurisdiction between law and equity. The power in equity, warned Brutus, would allow the judges to "explain the constitution according to the reasoning spirit of it, without being confined to the words or letter," thereby granting them the power to "mould the government into almost any shape they please."[46]

The Federal Farmer was equally shrewd in his appraisal of the judiciary. In his view, his countrymen were "more in danger of sowing the seeds of arbitrary government in this department than in any other." The lack of precision in defining the limits of equity in the Constitution was a serious defect that would contribute to "an arbitrary power of discretion in the judges to decide as their conscience, their opinions, their caprice, or their politics might dictate." For if a judge should find that the "law restrain him, he is only to step into his shoes of equity, and give whatever judgment his reason or opinion may dictate."[47]

To defend the power of federal juridical equity against the anti-Federalist attack, Alexander Hamilton insisted that the power was both essential and severely limited. Its purpose, he said, was to provide relief

45 This section draws generally from Gary L. McDowell, *Equity and the Constitution: The Supreme Court, Equitable Relief, and Public Policy* (Chicago, 1982).

46 Brutus, in Herbert J. Storing (ed.), *The Complete Anti-Federalist* (7 vols.; Chicago, 1981), 2. 9. 145.

47 The Federal Farmer, *ibid.*, 2. 8. 185.

to those who suffered the consequences of "hard bargains." Such hard bargains were those dealings between individuals that might, for whatever reason, involve the elements of *"fraud, accident, trust,* or *hardship."* In general, Hamilton argued, "the great and primary use of a court of equity is to give relief in *extraordinary cases*, which are *exceptions* to general rules."[48]

In the Judiciary Act of 1789 and the subsequent Process Act, Congress (whose key committees contained some of the leading anti-Federalist doubters) effected something of a balance between those who advocated a hard separation between law and equity and those who wished for equity to be an unfettered judicial tool in every federal court. Although the acts extended equity to all federal courts, they simultaneously established the principle of a rigid procedural separation between the two actions. The drafters of these bills saw this procedural distinction as necessary if equity was to be kept from becoming a dangerous source of unfettered judicial discretion.

By combining the procedures of law with procedures in equity, the Rules of Civil Procedure of 1938 in effect ignored the dangers of equity that had always lain at the core of its procedural arrangements. The rules made it convenient for judges to switch from their shoes of law to their shoes of equity whenever they found the law too restrictive, as the Federal Farmer had warned they would if they could. In its effort to reduce equity to a safe and more certain code, the rules opened the door for the power of equity to be exercised with a disregard for precedent or procedure.

An underlying assumption of American constitutionalism is that there is an intimate connection between procedure and substance, that the institutional arrangements of a polity have a direct bearing on its substantive actions. This understanding lay at the heart of the original separation of law and equity. By maintaining a procedurally distinct judicial system, equity would be kept from flowing over and giving the law an undue liberalism, and law would be kept from rendering equitable dispensations too rigidly bound. Each had its place in the American system, and to maintain that system's authority, each had to be kept in its place. The merging of equity procedures and legal procedures had one overwhelming effect. Without the rigid separation of pleadings it was only a matter of time until equity would no longer be held as a nec-

48 *The Federalist*, No. 80, p. 538; No. 83, p. 569.

essary substantive body of law and would be viewed as merely another set of remedies available to the court for any purpose. Restraint through adherence to principle and precedent would be lost.

In *Porter* v. *Warner* (1946), the Court seemed to be on the verge of giving equity a radical expansion by arguing that when the "public interest is involved in a proceeding" the equitable powers of the federal district courts "assume an even broader and more flexible character than when only a private controversy is at stake."[49] But it was not until 1955 that it became clear just how fluid equity had become. The Court, in the second *Brown* v. *Board of Education at Topeka, Kansas* case, fashioned a new understanding of the Court's equitable remedial powers. The central thrust was that in place of an individual adverse litigant the Court placed an aggrieved social class. Its remedies would no longer be decreed for the individual who had been injured by the generality of the law, but rather for whole classes of people on the basis of a deprivation of rights—a deprivation that was provable only by resort to the uncertain turf of psychological knowledge and sociological inference. Further, the Court went beyond decreeing discriminatory laws unconstitutional and restricting their operation, and attempted to fashion broad remedies for those so deprived.

What is particularly striking about Chief Justice Warren's invocation of the federal equity power in the second *Brown* case is that although he spoke of the "traditional attributes" and guiding "principles" of equity being controlling, he then ignored most of the more substantial equitable principles in writing his decree. The effect was to present the lower federal courts with a virtual blank check for restructuring American political and social institutions.

The new "sociological" understanding of equity expressed in the second *Brown* case and its progeny differs from the traditional understanding in seven essential ways:

OLD	NEW
Equitable and legal procedures separated	Equitable and legal procedures merged
Applied to specific individuals	Applied to broad social groups
Focused on specific concrete rights, especially property	Focuses on more abstract rights, especially equality

49 *Porter* v. *Warner*, 382 U.S. 395, 398 (1946).

Usually exercised in a *proscriptive* way to block the enforcement of an unjust law or action	Greater emphasis on broad remedial mandates, hence generally exercised in a *prescriptive* way
Largely bound by precedent	Largely unbound by precedent
Required an irreparable injury that was immediate, great, and clear	Irreparable injury generally proved by a resort to social science hypotheses
Restricted by the federal principle	Not restricted by the federal principle

Since *Brown*, the Court has continued to expand, and to confuse the public perception of, its power of equity. The result has been the replacement of precedent and principle as the standards of constitutional meaning and equitable relief with social science speculation. This new tradition of sociological equity has baffled even its defenders who have sought to define its scope. Chief Justice Burger thus was driven to conclude in *Swann* v. *Charlotte-Mecklenburg Board of Education* (the 1971 school busing case) that "words are poor instruments to convey the sense of basic fairness inherent in equity. Substance, not semantics, must govern, and we have sought to suggest the nature and limitations without frustrating the appropriate scope of equity."[50] The problem, of course, is that words are all we have. One must at least suspect that if the limits of any governmental power cannot be clearly and forcefully articulated, then there is something desperately wrong with our understanding of that power.

With this "triumph of equity," as Abram Chayes describes it, it is no wonder that the city of Parma, Ohio, now finds itself obligated by the decree of Judge Frank Battisti to advertise in minority publications in order to recruit more minorities to move within its borders to effect his desegregation plan; or that the city of Boston in 1981, despite being fiscally strapped, was pushed by decrees from Judge Arthur Garrity into abandoning its earlier budget cuts because it seemed to Garrity that such belt-tightening measures as increasing youth fares on the Massachusetts Bay Transit Authority and charging youth groups for

---

50 *Swann* v. *Charlotte-Mecklenburg Board of Education* 402 U.S. 1, 15–16 (1971).

their use of public park facilities constitute "a very serious impeding of the court's desegregation orders." Through their equitable remedial powers the federal courts have come to exert an ever greater control over the public till. And one should at least pause to reflect on the promise made by the Federalists that the judiciary would be the institution least dangerous to the political rights of the Constitution because it would neither wield the sword nor control the purse strings of the polity.[51]

If the Court cannot speak with confidence about the limits of the equity powers, it is the responsibility of Congress to do so. It is clearly within the constitutional prerogatives of Congress to give some definition and hence limitation to the equitable powers of the federal courts. Political deference to judicial self-restraint may indeed be a sound policy — as long as the judiciary can articulate some meaningful standards for the exercise of its powers. When it cannot, or will not, then it is time for the Congress to assume its constitutional obligations. That is what the separation of powers is all about.

Congress can address the equity problem in a variety of ways. It could again separate the procedures in equity from the procedures in law. Although this might be awkward and cumbersome, it would at least serve to remind the court as well as the country that such procedural devices are frequently necessary to maintain the substantive integrity of a regime based upon the principle of the rule of law. Congress could also begin to refuse to grant equity jurisdiction as a part of many pieces of legislation. (The Fair Housing Act, for example, empowers the judiciary to enforce its provisions by injunctive relief.) There could also be a jurisdictional amount that sets a minimum of damages (ten thousand dollars, for example) before a federal court can exercise its equity jurisdiction. Congress could also place an upper jurisdictional limit on the amount of funds that can be ordered spent to fulfill an equitable decree.[52] A limit, say, of ten thousand dollars would certainly put something of a dent in most busing proposals. Or,

51 See Gerald E. Frug, "The Judicial Power of the Purse," *University of Pennsylvania Law Review*, CXXVI (1978), 718; and Robert F. Nagel, "Separation of Powers and the Scope of Federal Equitable Remedies," *Stanford Law Review*, XXX (1978), 661.

52 I am indebted for this suggestion to Laurence E. Silberman's remarks during the conference entitled "Judicial Power in the United States: What are the Appropriate Constraints?" held at the American Enterprise Institute, Washington, D.C., October 1-2, 1981.

more drastically, Congress can exempt certain cases from equitable relief, as it did with labor disputes in the Norris-La Guardia Act. Whatever the tactic, Congress can do a good many things in the area of equitable relief, as in the other procedural areas, to return the judiciary to a more constitutionally faithful exercise of its intended powers.

The movement from the concrete to the abstract in the procedural areas of standing, class actions, intervention, consent decrees, declaratory judgments, and equitable relief has been made possible by the diminution of the importance of the case or controversy requirements of the Constitution. This explicit requirement is the constitutional key to understanding the forms and limits of judicial power. Simply put, the doctrine restricts the jurisdiction of the federal courts to matters that are justiciable, to matters that *can* be resolved by judicial decision. Traditionally, the case or controversy requirement was understood to include a judicial power to resolve abstract legal and constitutional issues but only incidentally to the resolution of real disputes between well-defined adverse litigants.[53] This traditional understanding has been reversed so that the resolution of abstract legal or constitutional issues is very often the primary objective and the resolution of a particular dispute between individuals merely a by-product.

The characteristic features of this new model of public-law litigation are, as Abram Chayes has demonstrated, strikingly different from the features of traditional litigation:

> The party structure is sprawling and amorphous, subject to change over the course of the litigation. The traditional adversary relationship is suffused and intermixed with negotiating and mediating processes at every point. The judge is the dominant figure in organizing and guiding the case, and he draws for support not only on the parties and their counsel, but on a wide range of outsiders—masters, experts, and oversight personnel. Most important, the trial judge has increasingly become the creator and manager of complex forms of ongoing relief, which have widespread effects on persons not before the court and require the judge's continuing involvement in administration and implementation.[54]

Ultimately, the new constitutional jurisprudence is possible only if the Constitution is abandoned. Constitutional law has taken precedence over the Constitution; judicial prejudice has been allowed to

53 Brilmayer, "The Jurisprudence of Article III," 300.
54 Chayes, "The Role of the Judge in Public Law Litigation," 1283.

transform political principle. The novelty of the new jurisprudence and its resultant litigation actually lies in substance rather than in procedure: The move from the concrete to the abstract in the procedural realm is but a reflection of a deeper movement from the concrete to the abstract in the realm of substantive rights.[55] The courts have "found" in the Constitution guarantees for such "rights" as clean sheets for mental patients and hearings for prisoners before parole revocation, not to mention abortion and interstate travel. Yet, although the increasing abstractness on the procedural level may indeed be but a reflection of the deeper, more substantive movement, procedure in turn does have a bearing on just how far that movement can go. The relationship between procedure and substance is reciprocal. Proper legal procedures are necessary to a proper exercise of judicial power, for it is only through the erection of a few procedural fences that judges can ever be kept from roaming at large in the "trackless fields of their own imagination." Controlling the courts through procedural arrangements is an idea amply supported by both American legal theory and practice. From the beginning we have known, as Hamilton knew, that in order to "avoid an arbitrary discretion in the courts, it is indispensable that they be bound down by strict rules and precedents which serve to define and point out their duty in every particular case that comes before them."[56]

By resuscitating an appreciation for the relationship between procedure and substance, and by providing more concrete rules for the administration of judicial business, a more principled foundation for judicial power can be laid. More precisely, the now-crumbling foundations of principle can be shored up. Procedure is, and must be understood to be, an "epistemological device" that is necessary to guide the judiciary toward a more constitutionally legitimate and institutionally capable exercise of its powers.[57] Judges, after all, were intended to be judges, not legislators, policy planners, managers, or Platonic guardians.

---

55 See Theodore Eisenberg and Steven C. Yeazell, "The Ordinary and the Extraordinary in Institutional Litigation," *Harvard Law Review*, XCIII (1980), 465, 510-11.
56 *The Federalist*, No. 78, p. 529.
57 Brilmayer, "The Jurisprudence of Article III," 314.

EPILOGUE
RIGHTS, REMEDIES, AND RESTRAINT:
THE CONSTITUTION AND THE
LIMITS OF JUDICIAL POWER

Every instance of judicial activism from *Dred Scott* to the present has been animated by a common sentiment. The notion of "vested rights" alluded to by Chief Justice Taney in *Dred Scott* leads historically and analytically to the idea of substantive due process that dominated judicial thinking and constitutional interpretation from 1890 to 1937, and to the later new substantive due process and substantive equal protection of the present. Judicial power since *Dred Scott* has been administered more or less regularly by judges and justices who are more concerned with natural than with legal justice.[1] The unifying sentiment of both proscriptive and prescriptive activism has been referred to as the "Rule of Reason." What is constitutional is what the jurist thinks is reasonable or just, and the basis of judicial power is understood to be an active concern for vindicating notions of abstract justice or for advancing a particular jurist's view of what constitutes "human dignity."

At the core of the new jurisprudence lies a new understanding of how rights and remedies are related. The older, traditional jurisprudence understood rights as limitations against governmental power for the protection of the individual; the new jurisprudence understands rights to be entitlements that the individual is owed by the government. In the earlier view, rights were derived from the letter of the Constitution; in the new, they are derived from its presumed spirit. The traditional jurisprudential view was that a remedy was a formally deduced response to the legal wrong in question (for example, in contract law, the payment of money due). In the new view, the remedy is understood as instrumental rather than formal; it is not deduced from the specific wrong but rather aspires to be the "actualization of the right." Under the new understanding rights and remedies "jointly constitute the meaning of a public value."[2]

---

1   There have, of course, been important exceptions, most notably justices Oliver Wendell Holmes, Hugo Black, and William Rehnquist.
2   Owen Fiss, "The Forms of Justice," *Harvard Law Review*, XCIII (1979), 1, 52.

A remedy has become the judicial effort to give meaning to a public value "in practice." A remedy is more "specific," more "concrete," more "coercive"—in short, it is "more tangible, more fullblooded than a mere declaration of right." Blurring the line between right and remedy has led to the belief, for example, that busing in order to achieve a desegregated school system is constitutionally mandated and above political challenge; the older jurisprudence, maintaining a sharper distinction between right and remedy, would have viewed busing as being merely judicially mandated and hence more readily subject to political adjustment.[3]

The constitutional and political dilemma posed by the new jurisprudence is that the declaration of a public or constitutional value is now a highly intuitive and personal judicial matter. A constitutional value depends more upon a creative judicial imagination than upon constitutional text or intention. The declaration of a constitutional value is therefore considerably more difficult than the declaration of a constitutional right. It is so difficult in fact that even the most ardent proponents of the new jurisprudence concede that such values "can never be defined with great precision." What we are left with is an appalling state of affairs in which "the judge must search for the 'best' remedy, but since his judgment must incorporate such openhanded considerations as effectiveness and fairness, and since the threat and constitutional value that occasions the intervention can never be defined with great precision, the particular choice of a remedy can never be defended with any certitude."[4] This is hardly limited constitutional government.

The purpose of the Constitution was not merely to achieve popular government; its object was *good* popular government. The members of the Constitutional Convention of 1787, an aged James Madison would recall, were committed "to the object of devising and proposing a constitutional system which should . . . best secure the permanent

---

3 *Ibid.*, 52, 46. Consider, for example, the psychological foundation of the right articulated in *Brown* v. *Board of Education* and the resulting "remedies" created in the judicial attempt to enforce the right. See Gary L. McDowell, *Equity and the Constitution: The Supreme Court, Equitable Relief, and Public Policy* (Chicago, 1982), 97-122. The idea of a right of psychological equal protection (a right against a "feeling of inferiority") blurs into the idea of a sociological remedy (integration as opposed to desegregation). Thus, the right declared in *Brown* led logically to the remedy upheld in *Swann*. See Ralph A. Rossum, "*Plessy, Brown,* and the Reverse Discrimination Cases," *American Behavioral Scientist*, XXVIII (1985), 785.

4 Fiss, "The Forms of Justice," 49.

liberty and happiness of their country."[5] The framers believed that good government could only be gained through a constitution that created a government at once powerful and energetic yet limited and stable. The key was to render the government responsive to the permanent and aggregate interests of the community, rather than to every transient impulse or passion that might capture and convulse popular opinion. These deeper interests can only be drawn out and made politically operative by an institutional arrangement that fosters deliberation over important issues between as well as within the various representative national councils.

The framers believed that the opinions, passions, and interests of the community could be channeled through a complex of institutions in a series of "successive filtrations" so that most of the "factious tempers," "local prejudices," and "sinister designs" would be drawn off. The end product would be a view of the public good that was both refined and enlarged; the process would secure a more elevated view of the public good than could be had by any simple calculus of popular opinion measured at any given moment. The framers were convinced that their Constitution could secure the public good and private rights while simultaneously preserving the spirit as well as the form of popular government. Their republican remedy for the diseases most incident to republican government was a Constitution designed to secure a qualitative instead of a merely quantitative majority rule. It was this process, not the desires of judges and justices, that would produce "public values."

According to the Constitution, the Congress, the president, and the Supreme Court were intended to play essential deliberative roles in the framers' great experiment in popular government. Differing in their modes of election, tenures of office, and constituencies, each branch of government would contribute to the deliberations over public issues in different ways. From the frequently elected and numerous House of Representatives, to the "more august" Senate standing a step removed from the hustle and bustle of popular election, to the single, nationally based president, to the appointed and life-tenured Supreme Court, each branch was to be a significant and indispensable voice in the republican chorus. But that was not all. Each of the branches was in-

5   James Madison, "The Necessity of the Constitution," in Gary L. McDowell (ed.), *Taking the Constitution Seriously: Essays on the Constitution and Constitutional Law* (Dubuque, Iowa, 1981), 16.

tended to play an important role in the Constitution's implicit scheme for political safety. For the framers had sought to limit political power "by so contriving the interior structure of the government, as that its several constituent parts may, by their mutual relations, be the means of keeping each other in their proper places." In the science of politics of the Constitution, the "fundamental principles of good government" demanded that each branch "be subordinate to the laws." And only by a system of checks and balances could this subordination be secured.[6]

The judiciary was understood to fit into the constitutional plan as nothing less than "the citadel" of public justice and public safety. Independent, largely politically immune, and institutionally weak (with no immediate control over either the sword or the purse of the community) the courts were praised as the "bulwarks" of the framers' limited Constitution. As the "faithful guardians of the constitution" the courts were expected to keep the other branches and the states "within the limits assigned to their authority."[7]

The courts were to effect their appointed task by declaring the "sense of the law" in certain cases and controversies that would inevitably arise under any written constitution and, in those extreme cases, by declaring "all acts contrary to the manifest tenor of the constitution void." The courts would contribute essentially to "a steady, upright and impartial administration of the laws" by their power to declare laws unconstitutional and by their power to confine the operation and mitigate the severity of "unjust and partial laws" that might seek to injure the private rights of certain classes of citizens.[8]

This necessary judicial power of constitutional and legal interpretation was understood to not be so vast as to be at odds with the basic premises of popular or republican government. Interpretation was not to be simply a matter of "arbitrary discretion" by a judge in resolving disputes of either a public or a private nature. The discretion necessary to the task was what Joseph Story described as judicial discretion—a discretion "bound down" by strict rules and precedents that serve to define and point out the duty of judges in all the cases that come before them. Such a tempered discretion demanded at the very least a "competent knowledge" of the precedents that would be binding; and,

6 Jacob E. Cooke (ed.), *The Federalist* (Middletown, Conn., 1961), No. 51, pp. 347–48; No. 71, p. 483, hereinafter cited as *The Federalist*.
7 *Ibid.*, No. 78, pp. 524, 526; No. 80, p. 535; No. 78, p. 525.
8 *Ibid.*, No. 83, p. 560; No. 78, pp. 524, 528.

further, an appreciation for the limitations placed on the exercise of judicial power by procedural regulations. Flowing between the banks of precedent and procedure, judicial interpretation would, it was anticipated, be characterized as reflecting the "rules of *common sense.*"[9]

In interpreting the Constitution and the laws, "the natural and obvious sense of its provisions, apart from any technical rules, is the true criterion of construction."[10] The underlying premise of a written constitution, after all, is that it can be read and understood by those it governs. Plain, simple language and straightforward, commonsense provisions for rights and rules require no special mystical powers of divination. The judges were intended to be politically independent but constitutionally bound arbiters of any dispute that might arise; they were nòt intended to be either seers or soothsayers probing into the darkest mysteries of nature and her laws.

The judiciary could be safely entrusted with the power of interpretation for two reasons. First, judicial authority is "declared by the constitution to comprehend certain cases particularly specified" that mark "precise limits beyond which the federal courts cannot extend their jurisdiction." Second, the appellate jurisdiction of the Supreme Court is constitutionally subject to "any *exceptions* and *regulations*" Congress might think "will best answer the ends of public justice and security"; the total jurisdiction of any inferior courts Congress might see fit to create is "left to the discretion of the legislature." Thus, if judicial "misconstructions and contraventions of the will of the legislature" do occur, there is a constitutional means of political redress. For even though the legislature cannot legitimately "reverse a determination once made, in a particular case," it can "prescribe a new rule for future cases."[11]

Judiciously empowered and prudently restrained, the judiciary, it was hoped, would serve to ensure the constitutional integrity of the republic. Without courts, it was widely agreed, all the particular rights and privileges of the Constitution "would amount to nothing."[12] But those rights and privileges — the true constitutional values — were constitutionally and not judicially created rights and privileges. For a judicial restructuring of society by the manipulation of the Constitu-

9 *Ibid.*, No. 83, p. 559; Story quoted in McDowell, *Equity and the Constitution*, 73.

10 *The Federalist*, No. 83, p. 560.

11 *Ibid.*, No. 83, p. 560; No. 82, p. 557; No. 81, p. 545.

12 *Ibid.*, No. 78, p. 528.

tion in the name of a minority is no more just in the republican sense than a legislative restructuring of society by the manipulation of the Constitution in the name of the majority. Strictly enforced constitutional language—rights, privileges, and limitations—results in a regime wherein the interaction of the several institutions produces the legitimate consensus on public values that lies at the heart of any popular form of government.

The emergence of the "reforming judiciary" is the result of the judicial shift from a concern for constitutional rights to a concern for constitutional values. When a judge sees an evil it is now considered appropriate for him to use all his powers to remedy it in the name of protecting what he considers to be a constitutional value. But a strong desire, however morally noble, to correct an evil and the legitimate constitutional power to do so are two very different things. A judge who assumes "a roving commission to do good" loses the ability—or at least the willingness—to distinguish between a social evil and a constitutional violation.[13] But this distinction is essential to the maintenance of limited constitutional government. As James Wilson stated at the Constitutional Convention, "laws may be unjust, may be unwise, may be dangerous, may be destructive and yet not be . . . unconstitutional."[14] By the same token, laws that create such public institutions as schools, prisons, and mental hospitals do not *on the basis of the Constitution* create new rights and entitlements unless they are specifically so worded. It seems fair to say that Wilson, a preeminent lawyer, professor of law, and justice of the Supreme Court, would find such rights as the "right to treatment" of patients in a mental hospital discovered by Judge Frank Johnson more than a little puzzling.[15]

The older constitutional jurisprudence was in part based on the notion that "the written Constitution of 1789 must be what those who brought it into being and gave it the sanction of their ratification believed and knew it to be, and cannot be changed by what men . . . thereafter choose to think it ought to have been." It was this funda-

13 Paul Mishkin, "The Reforming Judiciary" (Paper presented at a conference entitled "Judicial Power in the United States: What are the Appropriate Constraints?" held at the American Enterprise Institute, Washington, D.C., October 1-2, 1981). See also Mishkin, "Federal Courts as State Reformers," *Washington and Lee Law Review*, XXXV (1978), 949.

14 Max Farrand (ed.), *The Records of the Federal Convention of* 1787 (4 vols.; New Haven, Conn., 1936), II, 73.

15 See *Wyatt* v. *Stickney*, 344 F. Supp. 387 (MD Ala. 1972).

mental assumption of textual permanence that made the Constitution legitimate; it was this premise upon which the faith of the founding generation was based that a written constitution was indeed a "peculiar security" in the political history of the world. If this original understanding is not the guide in expounding the Constitution, James Madison cautioned, "there can be no security for a consistent and stable, more than for a faithful exercise of its powers."[16]

In the traditional jurisprudential view, should the judiciary (or any other branch, for that matter) take it upon itself to transform the Constitution by seeking "the meaning of the text . . . in the changeable meaning of the words composing it," it would be constitutionally legitimate for the coordinate branches to return the wandering courts to the republican fold. By prescribing "the content and guiding the exercise of judicial power" Congress can draw the attention of the judiciary back to the Constitution. By restructuring the procedures of the courts — "the mechanism of the law" — and positing unambiguous rules designating "what courts are to deal with which causes and subject to what conditions," Congress can go far in fencing the courts out of the politically risky business of attempting to declare constitutional values and keeping them in the judicially sound business of resolving disputes and vindicating constitutional rights.[17]

By fashioning judicial procedures in light of the constitutional principles of federalism and the separation of powers, Congress can effectively harness the judicial enthusiasm to do good by placing statutory restrictions on how judicial power is to be administered. By placing restrictions on the power of the courts to mandate the expenditure of public funds, or on their power to interfere with the internal administration of the state governments, or by articulating clear limits to their power to assume administrative oversight of public institutions, Congress can take a principled stand against contemporary judicial activism.

The "reforming judiciary" can be argued against on separation of powers grounds, in that the administration of an agency is an inherently executive, rather than judicial, function. Additionally, judicially

16 John R. Tucker quoted in Mishkin, "Federal Courts as State Reformers," 961; James Madison to Henry Lee, June 25, 1824, in Gaillard Hunt (ed.), *The Writings of James Madison* (9 vols.; New York, 1900–1910), IX, 191.

17 *Ibid.*; Felix Frankfurter and James Landis, "The Power of Congress Over Procedure in Criminal Contempts in 'Inferior' Federal Courts — A Study in Separation of Powers," *Harvard Law Review*, XXXVII (1924), 1010, 1018. See also William Kristol, "The American Judicial Power and the American Regime" (Ph.D. dissertation, Harvard University, 1979) 40–60.

monitored institutional reform inevitably will lead to the courts having power over the public purse, a power inherently legislative. The new prescriptive activism can be argued against with equal force by invoking the fact that federalism is a constitutionally mandated scheme that demands that the federal courts exhibit a "scrupulous regard for the rightful independence of state governments." Even as expansively as the Fourteenth Amendment has been interpreted, it does not give carte blanche to the federal courts to poke too far into the internal administration of a state's domestic affairs.[18]

In our time the Constitution qua constitution has been almost lost in the political and legal shadow cast by the Bill of Rights and the Civil War amendments. The commonly held view of American constitutionalism is that "the heart of American liberty is to be found in the Bill of Rights" and in its application to the states through the Fourteenth Amendment.[19] This view encourages the belief that the protection of liberty is an inherently judicial function and that the judiciary not only may but must do all it can in this noble cause. The zeal displayed by the courts in serving the cause of freedom has been rendered even more problematical by interpretations of rights that are increasingly abstract. For example, the rather straightforward First Amendment prohibition against Congress abridging the freedom of speech has been expanded to mean that neither Congress nor the states can inhibit "expression"; the Eighth Amendment's prohibition against cruel and unusual punishment has been expanded to demand humane treatment; and the Fourteenth Amendment's guarantee that the states cannot deny any person the equal protection of the laws has been stretched to embrace a value of equality that goes far beyond the notion of equal political liberty it originally meant.

However popular the common view may be, it is wrong. The true basis of American liberty lies not in a mere bill of rights and especially not in any natural-law interpretation of those rights by the judicial branch of the government. The true substance of American civil and

---

18　Justice Stone in *Matthews* v. *Rogers*, 284 U.S. 521, 525 (1932). See also Gary L. McDowell, " 'A Scrupulous Regard for the Rightful Independence of the States': Justice Stone and the Limits of the Federal Equity Power," *Harvard Journal of Law and Public Policy*, VII (1984), 507.

19　Herbert J. Storing, "The Constitution and the Bill of Rights," in M. Judd Harmon (ed.), *Essays on the Constitution of the United States* (Port Washington, N.Y., 1978), 34.

political liberty lies in a Constitution designed "with powers to act and a structure designed to make it act wisely and responsibly."[20] A Constitution of explicitly limited and mutually controlling powers is the best source of political freedom. The commonplace assumption that it is naïve to believe that the judiciary is limited by the Constitution is the most naïve assumption of all, for it ignores the fact that any political power without definite limit is a danger to any sound political order.

James Bradley Thayer captured the essence of the problem clearly: "If it be true that the holders of legislative power are careless or evil, yet the constitutional duty of the court remains untouched; it cannot rightly attempt to protect the people, by undertaking a function not its own. On the other hand, by adhering rigidly to its own duty, the court will help, as nothing else can, to fix the spot where responsibility lies, and to bring down on that precise locality the thunderbolt of popular condemnation."[21] There are limits — *constitutional* limits — to judicial power, and any attempt to curb the courts must take those limits as its point of departure. To do otherwise is to risk a remedy worse than the disease. Constitutional restraint, not an empty reliance on self-restraint, is essential to ensure that the judiciary will continue to be viewed as the boast of a Constitution dedicated to achieving good popular government and the republican idea of justice.

20 *Ibid.*, 280.
21 Thayer quoted in Felix Frankfurter, "A Note on Advisory Opinions," *Harvard Law Review*, XXXVII (1924), 1002, 1008.

CASE INDEX

Case Index

316 (1819): 26, 63, 103, 132, 133, 136, 155
Maher v. *Roe*, 432 U.S. 464 (1977): 165
Mallory v. *United States*, 354 U.S. 449 (1957): 157
Marbury v. *Madison*, 1 Cranch 137 (1803): 36, 41, 60, 97, 105, 136, 189
Ex parte Merryman, 17 Federal Cases 144 (No. 9487) (1861): 138, 139
Ex parte Milligan, 4 Wallace 2 (1867): 10, 138, 139, 140
Miranda v. *Arizona*, 384 U.S. 436 (1966): 13, 34, 157, 158
Mississippi v. *Johnson*, 4 Wallace 475 (1867): 140
Muskrat v. *United States*, 219 U.S. 346 (1911): 174

National Mutual Insurance Co. v. *Tidewater Transfer*, 337 U.S. 582 (1949): 125
Northern Securities Co. v. *United States*, 191 U.S. 555 (1904): 143

Pollock v. *Farmers' Loan and Trust*, 157 U.S. 429
158 U.S. 601 (1895): 144
Porter v. *Warner*, 382 U.S. 395 (1946): 192
Prigg v. *Pennsylvania*, 16 Peters 539 (1842): 136

Reagan v. *Farmers' Loan and Trust*, 154 U.S. 362 (1894): 142
Reynolds v. *Sims*, 377 U.S. 533 (1964): 13
Roe v. *Wade*, 410 U.S. 113 (1973): 18, 35, 36, 63, 155, 162, 163, 164, 165, 166, 188

Schecter Poultry Corp. v. *United States*, 295 U.S. 495 (1935): 146
Slaughterhouse Cases, 16 Wallace 36 (1873): 142
Smyth v. *Ames*, 169 U.S. 466 (1898): 142
Swann v. *Charlotte-Mecklenburg Board of Education*, 402 U.S. 1 (1971): 159, 160, 163
Swift & Co. v. *United States*, 196 U.S. 375 (1905): 143

Thornburgh v. *American Colle:.* of *Obstetricians and Gynecologists*, 54 U.S.L.W. 4618 (1986): 163, 164, 165

United States v. *Armour & Co.*, 402 U.S. 673 (1971): 184, 185
United States v. *Butler*, 297 U.S. 1 (1936): 146
United States v. *Carolene Products Co.*, 304 U.S. 144 (1938): 32, 36, 37, 147, 151
United States v. *DeWitt*, 9 Wallace (76 U.S.) 41 (1870): 141
United States v. *E. C. Knight Co.*, 156 U.S. 1 (1895): 143
United States v. *Klein*, 13 Wallace 128 (1872): 125, 141
United States v. *More*, 3 Cranch 159 (1805): 124
United States v. *Richardson*, 418 U.S. 166 (1974): 178
United States v. scrap, 412 U.S. 669 (1973): 177, 178
United States v. *Wade*, 388 U.S. 218 (1967): 147
United Steelworkers v. *Weber*, 443 U.S. 193 (1979): 34

Wallace v. *Jaffree*, 472 U.S. 36 (1984): 157
Watkins v. *United States*, 354 U.S. 178 (1957): 13, 154
Wesberry v. *Sanders*, 376 U.S. 1 (1964): 34, 155
West Coast Hotel v. *Parrish*, 300 U.S. 379 (1937): 146
Wiscart v. *Dauchy*, 3 Dallas 321 (1796): 123, 124
Wolff Packing Co. v. *Kansas Court of Industrial Relations*, 262 U.S. 522 (1923): 145, 146

Yakus v. *United States*, 321 U.S. 414 (1944): 125, 150
Yates v. *United States*, 356 U.S. 363: 154
Ex parte Yerger, 8 Wallace 85 (1869): 125, 141

INDEX